Rethinking the Third World

Rethinking the Third World:
Contributions
Toward A New Conceptualization

Edited by
Rosemary E. Galli

CRANE RUSSAK
A member of the Taylor & Francis Group
New York • Philadelphia • Washington • London

USA	Publishing Office:	Taylor & Francis New York Inc. 79 Madison Ave., New York, NY 10016-7892
	Sales Office:	Taylor & Francis Inc. 1900 Frost Road, Bristol, PA 19007-1598
UK		Taylor & Francis Ltd. 4 John St., London WC1N 2ET

RETHINKING THE THIRD WORLD: Contributions Toward a New Conceptualization

1 2 3 4 5 6 7 8 9 0   E B E B   9 8 7 6 5 4 3 2 1

This book was set in Times Roman by Hemisphere Publishing Corporation. The editors were Carol Clark and Michael Folker; the production supervisor was Peggy M. Rote; and the typesetter was Phoebe Carter. Cover design by Debra Eubanks Riffe.
Printing and binding by Edwards Brothers, Inc.

A CIP catalog record for this book is available from the British Library.

Library of Congress Cataloging-in-Publication Data

Rethinking the Third World: contributions toward a new
  conceptualization / Rosemary Galli, editor; [essays by] Leonard
  Bloom . . . [et al.].
      p.   cm.
    Includes bibliographical references and index.
    1. Developing countries—Social conditions.   2. Economic
development—Social aspects.   I. Galli, Rosemary.   II. Bloom,
  Leonard, date.
HN980.R448   1991
306'.09172'4—dc20   91-9437
                                                                     CIP

ISBN: 0-8448-1711-2 (case)
ISBN: 0-8448-1712-0 (paper)

To my co-authors and
the many people who
helped us in Africa,
Latin America, and elsewhere.

Contents

Preface

As we collectively stumble toward the 21st century and into yet another war, we must gather the courage to ask what this century of world wars and failed social experiments has taught us. We must allow ourselves the intellectual freedom to evaluate the systems of thought that have governed our lives. Jewsiewicki (1989) reminds us that those committed to fundamental social change "cannot escape Marxism," the 19th century theoretical perspective upon which revolutionary praxis has been based. This volume was conceived as a project to rethink the relevance of the social sciences, both Marxist and liberal, to social change in the Third World.

The authors are concerned with the failure of contemporary development theory to explain and take seriously the dynamic histories of the peoples of Latin America, Africa and Asia. Breaking with unilinear, ahistorical approaches in economics, sociology, political science and psychology, they explore a broad range of issues in an attempt to break new ground. They offer insight into the link between democracy and raising productivity; the respective influence of technology and social relations in industrialization; the contribution to and participation in development of peasants, primitives, and other, often ignored, stereotyped peoples; the conflict between individual freedom and authoritarianism; the changing relations of governments and bureaucracies to other governments, institutions and subject populations, and the political alliances formed around development issues.

We owe an enormous personal as well as intellectual debt to many people, especially in the Third World, who contributed across the years to our understanding. We dedicate this book to them and to the special others who have given us moral and other support. Especial thanks go to Ron Chilcote for his commitment to the Comparative Studies in Political Economy and Society Series which this book was meant to introduce and for recommending our work to

Jewsiewicki, Bogumil. 1989. African Historical Studies: Academic Knowledge as "Usable Past" and Radical Scholarship. *African Studies Review* 32:3 (December):1–76.

Taylor and Francis. Many thanks are due to Lionel Cliffe and Peter Meyns for helpful, constructive, and timely criticisms. We are grateful, too, to Ralph Salmi, Todd Baldwin, and Michael Folker for their enthusiasm and guidance through the publication process.

Rosemary E. Galli
Christmas, 1990

Introduction

The original purpose of this volume was to set an intellectual agenda for a series of books on the comparative political economy of the Third World. The authors were invited to raise the most important questions that they believed needed to be asked or that were still unanswered with regard to social change and development. They were selected because they represent most, though by no means all, of the disciplines engaged in research on the Third World. Frederick Weaver is an economist and historian, Lars Rudebeck is a political scientist, K. P. Moseley is a sociologist, Leonard Bloom is a social psychologist, and Rosemary Galli is a student of international relations. The importance of having insights from all these fields in the search for alternative approaches to Third World problems is obvious. Synthesis of these insights and approaches, however, remains for the future. For the present, the objective of this work is to engage the reader in taking a fresh look at the contemporary historical process and how it has been interpreted.

The book is about rethinking what has been previously understood as development. Frederick Weaver offers an explicitly historical, comparative definition of the process of industrialization. Lars Rudebeck argues the case for linking democracy with development by referring to the recent experiences of Guinea-Bissau and Mozambique. Leonard Bloom defines a developmental psychology relevant to the Third World as one that focuses on what motivates people in their everyday lives. He links postcolonial struggles for economic and political independence with those for emotional independence. K. P. Moseley exposes the dilemma that the existence and resistance of what she calls (after Stanley Diamond) "the primitive" pose for contemporary notions of development. Galli recalls the myopia of social science theories in regard to rural producers. While some theories acknowledge their importance in the birth process of capitalism, most see rural cultivators as obstacles to change in a world, or mode of production, apart. Galli attempts to redefine this image.

As a whole, the book underscores the contradiction and crises inherent in contemporary Western models of development. The contradiction is expressed in a competitive market ideology and a statist practice. The chapters by Weaver, Galli, and Rudebeck are most explicit on this point. The crises, which explode the myth of development, are capitalism's wholesale waste of human beings and destruction of the environment discussed in the chapters by Moseley and Bloom. As a group, the authors share a general dissatisfaction with contemporary social science, particularly liberalism as it is expressed in modernization theory, mainstream development economics, and behavioralism for its lack of a critique but also dependency theory, world systems analysis, modes of production analysis, and so on. They emphatically reject the notion of historical necessity that characterizes most of these conceptualizations of development.

In the chapter by Weaver, it is clearly demonstrated that societies do not retrace the trajectory of others. He forcefully argues that the path taken toward industrialization depends upon the kinds of technology available and the state of social relations in a country. Weaver suggests an alternative, comparative history of industrialization. The examples he gives of Great Britain, the United States, Germany, and Brazil show the industrial process to be both cumulative and specific to the industrializing society. Because of the availability of advanced techniques, Brazil has not had to repeat the early experience of industrialization of either Great Britain or Germany. Nevertheless, its social structure prevents widespread mass consumerism on the pattern of the United States. Weaver also shows that the choice of technology can enhance certain kinds of social relations. The economic and social costs of Brazilian industrialization have reinforced the dominant position of the state and the military.

Galli's chapter attacks the uncritical acceptance of the dominance of the state in late industrialization apparent in recent liberal and neo-Marxist interpretations. She argues that theories of social change that portray the state as the primary agent of industrialization, but fail to consider the social conditions that produce this phenomenon, serve as an ideology for, and instrumentality of, so-called modernizing elites. Wittingly or unwittingly, these theories legitimize a particular set of social and political relations that foster particular forms of development.

Galli argues that the choice of development strategy is a political choice. There is no inevitability involved. Not all countries have to follow the state-led path toward industrialization forged by Germany, Japan, Brazil, and Mexico. She contends that a dynamic small-scale agriculture can be the basis for decentralized industrialization. Nor do countries have to industrialize. The choice of strategy is related to the balance of forces in the society. Social science theories throw their weight into the political balance by defining some groups as pro-

throw their weight into the political balance by defining some groups as progressive and others as backward—the winners and losers in the title of Galli's chapter.

Moseley calls attention to the unease, tension, and ambivalence of social science theory in trying to assess the significance of communal groups, also considered as losers in the historical process. She asserts that the very existence of communal societies has subversive implications for contemporary theory since it embodies both a moral and cognitive critique, and a challenge to that theory. The critique is cognitive in the sense that communal regimes imply models of steady-state development rather than continual economic growth upon which both capitalism and socialism are based. It is moral in that the struggle for survival of such groups draws attention to the violent, destructive aspects of contemporary overconsumption models of development.

How social scientists characterize the historical process is crucial. Pierre Bourdieu points out that "the theory of knowledge is a dimension of political theory because specifically symbolic power to impose the principles of the construction of reality—in particular, social reality—is a major dimension of political power" (Ashley, 1984:225). In the same vein, Claude Ake warns that the "social scientist has an enormous responsibility, for his or her work defines in an important way the possibilities of progress" (Ranger, 1988:479). Galli and Bloom take the position that social scientists are too easily coopted in defining reality from the perspective of those in power. They argue for a critical perspective—even one that identifies closely with subject populations. Moseley and Rudebeck both realize this in their chapters in different ways. As one step toward a more critical social science, Moseley suggests replacing insidious dichotomies such as backward/advanced and primitive/civilized with more precise concepts. In terms of political choice, she argues for "greater self-management at various levels of organization" as one way of legitimizing the reality of subject populations and as an alternative form of development.

The strength of Rudebeck's essay lies in his intimate knowledge of the peasants and state officials (particularly in Guinea-Bissau) who made the revolutions that are the subject of his case studies. He presents fascinating insights into their differing perceptions of development, democracy, and power. Of all the authors, Rudebeck is the most explicit in redefining development as people's development, which he conceives as a better life for people, including social and material security (Bloom adds emotional security), and human dignity. Most important, Rudebeck insists that the concept of a better life be defined as people themselves define it, which would democratize development theory as well as practice. On the level of practice, Rudebeck echoes Moseley's suggestion for people jointly assuming "control of their life situations."

Bloom's chapter also resonates with the notion of self-management for individuals. He recalls Frantz Fanon's efforts in the 1950s to encourage self-reliance in people living under colonialism. Bloom maintains that the psychology of self-reliance is the most crucial problem for a relevant psychology. In this perspective, development, both for individuals and groups, is liberation from domination.

In contrast to the social science approaches of the 1970s and 1980s that presented overarching frameworks of analysis—macro-theories of capitalism and socialism—these chapters underline the fundamental importance of studying social formations in their concreteness and in relation to other formations. The chapters examine relationships between individuals, social groups, classes, and institutions within and across social formations. Some look at attitudes and perceptions as well as ideologies.

Bloom looks specifically at the interplay between individuals and Third World societies and between these and Western societies. He calls for a psychology that pays attention to the stress caused by dizzying social change but also to the rich, complex world of myths and symbols that individuals and social groups use to make sense out of change and to deal with its uncertainties. There is no inevitability here, either; rather, a large variety of responses. For Bloom, behavioralist theories of conditioning are "too tidy and deterministic, too static and unable to make sense of the human propensity to novelty." He suggests psychoanalysis—which he sees "permeated by the theme of how social relationships and structures" shape individual lives—as a countermethod.

In his chapter, Bloom does not debate the challenge to psychology of the other social sciences that maintain the primacy of groups in the historical process over the individual. This point of departure informs the other essays that examine tensions between dominant and other groups. Rudebeck focuses on the mutual alienation of national and subnational groups—state officials and villagers—in the context of two newly independent African countries. Weaver looks at the overall antagonistic patterns of social relations in specific examples of industrialization. Moseley discusses the challenge to dominant Western societies represented by the very endurance of communal regimes. The array of experiences and groups explored in the essays as a whole cautions against hasty generalization. Galli recalls Polly Hill's admonition regarding peasants, ". . . and at all costs we must avoid generalizations about different types of peasants who are as different as chalk from cheese" (1970:28). She describes a range of peasant responses to a general lack of economic opportunities and attempts to explain the multiple actions and reactions of rural producers in terms of the human search for security and well-being under unequal, often limited, exploitative conditions.

This book thus presents a variety of themes and approaches that extend the range of social inquiry to include forms of everyday life and levels of reality that have too often been ignored in the general theoretical construction of social life. Nevertheless, the authors do not overlook the force of ideas and impersonal structures such as modes of production/social organization in shaping peoples' histories. Rather, there is an attempt to understand the complex interaction between them—individuals, social groups, and modes of social organization—as a counterweight to the trend in social science to investigate dominant modes and consciousness.

The chapters in this volume hold the premise that one learns more about a particular social formation by confronting it with others. A brilliant example of this type of analysis is T. Ranger's *Peasant Consciousness and Guerrilla War in Zimbabwe,* which illuminates the birth and development of the resistance movement in southern Zimbabwe by comparing it with the experiences of the Mau-Mau in Kenya and FRELIMO (Frente de Libertação de Moçambique) in Mozambique. In this volume, Frederick Weaver and Lars Rudebeck write from explicitly comparative frameworks to argue the case for a cumulative historical approach to the study of industrialization (Weaver) and to explicate and illuminate the negative developmental consequences of the alienation of states and peasantries (Rudebeck).

The term *Third World* appears in the text for convenience only. It is problematic because it groups together social formations from Asia, Africa, and Latin America that have less in common than is generally assumed. Although most of these countries shared an experience of colonialism and, today, are subjected to the only slightly less onerous control of the World Bank and International Monetary Fund, the differences rather than similarities between countries are primary and demand attention. Although this assertion may appear self-evident to researchers in the field, decision makers in Western development agencies, who are looking for quick and easy solutions to complex problems, impose another perception.

The failure of most development programs, projects, and loans stems from the assumption that economic and social problems are virtually the same in Third World countries and can be solved through standardized policy packages such as structural adjustment programs and through technologies such as the green revolution. These formulas and the capital and personnel they bring in their wake add an international dimension to a country's political economy as described by Rudebeck and Galli. The fact that they almost always end in failure has been shown by Piotr Dutkeiwicz and Robert Shenton (1986) to benefit certain social groups such as national bureaucracies and the armies of experts, consultants, and officials of international "donor" agencies. These are

Third World, industrialization, and development because it legitimizes their position as agents of social change.

The assumption that the many societies of the southern hemisphere form a world apart is also objectionable. This idea is discussed in Bloom's essay. A recent text implies this in its title, *The Other World*. It is too easy to think of ourselves as the "developed" we and others as the "underdeveloped" or "newly industrializing" they. Bloom shows that this is a particularly insidious type of thinking that can easily degenerate into prejudice or, even worse, racism. He cites those who maintain that there are such great differences in affective and cognitive processes between peoples that understanding is difficult. He also cites Third World psychologists who maintain that Western theories and methods are alien to African thinking. This he calls cryptoracism. Bloom maintains that understanding is possible because affective-emotional and cognitive-intellectual processes are essentially universal, although influenced by social and cultural variations. These very differences between groups, however, enrich the human experience. Moseley and Rudebeck also call attention to the importance of maintaining social and cultural variations in the interest of human survival (Moseley) and democracy (Rudebeck).

Although writing from a wide variety of disciplines, the authors stress the importance of the social relations that underly the production and distribution of goods and services as well as knowledge and consciousness (culture and identity). The fact that some individuals and groups are dominant derives from their access to and control over means of production and reproduction, both material and cognitive. The struggle to maintain this position translates into political interests and alliances across local, national, and global arenas. Within this context is the industrialization described by Weaver, the social struggles described by Rudebeck, Galli, and Moseley, and the social psychology described by Bloom.

This book is different from others in that it is about *how* to think rather than *what* to think about the Third World. Its aim is to help readers engage for themselves the individuals, groups, and social formations and to formulate their own hypotheses. The authors, therefore, invite readers to make this a cooperative enterprise. In the expectation that the essays in this volume will stimulate controversy, comment, and criticism, the authors are excited by the prospect of publishing a companion volume to include readers' responses.

Rosemary E. Galli

References

Ashley, R. K. 1984. "The Poverty of Neorealism." *International Organization,* 38(2) (Spring).

Dutkiewicz, P. and R. Shenton. 1986. "The African Crisis." *Review of African Political Economy,* No. 3 (December).

Hill, Polly. 1970. *Studies in Rural Capitalism in West Africa.* Cambridge: Cambridge University Press.

Ranger, T. 1985. *Peasant Consciousness and Guerrilla War in Zimbabwe.* Berkeley, California: University of California Press.

Ranger, T. 1988. "Review Article: Africa Looks at Southern Africa: A Review of Journals." *Journal of Southern African Studies,* 14(3) (April).

Weatherby, J., Jr. *et al.* 1987. *The Other World: Issues and Politics in the Third World.* New York: Macmillan.

Chapter 1

Winners and Losers in Development and Antidevelopment Theory

Rosemary E. Galli

INTRODUCTION

There is a convergence in liberal and Marxist scholarship that development means industrialization and that the process involves a more or less clean sweep of all previous patterns and relations of production. History is conceived as the working out of social laws whose outcome is always the same: rationalism, industrialization, modernity, and eventually postindustrialism (Williams, 1979). The objective of development theory is to comprehend the process to accelerate the change from so-called underdevelopment to development, from traditionality to modernity and, for Marxists, from capitalism to socialism. This chapter argues that social science in the service of developmentalism loses its critical faculty.

The notion of progress originated during the Enlightenment. The rationalization of human relations was perceived to be leading mankind toward the end of all that had been known previously. Marx theorized the process in the economic sphere through the laws of motion of capital, while Weber traced its political development. The idea that progress could be directed from above was behind Jacobin optimism and Napoleonic reforms. Lenin in Russia, Taylor in the United States, and the Fabian Socialists of Great Britain refined and legitimized the practice. The principal beneficiaries have been administrators in the ministries and armies of centralizing nation-states and managers in expanding industries.

I originally drafted this essay in 1987 when I spent a summer at the Fernand Braudel center of the State University of New York, Binghamton. The center's on-going challenging theoretical work made me feel a need to articulate the importance of incorporating the perspective of social history, that is, the life and perceptions of those without a voice, into theories of social change. I would also like to thank Professor Scott Shrewsbury for asking me whether the Scott-Popkin debate had relevance for Africa.

1

Development theory—whether in the guise of development economics, sociology, or comparative politics—categorizes social groups in the Third World according to their capacity and willingness to rationalize their economic and social behavior along Western lines. The "forward-looking," "modernizing," agents of history—the winners of the title—are government officials, military, international bureaucrats, and national and international capitalists who are strategic economic and political actors. Their positions and interests have moved center stage in the development literature, ". . . the banks provide the capital, the state provides the muscle and brains to force-march the countries into the industrialized world" (Frieden and Lake, 1987:299). The losers, by definition "backward-looking" and "traditional," tend to be peasants,[1] small-scale traders, and artisans.

There is very little room in development theory for the notion that small-scale agriculture can be efficient; that is, highly productive and ecologically sound over the long-term. Such ideas are labeled romantic, archaic populism, and bad economic policy (Kitching, 1982). The argument that simple commodity producers and petty traders along with other social groups should be involved in making agricultural policy (at least) is branded unrealistic. Peasants, artisans, and traders are expected to disappear—hopefully quietly.

The first section of this chapter demonstrates that both development and antidevelopment theories deny peasants and others historical importance and give prominence instead to the state. In so doing, various stereotypes are constructed that oversimplify the historical process. The second section reviews recent literature about peasants to try to find a balanced view. It argues that the image of peasants as "backward" is counterproductive, and that those who promote it, wittingly or unwittingly, support a structure of economic and political interests that threatens to overwhelm the agricultural base of most Third World countries.

THE THEORIES

World systems analysis and dependency theory are characterized as antidevelopment theories because they understand the fate of the Third World under capitalism as "immiseration." In Immanuel Wallerstein's conceptualization (1983), capitalism is a self-generating and expanding system that creates and recreates an international division of labor through market relations. It benefits

---

[1]The term "peasant" is used for convenience only. As shall become clear from the exposition, I do not subscribe to the notion that there is a universal category of rural cultivators.

mainly those in core or central areas of the system and those allied to them in other areas. For those in peripheral areas, however, there is mainly misery.

The earliest agents (and beneficiaries) of capital were merchants, bankers, landed elites, and yeomen turned entrepreneurs, and entrepreneurs of all kinds, along with the officials of the European states at the center. Today, a world bourgeoisie and state structures in the core of the world economy have the greatest influence within the system. Wallerstein signals a special relationship between capitalists and states over the past 400 years, ". . . the state has been a crucial mechanism for the maximum accumulation of capital. . . . in historical capitalism, capitalists relied upon their ability to utilize state-machineries to their advantage. . . ." State machineries were useful because of their power to (1) modify the social division of labor; (2) expand by swallowing up other territories, thus extending markets; (3) regulate and enforce social relations of production; (4) assist accumulation through taxation, subsidies, services, redistribution of income, and finally; (5) enforce law and order through the monopoly of legitimate force (Wallerstein, 1983:49–56).

Contradictions and conflicts among world capitalists and states move the system across time and space forcing it to expand and polarize. Productive forces develop endlessly in the center, which also shifts in time and space. For social groups in the periphery, there is nothing but increasing marginalization and immiseration. Rural populations in particular have no autonomy and are, in effect, prisoners of the system.

Arrighi, Cardoso, Evans and others (including Wallerstein) identified an intermediate position between core and periphery, a semiperipheral capitalism, in such countries as Brazil, Mexico, and other so-called newly industrializing countries. More than mere description was involved. For Cardoso and Evans, a "strong" state had helped to redefine their countries' place in the international division of labor. This signified that at least some states and some social groups had relative autonomy within the capitalist world system and that change and development could occur outside the center.

A much greater challenge to world systems analysis and dependency theory came from those who defined development and underdevelopment in terms of internal relations of production rather than an international division of labor based on market relations. Ernesto Laclau (1977) and Robert Brenner (1977) defined capitalism as a mode of production in which capitalists appropriate relative surplus value from wage laborers. They explained the fact that this type of labor organization was not universal by the persistence of other modes of production, characterized variously as precapitalist, feudal, semifeudal, peasant, colonial, African, Asian, and so on. These modes come into contact with the capitalist mode through the mediation of the state in the international relations of trade, indebtedness, and so on. Contact produces a variety of social formations, not simply the main three of core, semiperiphery, and periphery. Wallerstein describes the many varieties of labor organization, including peasant agriculture as capitalist, and explains their persistence by the need for cheap labor within the international division of labor.

While the modes of production theorists broadened the range of social inquiry by focusing on both internal and external relations of production and distribution, they were no more successful than world systems theorists in describing the various forms of articulation and interaction of individuals and groups with dominant modes. Moreover, they too were pessimistic about the outcome. Much of their analysis at field level also tended to be structuralist and abstract. Individuals tended to be treated as representative of certain stereotypes, which is apparent in the analyses of James Scott and Goran Hyden reviewed in the next section.

The early work of Henry Bernstein (1979, 1981) is noteworthy among Marxist scholars for its portrayal of rural producers as neither backward nor traditional nor isolated in their own separate mode of production. Rather, Bernstein saw simple commodity producers as full but very unequal participants in the capitalization of agriculture. The struggles between rural producers, states, and other agents of capital determined the relations of production and distribution, which, in turn, distinguished various social formations rather than the other way around. The upshot of his analysis was that the so-called capitalist transition took a variety of concrete forms, none of which was predetermined.

Outside an explicitly Marxist framework, Barrington Moore (1966) identified the commoditization of agriculture (a key concept in Wallerstein and Bernstein also) as the essential initial step in the process of industrialization and modernization of societies, whether European or Third World. For Moore, peasants along with state officials, landed elites, and bourgeoisie are pivotal groups in determining whether the path to industrialization becomes a capitalist, fascist, or communist one—three variations that he identified as successive stages of the same process. Yet, regardless of which path is followed, peasants, small traders, and artisans are portrayed as doomed once industrialization takes hold.

Liberal scholarship goes to the opposite extreme of describing development as an open process involving all groups regardless of their structural position in production or exchange. Economic development is characterized as dependent upon the initiative of individuals (rather than social relations)—producers, employers, traders, bankers, and so on—all of whom, are theoretically equally free to buy and sell in the marketplace. Liberal theory not only does not account for power and privilege in markets, it also endows all humans with the same economic logic regardless of their role in production or exchange. A further discussion of this point occurs in reference to Samuel Popkin's characterization of peasants, in the next section.

The traditional liberal view was one of a dominant civil society with the state in a minimalist role. Yet, even for classical theorists, political authority had a crucial role in legalizing property rights, legitimizing the existing division of labor and maintaining social order. Moreover, they recognized that states perform other tasks essential to a functioning economy such as establishing a social and economic infrastructure—roads, railways, ports, educational systems, health facilities, the tax structure, and subsidies—that motivates and supports private enterprise and maintains a healthy and productive workforce.

Thus, liberals and Marxists both recognized that states have a strategic function in a capitalist economy and downplayed the importance of peasants. They differed insofar as the extent to which they were willing to recognize an autonomous role for the state. In the late 1960s and 1970s, as peasants, workers, and intellectuals throughout Latin America, Asia, and Africa took up arms in anticolonial, anti-imperialist wars and movements, liberal social scientists were willing to extend the powers of states. Samuel Huntington (1968) was typical when he observed that centralized power was necessary to promote order in Third World societies—an order that he maintained was essential to their industrialization and development.

Non-Marxist structuralists (Prebisch, Furtado, Seers, Singer, and others) were even more explicit about the importance of the state for industrialization and development. One point of departure from both liberal and Marxist theory was their almost exclusive focus on the state as the agent of social change. The objective of structuralists was to reinforce national capital in opposition to international capital. Empirical analysis was openly prescriptive. Theory blended with ideology.

Structuralists shared with dependency theory the view that capitalist development was blocked in the Third World because of the hegemonic structure of international trade, investment, and aid, which they considered operated in the interests primarily of multinational corporations, banks, and the wealthy countries. During the 1970s, they advocated a restructuring of the international economic order through international institutions, invoking an image of collective bargaining between governments of the Third World banded together (in the Group of 77, for example) and the governments of the major capitalist countries. In regard to domestic policy, structuralists advocated a strong state armed with both Keynesian and supply-side policies to break down what they saw as structures of underdevelopment. The latter were identified mainly with a lack of national investment that was attributed to a stranglehold of "nonproductive" landed elites and "backward" peasants and the monopoly hold of multinational corporations on industry.

None of the foregoing analyses attach importance to small commodity producers and traders. In some theories, peasants are important in the birth processes of capitalism or socialism but they are then condemned to disappear from the stage of history. There is, however, a convergence of views about the pivotal position of states, whether as instruments of national or international capital, or as actors in their own right (see also Kohli, 1986 and Bates, 1988).

The major difference between the views characterized above is between those who explain Third World societies in terms of a blocked or incomplete capitalist transition or a separate capitalist development (Amin, 1976) and those who view the transition as just a matter of time and correct policy. For the former, socialism is evoked as the only alternative historical path. Yet, in most views, socialism also entails the forced separation of the means of production from direct producers, the transformation of rural cultivators into wage laborers and the vesting of the means of production in a separate class, whether private or public.

History, however, has not been as neat as theory—as the events in the Soviet Union and Eastern Europe clearly show. What one sees, once the blinders of ideology are removed, is an incomplete transition everywhere. Neither capitalism nor socialism exist as universal, exclusive systems. A reconceptualization of the process of social change and the respective roles of the actors is long overdue.

Geoffrey Hodgson (1984) eschews the notion that class struggle between two major polarized classes moves history forward. He sees the lines as more complex, the social actors as many, the interaction between system and actor as mutual. Hodgson treats the existence in highly industrialized and postindustrial societies of such noncapitalist forms as the family, the corporation, the grant economy, and so on, not as a sign of prevailing capitalism (as per Wallerstein) but as evidence of what he calls the "impurity principle." Although there is support and antagonism between capitalism and the other forms, their overall relationship is structured by power.

Hodgson's view suggests a more dynamic way of approaching development and underdevelopment than the overly abstract deductive approach of the macrotheorists just discussed. If small commodity forms of production have a contradictory and conditioning relationship of support and antagonism with dominant mode, it makes little sense to focus history solely on the so-called agents of capitalism. We turn now to the literature on peasants to examine how recent theorists deal with this relationship.

HISTORY'S VICTIMS?

The literature of peasant studies is, for the most part, sensitive to the relations of power between peasants, colonizers, and states. Yet, the image of peasants presented in three of the four case studies reported below seems unreal because the authors describe events from a distance rather than from the perspectives of peasants themselves. Their notions of rural cultivators are as abstract and over-generalized as those of the grand theories of social change.

Scott

In his study of the peasants of Burma and Vietnam, James Scott (1976) seeks to explain the reasons they rebelled in the 1930s in both countries. Initially, this appears to be a promising work because it takes peasants seriously and does not merely consider them objects of capitalism and the colonial state. It defends their values and rights in the face of capitalism; it acknowledges their history. In the end, however, this is not the image that emerges. Although Scott goes into great detail to recount the setting—the economic and political context for each rebellion and the events themselves—the peasants he describes appear as rein-carnations of seventeenth century French and other European peasants threat-ened by the commercialization and capitalization of agriculture. They are "peasants" in a universal sense and their history is predetermined. In his own words: "The peasant reaction to the transformation in Southeast Asia bears many of the marks of the European peasant's reaction to the shift from feudal to capitalist labor relations in the West" (Scott, 1976:67). The text is littered with such allusions.

According to Scott, timing distinguishes what happened in Europe during the transition from feudalism to capitalism from what happened in Burma and Viet-nam in the 1930s and from what is happening throughout the Third World today. What previously took three centuries to accomplish is now taking only a few decades all over the Third World. What it accomplishes is proletarianiza-tion.

Scott creates an ideal peasant, and builds a model of his behavior. He be-lieves his model is representative not only of Southeast Asia, but elsewhere as well. "While the evidence presented here is largely taken from Southeast Asia, I believe it may be representative of many peasant societies" (Scott, 1976:35).

The peasants in Scott's Burma and Vietnam are poor and middle-income rural cultivators—those with little access to land and capital, possessing mainly their family labor. They live close to the margin of existence; several bad harvests in succession can throw them off their land and over the edge. By preference, they are subsistence farmers, growing mainly their own food.

Scott's ideal peasant lives in a household that is both a unit of production and consumption.[2] Obsessed with subsistence needs, the household is willing to exploit family labor mercilessly, to pay any price for an extra piece of land, and to shun actively market involvement as too risky. This behavior Scott calls the "safety-first" principle. All other claims on the household, such as rent and taxation, are viewed in the light of this subsistence ethic. Rather than calculate the proportion of the total production that these claims take, Scott's peasant conceives of exploitation in terms of what is left over for consumption after the claims are met.

Scott's peasant surrounds himself with as many forms of social insurance as he can. He lives in a village which guarantees him a minimum of subsistence through access to communal lands, through the pooling of risks—that is, access to a communal granary—through a guaranteed right to work enough land to feed his family, through specific obligations of the wealthy to share their good harvests and good fortune, and so on. Such guarantees define the "traditional" village." If he has to enter tenancy arrangements, these, too, operate within the framework of a safety net.

The "traditional" landlord is a patron who looks after his tenants in times of need. He may remit or reduce rents after natural disasters and when yields are generally low. He may subsidize his tenants' need for credit and so on. Scott's portrayal of the "traditional" state is that of a "soft" state that collects fewer taxes during bad times, not necessarily out of charity, but because of its inability to collect them. In this passage, one gets the first glimpse of the peasants' own particular power over the state, but it is a fleeting glimpse. The overall portrait of traditional society is one of give and take. The village is conservatively egalitarian (Scott's own phrase).

Colonialism, for Scott, is the reverse image. The situation for the peasant is all give and no take. The situation for the landlord and colonial state is all take and no give. The stability of traditional village life succumbs to a state of perpetual insecurity because of (1) exposure to the wild fluctuations of prices and credit, (2) the unavailability of land as the result of its concentration in a few hands, (3) the instability of tenure under tenancy arrangements and the absence of patronage, (4) the erosion of kinship and village forms of social

---

[2] Scott cites no less an authority than Chayanov in support of this conceptualization of the peasant household, but he also takes inspiration from John Mellor, Hla Myint, Leonard Joy, and Jere Behrman.

protection, and (5) the rigidity and enforceability of state claims. The average per capita income of Southeast Asian peasants does not seem to have increased between 1910 and 1929, and may well have declined from 1900 to 1940 (Scott, 1976:560).

Yet, despite this gloomy picture, peasants flow in massive waves—from the late nineteenth century onward—into the pioneer areas of Lower Burma and Cochinchina, which are the two regions that form Scott's case study. They go in response to land improvements and expanding export markets for rice. Scott does not spend much time trying to explain this phenomenon; in fact, he devotes only one line to it (Scott, 1976:67). The reason is simple. The eager response of peasants to the opening up of export markets does not fit the image of the defensive backward-looking peasant that Scott devotes four chapters to describing. Nonetheless, these pioneers abandon the security of their traditional villages for the adventure of the unknown. Either life in them was not as stable or secure as Scott would have us believe or Southeast Asian peasants were not as subsistence-minded as he imagined.

From approximately 1911 to 1924, these pioneers work less and enjoy a higher income than their compatriots left behind, but they are subject to a great deal of uncertainty over prices and the availability of working capital and loans to tide them over bad years. Many lose their land and become tenants. Many lose their tenancy and become wage laborers. The figures do not lie; they are on their way to becoming the victims of capitalism. Under the impact of the Great Depression in the 1930s, they rebel.

Scott explains the rebellion in terms of the "traditional society": the pioneer, lacking a safety net, seeks to restore the social insurance of the society left behind. Yet, one cannot help wondering whether Scott's elaborate model of traditional society is all that necessary to explain the rebellion. Why would a pioneer have to look backward to rebel? The present was insecure whether or not the past had been secure.

A further question arises about the reason that Scott finds it necessary to homogenize the experience of the Lower Burmese and Vietnamese peasants with that of seventeenth and eighteenth century European peasants' and nineteenth and twentieth century Russian peasants' experience. The answer lies in the substance, or rather lack of substance—nowhere does Scott attempt to describe the experience from the point of view of the rural peoples who lived it. He merely tells the story in outline.

This is history from the point of view of the top down—from the perspective of colonial officials and colonists, who are the main sources of Scott's data. The fact that Burmese and Vietnamese pioneers appear as victims of capitalism in this story has more to do with Scott's interpretation of European history than with their history, which he sadly neglects.

Hyden

In his work on Tanzania (1980), Goran Hyden takes great pains to distinguish African peasants as an entirely separate and unique historical category. He attempts to explain them according to their own terms rather than from a Western perspective. Hyden is acutely aware of the problem for Western scholars who must confront other cultures and social structures armed only with abstract models and formal categories. Nevertheless, he, too, creates an overgeneralized image of the African peasant.

Hyden's starting point is totally different from Scott's. He is not impressed with the transformational and destructive powers of capitalism, at least not so far as Africa is concerned; rather, he maintains that capitalism has failed to affect African agriculture in the way it presumably affected European and American agriculture. It has not been able to expel peasants from the land nor turn them into landless tenants and rural proletariat. Nor have the colonial and postcolonial states been able to extract substantial surplus labor or value for development or other purposes. The reason lies in the power of peasant societies to maintain themselves.

Hyden's conclusions are neither drawn mainly from books, a study of colonial archives, nor the occasional visit to the field. They are the product of more than twelve years of intimate contact with East African urban and rural areas. The image of the African peasant that emerges is, therefore, even more surprising. Hyden's conceptualization is remarkably similar to Scott's.

Hyden also draws inspiration from Chayanov. He begins with the conception of a peasant mode of production to distinguish peasant society analytically from the capitalist mode of production. The household is the basic unit of production, and it is oriented almost exclusively around satisfying the consumption needs of its individual members. Households cooperate with one another, as in Scott's model, "in the belief that everyone has a right to subsistence" (Hyden, 1980:13). Most of the household's labor time is spent in subsistence farming. Although the peasant household plans for the future, its perspective is governed by what is necessary for reproduction rather than production. Hyden asserts that peasant society actively shuns both the marketplace and the modern state because it realizes that both develop at its own expense.

> History has demonstrated that the development of modern society is inconceivable without the subordination of the peasantry. As long as this process is unfinished,

the ruling classes, those who control the state, are bound to be dependent on peasants. The peasants cannot conceivably be in the forefront on the route to modern society, as such a development is bound to be at their expense. Therefore, it is only logical that the peasants resist state policies as well as a total absorption by the modern economy. Such is the logic of the peasant mode of production (1980:16).

Instead of depending on the market economy for its means of social reproduction, the peasant household depends on itself in the first place, and secondly on what Hyden terms "the economy of affection" which has a noteworthy similarity to Scott's notion of social insurance.

In the economy of affection, economic action is not motivated by individual profit alone, but is embedded in a range of social considerations that allow for redistribution of opportunities and benefits in a manner which is impossible where modern capitalism or socialism prevails and formalized state action dominates the process of redistribution (1980:19).

Both Scott and Hyden derive these notions from Karl Polanyi's concept of the reciprocal mode of economic organization in simple agrarian societies. Polanyi's notion has come under attack in recent studies of Dahomey, the agrarian society on which he based his conceptualization (Metcalf, 1987).[3]

The crux of Hyden's argument is that African peasant societies have been relatively successful in resisting the capitalist mode of production. The economy of affection has helped them preserve a measure of autonomy. It has helped them preserve their independence vis-à-vis the market and the state, and it has also had an influence on the operation of the market economy in Africa. With this argument, Hyden appears to be staking a claim for the African peasant as arbiter, manager, controller of his own history, if not destiny. The arbiter, or at least mediator of development, in Hyden's scenario, however, turns out to be the state. Hyden laments the power of African peasants to ignore its claims. He calls this the "exit option" after A. O. Hirschman (1970) and feels that it has to be eliminated. "Development is inconceivable without a more effective subordination of the peasantry to the demands of the ruling classes. The peasants must be made more dependent on the other social classes if there is going to be social progress that benefits society at large" (Hyden, 1980:31).

Hyden's conception of the African peasantry has been roundly criticized by Nelson Kasfir (1986). Another study of Guinea-Bissau (Galli and Jones, 1987)

---

[3]George Metcalf (1987) also questions its validity in regard to Fante society in the eighteenth century where "the people had imbibed entrepreneurial attitudes at an early stage and where there was no state trading as in Dahomey or Asante" (Metcalf, 1987:34).

showed its inappropriateness there on several counts. First, Guinean producers eagerly responded to world markets from at least the thirteenth century, whenever terms of trade seemed favorable. Secondly, some producers were willing to uproot themselves from village settlements to farm groundnuts on a contract basis, far from any social protection or insurance. Moreover, since the nineteenth century, youths have participated in the massive seasonal labor flow from all over the Senegambia to work in the Senegalese groundnut harvests. Finally, research into contemporary households in one region of the country (Caio) showed that the typical household consisted of a female and her children during the seven to ten years when her husband was out of the country. The woman alone was totally responsible for the basic subsistence needs of the family. She often hired the labor of young boys to help her or had recourse to the help of other women in similar situations. None of these situations can be explained by the concept of the peasant mode of production.

The most disturbing aspect of Hyden's analysis is that he is willing to sacrifice what little independence African peasants still have on the altar of social progress and in the name of socialism. Hyden's work is the example par excellence of social science in the service of developmentalism.

Popkin

Samuel L. Popkin's work, *The Rational Peasant* (1979), begins where James Scott's book left off. It is an analysis of the Vietnamese struggle for independence. Popkin disputes the narrow conception of peasant society that arises from Scott's and Hyden's works. He labels their approach (and that of others like it) the "moral economy" approach. Popkin argues that because moral economists neglect a whole range of peasant behavior, their interpretation of what is happening in peasant society is limited and sometimes distorted. His view is that:

1. Peasants are not simply security-minded; they do take risks. They make both short- and long-term investments.
2. Investments are not solely in village forms of social insurance such as in irrigation schemes; they may be private investment such as in having an extra child.
3. The forms of social insurance found in villages are often precarious because conflict as well as cooperation obtains in villages.
4. Patron-client relations are not necessarily beneficial because a power relationship is involved.

5. The notion of a minimum of subsistence is not necessarily fixed culturally but may be subject to collective bargaining.
6. Market involvement is not always harmful to peasants.

Popkin's approach is to place the peasant in a Hobbesian world of striving individuals whose primary concerns are survival and the well-being of self and family. Village, friends, and relatives are also important, but they cannot claim priority.

Popkin's village is an insecure place that provides the peasant with identity, land, and other elements of the patrimony as part of the privileges of membership. The village underwrites procedures for settling disputes and grants a measure of social protection. This is not necessarily enough to guarantee subsistence because the village is an institution based on the principle of inequality so that some members have more access than others to all of the above. This is the dynamic principle of village life that makes Popkin's peasant an insecure, self-interested, seeking individual, always trying to better his own and his family's situation. Position in the social hierarchy is the key to material well-being which is what makes him adhere to political and religious movements that offer a vision of a new and more secure form of village organization. Social position is also what opens him up to alliances with others outside his own village.

Popkin formulates two types of peasant society: the corporate village—akin to the European village until the nineteenth or early twentieth century, and still found in parts of Asia and Latin America—and the "open" village which is found in most of the Third World today. Whereas the moral economists assume that colonialism and capitalism penetrated the corporate setting and broke down its institutions to the detriment of the poor peasant, Popkin resists this characterization. For him, the changes that occurred affected neither the welfare nor the mentality of peasants in a unilinear fashion. Things did not just go from bad to worse for all peasants, nor did their behavior alter from a collective to an individualistic one. While inequality increased under capitalism, people still strove to improve their material situation, and some succeeded in doing so. For Popkin, peasants apply an "investment logic" in all social situations regardless of time or place.

Popkin's notion of peasant is, thus, as ahistorical as is Scott's. It is not derived inductively from a study of Vietnamese peasants. Popkin also begins with a deductive model and applies it in his investigation of Vietnam. He invents a universal category whose pedigree originates neither with Chayanov nor Polanyi but rather with Hobbes and liberal, neoclassical, economics.

> . . . I am above all seeking a different strategy of inquiry, one which emphasizes individual decision making and strategic interaction. As Brian Barry has stated,

economic theory (roughly equivalent to the political economy approach) is a
method of analysis: the postulation of a number of actors with certain ends and a
deductive attempt to work out how persons will act in situations which present
certain alternatives, "on the assumption that they pursue their goals
rationally." . . .

Further, I specifically focus on rationality from the point of view of the individual, for what is rational for an individual may be very different from what is
rational for an entire village or collective. I shall point out the difference between
the two views of rationality and show the conflicts between them. Indeed, it is
frequently the case that the actions of individually rational peasants in both market
and nonmarket situations do not aggregate to a "rational" village
(1979:30, 31). . . .

As already noted, the liberal view sees society as the outgrowth of individual
initiative and interactions. It is "homo economicus" writ large. It is not something apart from individuals that conditions and structures their behavior, but,
rather, it is the result of their behavior.

Instead of the (functional) view that the villages overcome and shape individual
interests of its members, I have argued that the individual interests of the villagers
shape and determine the nature and scope of village-level cooperation. The
changes that occurred during the colonial period therefore can be analyzed in
terms of structural changes introduced by the French. There is no need to posit a
change from village (or altruistic) to individual (or selfish) orientation (Popkin,
1979:132).

Implicit in Popkin's model is the notion that every individual has the same
opportunity for making decisions about investments that will secure and better
his position, yet Popkin's description of Vietnamese life is literally peppered
with instances that indicate a qualitative as well as quantitative difference in the
opportunities for betterment between rich and poor. Popkin ignores distinctions
because he says "nearly everyone, including the notables were poor and faced
constant problems of economic and physical insecurity" (1979:87). Nevertheless, he later states that ordinary peasants were barred from high positions
(page 99), that investments in the feasts that secured power and prestige were
available only to the rich (p. 100), that there was a veritable privileged class (p.
101), that notables seized communal lands for themselves (p. 103), that the
council of notables was a self-perpetuating elite (p. 106), that ordinary peasants
did not normally speak in open village meetings (especially not against notables
(p. 108)), and that the wealthier and most educated administered villages (p.
110). These statements were made in the chapter on the corporate village but
such privileges obtained in both corporate and "open villages."

The structural barriers separating rich from poor were reinforced by cultural barriers emanating from the official religion and the educational system (pp. 116, 122). Political cleavages between the emperor and his court—the mandarinate and the notables—helped put pressure on the notables to function as a group (p. 114). These, too, worked against the poor.

Popkin's characterization of the corporate village covered mainly its power structures and culture rather than its economy. For Popkin, status gave economic advantage, not the other way around. This exempts him from entering a detailed discussion of the economy of the village. There is thus no examination of the material relationship between rich and poor nor commentary on exploitation. The one paragraph he devotes to sharecropping in Tonkin, moreover, seems to come straight out of Scott (1976:156).

Nor does one get an adequate understanding of the economic relations between villages or between Vietnam and her neighbors. Popkin makes it plain that the emperor's relationship with China is significant. One is left wondering about the impact of these relations on the security, stability, and life chances of the village and each villager. For example, were there no wars during the precolonial period?

In his discussion of colonialism, Popkin attributes wealth to large landholdings and concentration of land increases during colonial rule. In Annam and Tonkin, the rich get richer and the poor get poorer while in Cochinchina, the rich get richer and the poor improve their income but hardly their position; the barrier between rich and poor remains firmly in place. Yet, in this discussion as well, the rich seem to get richer only through political manipulation. The economic basis for accumulation is barely broached. What landowners did with the land, how they organized their labor forces, how the export market was created, expanded, and so on is scarcely touched. Again, there is no discussion of exploitation. Popkin dismisses these subjects with this statement: "Economics shapes village institutions. But economics should be understood to mean not only land, labor, water and capital, but also the infrastructure of the economic system, including land titles, taxes, methods of conflict resolution and the provision of security for persons and property" (1979:182).

Without a description and analysis of the relationships between land, labor, water, and capital in the three regions, Popkin's picture of Vietnam remains incomplete. Yet, it is this very unequal structure that is the key to the politics of the villages within the three regions—the focus of Popkin's history. Because the rich and notables, the emperor, the mandarinate, and the French controlled economic resources, they dominated politics, rather than the other way around. Most of the politics Popkin describes is that of the rich and would-be rich from which he derives his model of peasant behavior—that is, those who had the opportunity for securing and bettering their position within the given structure. The point at which the ordinary peasant is able to influence his position in life and exercise any freedom of choice is in the revolutionary situation when he or she perceives the possibility of eradicating the structures that normally inhibit decisionmaking.

Popkin's work is significant because it emphasizes the continuing influence of national and subnational groups on the history of Southeast Asia despite, or rather because of, their contacts with capitalism. The ability of Vietnamese notables to increase their power and position through the manipulation of the French, and the inability of the colonial bureaucracy to gain control over villages are phenomena that are part of the continuing history of many areas in the so-called Third World. Popkin's study demonstrates the durability and continuity of the Vietnamese social formations and argues persuasively against any interpretation of the Vietnamese peasants' struggle as a vindication of a mythical past.

Hill

Polly Hill's work (1970) embraces some of the very subjects that Popkin avoided. She evokes in detail the local disposition of land, labor, and capital in West Africa in the terms described to her by her informants. Her field research concentrated on the concrete conditions and realities of indigenous economics (her own term); she eschews the very idea of dealing abstractly with social and economic relations; in her own words, she leaves that to others.[4]

Hill considers her work to be that of filling in gaps of knowledge. She deals with areas that are ignored by macrotheories, government reports, national accounts, and, most conspicuously, by national plans. She begins her work with a quote from Tolstoy that merits repeating because it greatly supports the argument being developed in this essay (and book).

> The new arrangements on his farm absorbed him as completely as though there would never be anything else in his life. He read the books lent him by Sviazhsky

---

[4]Stephen Hymer evaluated her work in *Studies in Rural Capitalism in West Africa* (1970) in this way:

> The central feature of Polly Hill's framework is the relationship between *capital* and *capitalists*. . . . As the studies in this book show, the forms of capital represented by cocoa trees, cattle, fishing nets, manure, lorries, and so forth, play a crucial role in indigenous economies. . . . Polly Hill's major discovery is that, contrary to the usual view of an amorphous peasantry, the accumulation of capital in indigenous West African economies has been accompanied by the emergence of specialists who own and manage the capital stock—a 'class' of rural capitalists. She has, therefore, concentrated on the behavioral characteristics of these capitalists. . . . (1970:xviii).

and, having ordered various others that he required, he read political economy and socialistic works on the same subject, but, as he had expected, found nothing in them related to his undertaking. In the political economy books—in Mill, for instance, whom he studied first and with great ardour, hoping every minute to find an answer to the questions that were engrossing him—he found only certain laws deduced from the state of agriculture in Europe; but he could not for the life of him see why these laws, which did not apply to Russia, should be considered universal. . . . Political economy told him that the laws by which Europe had developed and was developing her wealth were universal and absolute. Socialist teaching told him that development along these lines leads to ruin. And neither of them offered the smallest enlightenment as to what he, Levin, and all the Russian peasants and landowners were to do with their millions of hands and millions of acres, to make them as productive as possible for the common good (1970:iv).

Polly Hill's answer is that peasants already know. For her, West Africans are born entrepreneurs; that is, they know how to organize and manage capital and labor in response to market opportunities. (She offers no historical explanation for their capitalism nor does she postulate a presumed precapitalist natural or moral economy). West African capitalists not only exploit their own labor but, in most cases, hire that of others, and they reinvest in new technologies (most of them) and in expanding their businesses (all of them), whether in fishing, cattle-raising, or cash cropping.

Hill considers rural capitalism to be essentially an unequal phenomenon. In all the cases she examines, there is an unequal social structure with capital concentrated in a few hands. Unlike Popkin's study, however, Hill's work demonstrates the qualitative differences in behavior between the large and small Ghanaian migrant cocoa farmers, between the seine net owners of Ewe beach, the Accra plains kraal owners and their Fulani herdsmen, the Katsina tobacco growers, and the Batagarawa groundnut farmers:

The small cocoa-farmer, for example, works his own land with his own labour. The large cocoa-farmer, on the other hand, must acquire land over and above what he has rights over under the traditional system and he often must hire labour to work his land. He must thus usually develop the organizing and entrepreneurial skills of investing in land, managing labour, and co-ordinating production on a relatively large scale. In learning these techniques he also acquires certain flexibilities and skills which, along with his capital, enable him to diversify into new industries or introduce new techniques. . . . Economic producers in West Africa are, therefore, not *amorphous* but *differentiated,* and analysis of their behaviour must distinguish between the various categories: landless labourers, small capitalists, larger capitalists and, in some cases, substantial capitalists who differ in horizons and skills and, therefore, in performance (Hymer, 1970:xviii).

Hill, herself, generally avoids all questions of class distinctions and even goes so far as to deny the applicability of Western notions of class in regard to the Hausa farmers of Batagarawa. It is important, however, to note that she deliberately excludes the ruling class and the emergence of an elite based on higher education in her discussion. Hill's explanation of wealth among the Hausa farmers includes both objective as well as subjective factors. For instance, she cites such structural causes as inheritance of large farms and having a large family; that is, the primary labor force. Among the subjective factors are good organizational skills, good luck, trustworthiness, and, thus, access to credit, a capacity for hard work, and an ability to run off-farm enterprises.

The situation is the reverse for the poor farmers and those who lose their lands entirely. Hill acknowledges that the economic system is weighted in favor of those who start off with the above-mentioned structural advantages. She insists, nevertheless, that having such advantages is short-lived; that is, that they extend only over the life of the individual family head because, upon his death, the farms are divided among his sons.

One obvious limitation of Hill's work, then, is that it reflects only the contemporary economic situation of the groups that she studies. Although she collects data on the history of the institutions she is describing, her work in no way pretends to give a historical account of West African capitalism. A historical study of the Hausas of Batagarawa would, for example, include the origins of the continuously cultivated farms which were the material bases of wealth in the society; it would show to what extent lineages have been able to maintain this and other capital stock intact; to what extent a poor individual had a chance to better his position; and the way in which the very small ruling class, as well as the emerging, highly educated elite, evolved.

Hill also neglects the relationship of West African capitalists (and those who work with them and for them) to the state and to local authorities. As just noted, she deliberately excludes the ruling class from her study of the Batagarawa Hausas. Such aspects of West African society can be ignored, however, only at the expense of knowing the political dynamics of the economies she describes. As Popkin skillfully demonstrated, local elites in Vietnamese society reinforced their economic power through access to the higher echelons in their villages. The same may have been true for West African capitalists, or they may have secured their economic base through access to credit and patronage from outside the village.

Hill's researches are limited by her failure to include the external, including the international, context in which these rural capitalists operate, and which necessarily influenced their decisionmaking. Rural capitalists were not only affected by world market prices, which Hill notes, but also by the availability of credit or other inputs and by the organization of markets on a world scale. To summarize, Hill has shied away from a political economy approach to peasant history by restricting her horizon to the immediate setting of the West African capitalists. Although one can learn the minutiae of local economies, one can never have a complete understanding of their rationale without a knowledge of the historical, political, and international context in which they are set.

An Alternative Approach

Implicit in this critique of the researches of Hill, Popkin, Hyden, and Scott on rural cultivators is an alternative perspective, whose outlines are by now clear and can be summarized briefly in the following points.

First, there is no such thing as a peasant mode of production. Rural cultivators are a very diverse group. Their diversity is the result of the enormous variety of physical, economic, and social environments in which they live and the way in which they respond to them. Differentiation among individuals and groups derives mainly from unequal access to social, economic, and political opportunities. It makes little sense not only to lump such a diverse and stratified group together in one universal category for purposes of analysis, but also to analyze their behavior in the abstract. This is Hill's point. ". . . and at all costs we must avoid generalizations about different types of peasants who are as different as chalk from cheese" (1970:28).

Second, despite their differences, rural producers, as indeed all people, are interested in the security and well-being of themselves and their families and others close to them (including their villages). For this reason, they will undertake cooperative actions (including not only mutual aid but also revolts and rebellions) when individual action does not appear more effective. Such behavior is not generalizable, however, into a moral economy nor pure individualism as it is fundamentally conditioned by historical experience and contemporary institutions. Analysis must account for both.

For example, Stephen Orvis distinguishes peasant political activity in Africa from that in Asia and Latin America as being mainly "private and individual, operating within existing patron-client networks to obtain state resources for individual and/or community use" (1988:1). Such networks also occur in Latin America (Galli, 1981) but, in Africa as opposed to Latin America, national peasant organizations are rare. The reasons have more to do with history and institutions than with individual psychology.

Third, rural producers cannot be said, as a whole, to be psychologically, culturally, or otherwise predisposed toward subsistence and opposed to accumulation. Generally, as individuals and as groups, they seize the opportunities available to them. Galli and Jones (1987) used the term "survival strategies" to describe a range of peasant responses to the general lack of economic opportunities within Guinea-Bissau at the time of this writing. (In his study of the Kisii district of Kenya, Orvis (1988) coins the term "strategies of reproduction.") These responses included, among others, increasing production and smuggling it across the border, immigration to zones of opportunity, and reducing production. The differences had less to do with individual preference than to location of producers and numbers of active workers in their households.

With the opening of markets in Guinea-Bissau, a strata of rural capitalists has begun to plant fruit, cashew nuts, and even staple crops along river banks, but their enterprise is in danger of being strangled because of a lack of transport and credit (Galli, 1989b). Opportunities are not open to everyone. The basic structure of rural societies, as all societies, is unequal, which accounts for much of what is generalized as "peasant behavior."

Fourth, inequality perpetuates itself through privilege and power, which have historical as well as contemporary roots. In Hill's description of Hausa agriculture, the large farmers obtain their wealth by storing their grain and groundnuts until they can obtain the best price on the market, which is possible because their production of grain is large enough to sustain them throughout the year. Poor farmers, however, must sell their grain and groundnuts immediately after harvests to pay debts, taxes, and to meet other financial obligations. The prices they receive are the lowest prices of the year. They usually sell to the large farmers who have granaries and, during the lean season, buy grain from the very same farmers who charge them much above the price at which they sold the very same grain. In the case of groundnuts, the poor farmer does not have seed stored for planting and must buy it from the large farmers, paying this debt with double the amount of groundnuts at harvest-time. In these ways, the poor farmer effectively ends up working for the rich one. *Internal* exploitation, such as that just described, is often at the root of what otherwise might be seen as subsistence production, avoidance of the market, and so on.

Fifth, unequal, *external* structures that influence peasant opportunities and, therefore, behavior include the markets for credit, land, labor, technology, and transport organized at regional, national, and international levels. Political as well as cultural agencies such as religious officials intervene to support clients. The clients who receive economic privileges, however, tend to be a local elite rather than the majority of rural producers. In the case of Guinea-Bissau mentioned above, credit for agricultural inputs, machinery, and transport was being given to a group of government officials, their families, and friends rather than to the enterprising producers who were turning their small-scale plots into medium-size plantations (Galli, 1989b).

Robert Bates has persuasively argued that African states have generally brought havoc to the majority of African peasants by rigging markets and other economic opportunities in favor of clients and urban populations (1981, 1983, see also Williams, 1981). In their eagerness to secure revenues, African states squelch the dynamic elements in rural societies by turning the terms of trade against them, by ignoring production needs, and by cutting off supplies of essential consumer goods (see also Galli and Jones, 1987). What Hyden and others describe as moral economy, Bates (1986) and others attribute to resistance to state efforts at control and domination. Therefore, of the contemporary institutions influencing behavior, states and the international institutions that support them are among the most important.

In contrast to the expectations of the macrotheories analyzed in the first section, states in Africa effectively block rural capitalism. See, for example, the studies by Williams (1976, 1986), Berry (1984), Richards (1985), Galli and Jones (1987). According to Piotr Dutkiewicz and Robert Shenton:

> The post-colonial states of Africa and the ruling groups which govern them are not, as Hyden maintains, outgrowths of the family or household and its 'economy of affection.' Rather they have come into direct and intensifying contradictions with the family/household based units of agricultural production which provided the wherewithal to finance the activities of those states and ruling groups. In so doing, the ruling groups diminished the productive capacity of their own sources of social reproduction (1986:114).

A critical understanding of this apparent contradiction requires going beyond merely positing a peasant-state dichotomy. It means analyzing the relations of power between the various groups constituting state and society. These relations include alliances with other governments and international agencies that generally support the state with development loans, projects, and programs.

Sixth, despite the odds against them, rural cultivators have not slipped quietly away, either in Africa or elsewhere. Indeed, this is one of Hyden's major points. They are not, however, the obstacles to progress that he and others imply, which is the point of Hill's book (1970). Global evidence from the FAO show small-scale land holdings to be highly productive—more so than large land holdings (Cornia, 1985). Case studies reinforce this view (see above; see also Hartmann and Boyce, 1981, 1983; Clough and Williams, 1984; Hill, 1986, Bernal, 1986). In most of these studies, small land holders were in direct competition with large ones but did not receive similar support. Had they enjoyed similar access to capital, land, labor, technology, and transport markets that the local elite did, it is likely that their productivity would have been much higher.

In regard to *industrialization,* Weaver (in this volume) demonstrates that contemporary industrial technology does not depend upon masses of uprooted peasants for a labor force as of yore. Small-scale agriculture per se is, therefore, no obstacle to industrialization. Far from being a structural barrier, a prosperous agricultural sector can be a stimulant by providing a large market for a range of consumer and capital goods. It is, therefore, a prerequisite for a diversified, decentralized industrial program. This appears to one of the lessons of China in the 1980s (Riskin, 1987).

Gavin Kitching (1982) drew a very different conclusion in his analysis of the China of the 1970s. He argued that large-scale industrialization and urbanization was a necessary, prior phase to the creation of a "smaller-scale, more democratic and less alienated world under communism" (1982:180). These were needed to provide the high rates of saving and investment necessary to raise productivity. Kitching invoked Marx and the almost thirty years of Mao's rule to substantiate this thesis.

Shanin (1984) showed that Marx also conceived of alternative, even peasant paths to socialism, particularly in his writings on Russia. Riskin (1987) demonstrated that Mao's strategy was counterproductive and led to an undersupply of essential consumer and capital goods in the countryside and an oversupply of large-scale capital and intermediate goods. The result was severe underconsumption for both workers and peasants, including food shortages. There was, however, no shortage of funds for heavy industry.

By giving households the responsibility of producing the crops best suited for each area as well as locally needed goods and services, the Chinese leadership since Mao has been trying to stimulate a prosperous internal market for light consumer goods and, eventually, durables. Statistics for the initial period of change showed a dramatic rise in productivity in the rural sector, although most of the rise came from off-farm activity (see Riskin, 1987).

Seventh, rural producers have important physical and economic knowledge of their environment that bureaucrats, research scientists, and, often, extension agents lack. Recognition of this, however, threatens the structure of political, academic, and material interests that development theory supports (Richards, 1985; Galli and Jones, 1987).

Finally, rural producers have power. Because their struggles are perceived to be on the losing side of the world-historical process, macrosocial theorists make the mistake of ignoring the significance of the conflict between "modernizers" and rural cultivators. Power does not flow in one direction only. Popular struggles condition the activities of national and international bourgeoisie, state and international bureaucracies. One only has to recall the World Bank discovery of peasants in 1973, the FAO studies on their farming systems, and IMF support for their interests in many structural adjustment programs. This does not, however, mean that rural producers have won a victory. "Popular resistance may not represent sufficiently coherent forces to pose an effective alternative to the state as currently constituted. However, the crisis of the ruling class hegemony provides significant openings for advancing the positions of democratic organizations and influencing the direction of reconstruction" (Beckman, 1988:24). It has been argued in this essay that power relations are at the base of what is defined as development and who are seen as its principal actors. Conscious or unconscious adherence to mechanistic theories of social change, with their one-sided focus on bureaucrats, technicians, national and international bourgeoisie—the so-called agents of development—threatens to preempt new forms of social reconstruction and development.

CONCLUSION

That there is a thin line dividing theory and ideology is not a new argument. Writing in 1982, Eric Wolf made this point in an eloquent attack on social science in general and sociology and anthropology in particular. Wolf lamented the deliberate separation of social science from political economy and, as a consequence, the shallowness of theoretical constructs in anthropology:

> The concept of autonomous, self-regulating and self-justifying society and culture has trapped anthropology inside the bounds of its own definitions. Within the halls of science, the compass of observation and thought has narrowed while outside the inhabitants of the world are increasingly caught up in continent-wide and global change (1982:18).

Following Hodgson, this study suggests that the conceptualization of capitalism and socialism as autonomous and self-regulating systems has trapped political economy into misinterpreting the relationship of capitalism and socialism with other formations—and that the basis of these relationships is power. Moreover, it argues that such conceptualizations have served well a particular set of social groups within the world economy; in other words, more than tunnel vision has been involved.

Even Marxist theory, which demystifies capital and delegitimizes the so-called modern state, acts as an ideology when it is invoked to justify the role of the socialist state in "primitive socialist accumulation" (see Saith, 1985). It is one of the merits of world systems analysis that even though it focuses on state power, it neither legitimizes the role of the state under capitalism or socialism. Wallerstein (1983) takes the position that once the leaders of antisystemic (anti-capitalist and anti-imperialist) movements seize power they find themselves in the position of reinforcing the capitalist order through the exercise of the five functions outlined by him (above). They become caught in the system.

One does not need to take such a deterministic view to note that bureaucrats are easily caught in a logic of extending bureaucratic power and, by extensions, their own individual privileged status. State officials, international civil servants, and social scientists share with capitalists a stake in the system and subscribe to a conscious ideology that reinforces their position. That ideology, as noted in the introduction, derives from the notion that progress can and should be managed, which, in turn, derives from the separation of intellectual from manual work. The ideology sets cadres apart as guardians of the "national interest," encouraging them to think that they know better than producers what and how to produce. It justifies interventions by personnel from such agencies as the International Monetary Fund, the World Bank, and US AID, whose raison d'etre is to set standards for management, to supply training or monies for training and to supervise government and business administration.

The creators and promoters of developmentalism are legion and include not only those who aspire to office but also those who train, up-grade, or otherwise serve to expand state power. These include the social scientists who are engaged in research on the state; academicians who are involved in training future political leaders; consultants sent by international "donors" to advise on national budgets—to identify and prepare development projects and to man the projects; and, finally, the "donors" themselves, who finance the extension of the state through development projects. Instead of the populations who must live under them, the "donors" become the ultimate legitimizers of Third World governments through their financial and ideological support. The irony is that these populations show more ingenuity and initiative than their so-called rulers, as Polly Hill's work indicates. Despite the economic, political, and cultural domination of this structure of interests, rural populations show a remarkable resiliency. Contrary to what social scientists would have one believe, rural producers have not limited their options simply to resignation or rebellion.[5]

References

Amin, Samir. 1974. *Accumulation on a World Scale.* New York: Monthly Review Press.
———. 1976. *Unequal Development.* New York: Monthly Review Press.

---

[5]According to Margaret Levi (1987), James Scott's recent work, *The Weapons of the Weak* (1987), recognizes numerous forms of peasant resistance. Levi has also made this the subject of her own book. I comment on the applicability to Guinea-Bissau of the model she constructs (Galli, 1989).

Bates, Robert, 1986. "Some Contemporary Orthodoxies in the Study of Agrarian Change" In A. Kohli (ed.), *The State and Development in the Third World,* Princeton: Princeton University Press.

————. 1981. *Markets and States in Tropical Africa: the Basis of Agricultural Policies.* Berkeley: University of California Press.

————. 1983. *Essays on the Political Economy of Rural Africa.* Cambridge: Cambridge University Press.

————. (ed.) 1988. *Towards a Political Economy of Development: a Rational Choice Perspective.* Berkeley: University of California Press.

Beckman, Bjorn. 1988. "Peasants and Democratic Struggles in Nigeria." *Review of African Political Economy* (41).

Bernal, F. 1986. *The Sociology of Rural Life: Eastern Cundinamarca.* Draft D.Phil. thesis, St. Antony's College, Oxford University.

Bernstein, H. 1981. "Concepts for the Analysis of Contemporary Peasants" in R. Galli (ed.), *The Political Economy of Rural Development.* Albany: State University Press of New York.

————. 1979. "The Sociology of Development and the Development of Sociology" in D. Lehmann (ed.), *Development Theory: Four Critical Essays.* London: Frank Cass.

Berry, S. 1984. "The Food Crisis and Agrarian Change." *African Studies Review.* 27 (2).

Brenner, R. 1977. "The Origins of Capitalist Development: a Critique of Neo-Smithian Marxism." *New Left Review* (104).

Brett, E. A. 1985. *The World Economy Since 1945.* London: Macmillan.

Clough, P. and G. Williams. 1984. "The World Bank and the Rural Poor in Northern Nigeria," Oxford, (mimeo).

Cornia, G. A. 1985. "Farm Size and Land Yields and the Agricultural Production Function: an Analysis for 15 Developing Countries." *World Development* 13 (4).

Cumings, B. 1981. "Interest and Ideology in the Study of Agrarian Politics," *Politics and Society* 10 (4).

DeJanvry, Alain. 1981. *The Agrarian Question in Latin America.* Baltimore: Johns Hopkins University Press.

Dutkiewicz, P. and R. Shenton. 1986. "The African Crisis" *Review of African Political Economy,* 37 (December).

Frieden, Jeffry and D. Lake (eds.) 1987. *International Political Economy.* New York: St. Martin's Press.

Galli, Rosemary E. 1981. "Colombia: Rural Development as Social and Economic Control" in Galli (ed.), *The Political Economy of Rural Development.* Albany, NY: State University of New York Press.

————. 1986. "Amilcar Cabral and Rural Transformation in Guinea-Bissau: a Preliminary Critique." *Rural Africana* (25–26).

————. 1987. "On Peasant Productivity: the case of Guinea-Bissau," *Development and Change* 18 (1).

————. and Jocelyn Jones. 1987. *Guinea-Bissau: Politics, Economics and Society.* London and New York: Pinter Publishers and Columbia University Press.

————. 1989a. "The Political Economy of Guinea-Bissau: Second Thoughts." *Africa* 59 (3).

————. 1989b. *Development Strategy in Guinea-Bissau: the European Community's*

Contribution. Bissau: Government of Guinea-Bissau and Delegation of the Commission of the European Communities.

————. 1991. "Liberalization is not Enough: Structural Adjustment and Peasants in Guinea-Bissau." *Review of African Political Economy* (49).

Hartmann, B. and Boyce, J. 1981. "Needless Hunger" in Galli, (ed.), *The Political Economy of Rural Development.* Albany: SUNY Press.

————. 1983. A Quiet Violence. London: Zed Press.

Hill, Polly. 1970. *Studies in Rural Capitalism in West Africa.* Cambridge: Cambridge University Press.

————. 1986. Economics On Trial. Cambridge: Cambridge University Press.

Hirschman, Albert O. 1970. *Exit, Voice and Loyalty.* Cambridge, Mass: Harvard University Press.

Huntington, Samuel P. 1968. *Political Order in Changing Societies.* New Haven: Yale University Press.

Hodgson, Geoffrey. 1984. *The Democratic Economy.* Harmondsworth: Penguin Publishers.

Hyden, Goran. 1980. *Beyond Ujamaa: Underdevelopment and an Uncaptured Peasantry.* Berkeley: University of California Press.

Hymer, S. 1970. "Foreword" in Polly Hill, *Studies in Rural Capitalism.*

Kasfir, Nelson. 1986. "Are Peasants Self-Sufficient?" *Development and Change* 17 (2).

Kitching, G. 1982. *Development and Underdevelopment in Historical Perspective.* London: Methuen.

Kohli, Atul. 1986. *The State and Development in the Third World.* Princeton: Princeton University Press.

Laclau, Ernesto. 1977. *Politics and Ideology in Marxist Theory.* London: New Left Books.

Levi, Margaret. 1987. "Weapons of the Strong and How the Weak Resist Them." Chicago: Annual meeting of the Midwest Political Science Association.

Marx, K. and F. Engels. 1959. *The Marx-Engels Reader.* New York: Norton.

Metcalf, G. 1987. "Gold, Assortments and the Trade Ounce: Fante Merchants and the Problem of Supply and Demand in the 1770s" *Journal of African History* 28 (1).

Moore, Jr., Barrington. 1966. *Social Origins of Dictatorship and Democracy.* Boston: Beacon Press.

Mouzelis, Nicos. 1980. "Modernisation, Underdevelopment, Uneven Development: Prospects for a Theory of Third-World Formations," *Journal of Peasant Studies* 7 (3).

Orvis, S. 1988. "A Model of Peasant Response to State Policy: Social Reproduction and Development in Kenya." Washington, D.C.: Annual meeting of the American Political Science Association.

Popkin, Samuel L. 1979. *The Rational Peasant.* Berkeley: University of California Press.

Richards, Paul. 1985. *Indigenous Agricultural Revolutions.* London: Hutchinson.

Riskin, Carl. 1987. *China's Political Economy.* Oxford: Oxford University Press.

Saith, Ashwani (ed.). 1985. "The Agrarian Question in Socialist Transitions." *The Journal of Development Studies* 22 (1).

Scott, James C. 1976. *The Moral Economy of the Peasant: Rebellion and Subsistence in Southeast Asia.* New Haven: Yale University Press.

————. 1985. *Weapons of the Weak: Everyday Forms of Peasant Resistance.* New Haven: Yale University Press.

Shanin. T. 1984. *Late Marx and the Russian Road.* London: Routledge.

Skocpol, T. 1979. *States and Revolution.* Princeton: Princeton University Press.

Strange, Susan. 1988. *States and Markets.* London and New York: Pinter Publishers.

Wallerstein, Immanuel. 1983. *Historical Capitalism.* London: Verso.

Warren, Bill. 1980. *Imperialism: Pioneer of Capitalism.* London: Verso.

Weaver, Frederick S. 1991. in this volume.

Wharton, C. 1969. *Subsistence Agriculture and Economic Development.* Chicago: Aldine.

Williams, Gavin. 1976. "Taking the Part of the Peasants" in Gutkind, P. and Wallerstein, I., *The Political Economy of Contemporary Africa.* Beverly Hills: Sage.

————. 1979. "Imperialism and Development," *World Development.*

————. 1986. "Primitive Accumulation for Africa?". *Development and Change.* 18 (4).

Wolf, E. 1982. *Europe and the People Without History.* Berkeley, Calif: University of California Press.

World Bank. 1981. *Accelerated Development in Sub-Saharan Africa.* Washington, DC: World Bank.

Chapter 2

Conditions of People's Development in Postcolonial Africa

Lars Rudebeck

INTRODUCTION

Development and democracy are frequently considered to be somehow linked to each other. The validity of the assumption hinges on the way development is conceptualized. If development is viewed either strictly in terms of GNP per capita and related indicators or, more qualitatively, in terms of the level of the forces of production, then there obviously is no necessary connection between development and democratically legitimate state power. Both past and present history provide ample evidence that economic development and democracy do not necessarily go hand in hand.

If, however, development is conceived more in accordance with everyday life experience in terms of social and material security (less insecurity) and human dignity, then it cannot be disconnected from notions of democracy and freedom. The term "people's development" in the title of this chapter stands for development in this sense—a better life, as they themselves define it, for that majority of people who suffer from the present order of things in the Third World. Development, in this sense, necessarily includes equalization of economic and political power, both as a goal and as a method. Thus the focus, in this chapter, upon the role of democracy in development.

At the most general level, this text is intended as a contribution to the ongoing debate over the interplay between political action and the structural determinants of politics. The concrete focus is on the nature and significance of the political transformation that occurs in the transition from armed anticolonial liberation movement to sovereign state power in the juridical sense. The empirical section treats the cases of Guinea-Bissau and Mozambique, both of which countries placed the achievement of people's development through the exercise

29

of people's power (*poder popular*) at the top of the political agenda when independence was won. In both countries, however, things have so far turned out differently. Why, how, and with what implications for development?

The analysis proceeds in three parts. Part one is a note on the structure of the theoretical debate on the failure of states to develop post-colonial Africa[1] plus my own contribution of an analytical framework. Part two looks at what happens in Guinea-Bissau and Mozambique, in the transitional period, to the social basis of power, to the internal structuring of state power, to the policies resulting from its exercise, and to the links between those three levels of societal reality. Part three is a comparative discussion, concluding with a final note on development and democracy.

THEORETICAL CONSIDERATIONS

A Note on the Structure of the Debate

Two major strands of thought are discernible in current theoretical attempts to explain the general weakness of state power in transforming the social and economic basis of accumulation in postcolonial Africa. The two cut across the conventional social divide between actor and structure-oriented explanations. The first strand uses the concept of political culture perceived as the aggregate attitudes of individuals; the second uses the concept of socioeconomic group or class. Cross tabulating culture-class with actor-structure yields the following two-dimensional matrix (Fig. 1).

Block 1 stands for descriptions/explanations that focus on the cultural attitudes of actors as the primary independent variables in development. Within the modernization school of thought prevalent in political development studies, this type of description/explanation is typically combined with an emphasis on structural differentiation and specialization of political systems, as represented by block 3. Note that in this analysis even the structural characteristics of the social system are culturally defined in terms of the values, goals, and prefer-

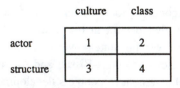

Figure 1   Cross-tabulation of culture-class and actor-structure.

ences of the actors making up the system. The earlier works of Gabriel Almond (1960; with G. Powell, 1966) and David Apter (1965, 1968) are characteristic of this kind of structural functionalism.[2] Despite two decades of critical discussion, the emphasis on culture and political structure, only weakly linked analytically to socioeconomic structure, remains the hallmark of western political science in regard of development.[3] Social scientists such as Richard Sandbrook (1986) and Göran Hydén (1980, 1983, 1986) may be characterized as straddling blocks 1 and 2/4 because of their laborious attempts to harmonize different approaches in trying to combine actor/culture oriented approaches with an interest in class-rooted determinants of political action. The institutional approach of Theda Skocpol's work (1979; with E. Amenta, 1986) suggests another way to achieve such a combination.

The class and structural perspectives of blocks 2 and 4 are characteristic of the political economy approach to the state in the Third World. Neomarxist analysis, dependency theory, and analyses taking the internal dynamics of different societies more directly into account have all contributed to these perspectives. See, for example, Hamza Alavi's article (1972) on the state in postcolonial societies, an early landmark in this theoretical development, and Elsenhans (1988), as possibly providing a new departure. Journals such as the recently established *African Journal of Political Economy* as well as the *Review of African Political Economy* exemplify efforts to bring the internal dynamics of societies into theoretical focus without overlooking the international context.[4] The theoretical point of departure of these perspectives is the class structure generated both nationally and internationally by the predominant system of production and accumulation, which by no means excludes an interest in political actors as important objects of analysis. Within this tradition, however, actors are not defined primarily in terms of cultural attitudes or positions in culturally defined systems, but rather in terms of their roles in the dynamics of confrontation between social (class) forces.

Block 3 represents, for instance, attempts to correlate positions along various types of democracy scales with selected socioeconomic and cultural variables. A model example can be found in Seymor Lipset's earlier work (1960).

Block 4 represents works that focus more or less deterministically upon socioeconomic structure variables in explaining development, thus tending to neglect the dialectics linking social structure and action. Moore (1966) is a classic historical sociology study of political transformation (not on Africa) within this tradition.

My own perspective is guided by the view that action occurs on a "stage" structured by class, institutions, and culture. At any given point in historical space and time, this structure limits the possible choices of political action and is, at the same time, affected by the choices actually made. This places my work close to the middle of the matrix, although paradigmatically rooted in the structure and class areas of the theoretical space captured by the two cross-cutting dimensions.

An Analytical Image

The following is an attempt to give an integral image of analytical levels crucial to the specific study of the development/political structure problem within a political economy perspective. This includes the crucial issue of democracy. The abstract image may appear simple. It is not intended to be simplistic, however, but a meaningful abstraction of real-life complexity.

Each level of the image is characterized by an analytically distinguishable quality, more or less clear-cut, more or less complex. Each quality varies (and is thus a "variable") along a dimension drawn as a rough scale.

The three levels (dimensions) included in the image are:

1. The social basis of the state
2. Political structure
3. Orientation of actual policies

Note that the factor of *state ideology,* socialist or other, is not included as a separate dimension. For our present purposes, it may be regarded as subsumed under "orientation of actual policies." It is tempting, however, to try to include two other dimensions in the image: namely the degree of *international autonomy* and *the cultural basis of the state.* Reasons for dealing separately with those two crucial dimensions will be given after presentation of the analytical image itself.

The Three-Level Image

The three levels/dimensions of our image are drawn from the bottom upward, which appears logical enough in a political economy perspective.

With the aid of Figure 2, we can do at least two things: (1) we can distinguish fundamental dimensions of actually followed paths of development or societal transformation, and (2) we can grasp relationships, supportive or contrary, between the various dimensions, both at given points in time, and as they change over time.

It is possible, too, to sketch a number of different types or models of societies and processes of transformation, where the differences between the types are defined in terms of different positions along the three dimensions.

An analytical image of important levels of societies

Orientation of actual policies	(world) market profitability			politically defined needs
Political structure: degree of power distribution	autocratic, elitist hierarchy	strong state, various kinds	popular mobilization	equal power distribution
	vertical power structure	of roots in society	democracy (people's power)	horizontal power structure
Social basis of the state	landlords,	intermediate strata		peasants, workers,
	capitalists			"marginalized" people

Figure 2   An analytical image of important levels of societies.

Certain types of relationships between different positions along the dimensions can be logically posited, should this be of interest. In reality, however, actually occurring interaction results in combinations that are neither mechanical nor one-way, but manifold and often unexpected. Let us begin by briefly discussing the three levels/dimensions one by one.

The Social Basis of the State

However complex the class structure is in real societies (and it is complex), the fairly simple bottom dimension of our image may still be good enough for our present, initial, purposes.

At the summits of many Third World societies, we may roughly discern large landowners of a more or less feudal type and/or various kinds of larger capitalists (including landowners), either national or international or both.

There are also richly diversified intermediate strata made up on the one hand of owners of medium and small enterprises, medium and small farmers, merchants, and artisans, and on the other hand administrative officials, military people, teachers, other intellectuals, and salaried employees at various levels. Most intellectuals belong in the category of salaried employees, but there are also lawyers, medical doctors, writers, artists, and so forth who function as independent enterprisers or freelancers.

Postcolonial societies without large landowners whose indigenous capitalist class is very small are also numerous, especially in Africa. Guinea-Bissau is an excellent example of this. Mozambique is another example, although not as representative. In such countries, politicians, bureaucrats, technocrats, and military people occupy the top positions in the hierarchies of power (and glory) through their monopolies of state power. Thus, they are not always "intermediate" in the strict sense of the world, if the perspective is limited to specific countries or societies. Still, their ancestry is most often in the intermediate strata of the not so distant colonial societies.

In some Third World countries, and not only in the so-called NIC ("newly industrializing" countries), there is also a large and growing working class. For African conditions, the Mozambican working class is quite large, although not growing in the 1980s. In many countries, however, including Mozambique, peasant producers still constitute the largest class, often dominated by large landowners or, as in large parts of Africa, including most parts of Mozambique as well as Guinea-Bissau, integrated into various more or less "traditional" forms of production. Although "traditional" in some respects, these forms of production have invariably been transformed by their contacts with colonialism through history. Whatever surpluses they produce are usually conveyed to the world market by way of complicated, and frequently extremely unequal, mechanisms of exchange.

In many societies, there are large and growing groups of marginalized people, who are living or barely surviving outside the officially established or recognized structures of society. The strength at the class level of these various groups and strata is related to their productive capacity and to their capacity to direct and control both production in a strict sense and social reproduction in a broader sense. Such capacity is transformed into political or state power, through confrontation with the capacities of others, by way of the political structure of society, and in ways affected also by specific cultural characteristics.

Political Structure

While the social *basis* of the state is "basic" in a literal sense, political structure is the crucial variable for our present purposes. Even in a simplified manner, it cannot be easily grasped by way of only one single dimension.

In my own attempt to grasp this dimension, I have been struggling with various combinations of expressions of qualities such as vertical/horizontal

(unequal/equal) power structure, degree of participation or popular mobilization, the strength of the state in different senses, the scope and direction of state
interventions (economy/non-economy) etc. . .—all directly or indirectly related
to the degree of democracy variously understood, but all also more easily talked
about than operationalized.[5] The variable does not lend itself easily to being
conceptually captured, loaded as it is with theoretical, philosophical, ideological, and political implications and undertones of all possible kinds.

Here, easy operationalizability is sacrificed for conceptual simplicity and
relative clarity, by letting degree of distribution of power (unequal/equal) be the
basic variable, following the "ideal type" way of reasoning. This can also be
formulated as the degree of equality (or inequality) of power, no distinction
being made as yet between different types of power (social, economic, political).

We are facing the classical paradox of democracy: necessary power versus
necessary freedom. At the one point of this scale, we find autocratic, elitist,
hierarchical, vertical structures of power—based, in the extreme case, on nothing but violence. Around the middle, we find structures combining a strong
power machinery with some kind of legitimate roots in society, more or less
democratic, more or less dictatorial. At the other extreme point, we may con-
ceive of direct democracy, egalitarian, horizontal distribution of power (certain
traditional societies, the communist utopia[6]).

Note that rule by democratically controlled organs of coordination is not
located at the horizontal end point of the scale, but somewhere in between pure
direct democracy and some kind of very strong state. The reason is that representative democracy and popular mobilization clearly presuppose the existence
of organs of power and coordination; that is, presuppose inequality with regard
to power. Democracy and manipulation are distinguishable by the degree of
institutionalized popular control of the leaders rather than by the degree of
inequality of power.

The distinction between economy and politics raises a difficult problem of
conceptualization with regard to power structure. The distribution of power in
society can hardly be equal without encompassing both economy and "polity"
(both production and rule). But it is a distinguishing characteristic of capitalism
as a societal system that separation is theoretically upheld between the economy
and the political system. Under the ideal model of capitalism, there are simply
two different systems of rule for the economy and the polity, respectively: the
economy is ruled by the supposedly impersonal and apolitical market, while the
political system is ruled either democratically or undemocratically. Under "actually existing capitalism," however, the two do naturally merge in practice.

This is different both from various traditional, feudal, precapitalist (or whatever we choose to call them) societies, and from socialist societies (without going deeply into the definition of socialism). In such types of societies, economy and polity are united much more immediately, even conceptually, than in the classical model of capitalism.

Thus, one can hardly conceptualize noncapitalist structures of power, even at the theoretical level, without also including power over and within production into the concept. This difference complicates the task of carrying out comparisons with regard to political structure across the lines between the various systems of society, although in reality the difference is much less distinct than under the ideal models of the systems.

Let us remain conscious of the problems of conceptualization now discussed, while still trying to use a simplified image of "political structure," where the basic variable, as stated above, is the degree of distribution of power, and where completely equal distribution of power naturally includes both economy and politics.

As already indicated, this means that democracy, in the usual sense of the term, can be combined with different degrees of distribution of power. It does not require full equality of power. This point will be discussed again.

In ideological and theoretical documents of liberation movements and socialist-oriented regimes in the Third World, the general democratic goal is often expressed through the concept of people's power (or popular power) rather than that of democracy. This was, for instance, very characteristic of the former liberation movements and subsequent post-colonial regimes of the Portuguese-speaking countries of Africa. In their documents, the two terms, up until the political liberalization of the 1990s, were actually quite often used interchangeably, without any serious effort being made to distinguish carefully between their conceptual connotations. Trying to do exactly that may, however, still be a worthwhile exercise in the context of our present discussion. The following is the result of an effort in that direction.

Democracy is about the regulation and organization of the power apparatus of the state and the participation of the citizens in that apparatus. There is no reason to confuse the concept beyond the conventional type of definition accepted by most political scientists: rule based on universal suffrage, guarantees for free discussion and opposition for everybody, the right to associate and organize freely, and safeguards against the arbitrary exercise of power.

We know that democracy, defined in this way, in reality exists primarily and then only in varying measure in certain advanced capitalist societies, where the majority of the citizens do not turn their equal rights to vote nor their juridical rights to speak, associate, and organize without state interference, against the rule of the market in the economic realm. We also know that democracy in this strict sense gives no guarantees against poverty, misery, social inequality, squandering of resources, war, and so forth, although making it more possible than under dictatorship to struggle against such ills.

Thus, concepts for other types of relations of power are needed besides those covered by the strict political science concept of democracy, which still belong to the same family of freedom-related political systems.

People's power is such a concept, genetically rooted in socialist theory, adopted and developed by various liberation movements. It figures prominently in the theoretical documents of the two movements we will be concerned with further on in this essay—FRELIMO (Frente de Libertação de Moçambique) of Mozambique and PAIGC (Partido Africano da Independência da Guiné e Cabo Verde) of Guinea-Bissau—where it is defined as an integral part of development for the people, simultaneously a necessary goal, a necessary means, and a necessary condition of such development. At this conceptual stage of our discussion, it is unnecessary to raise the well-known fact of serious gaps between theory and practice.

The following is a simple working definition of people's power—an attempt to sum up the substance of that concept as worked out by the liberation movements in the former Portuguese colonies in Africa: power exercised in close connection with the working people and legitimized by the fact that it meets concrete and fundamental interests of the people as experienced by them. Elements of such people's power did develop in practice during the independence struggles, as necessary and natural components of the process of unification against the colonial enemy.

This means that people's power and democracy (in English: people's rule) are closely related but not identical concepts, both at the analytical level and at the level of concrete, historical practice. They condition each other mutually, at the same time as they overlap.

In actual historical situations, people's power and democracy do not always appear simultaneously, but still condition each other strongly. It is, for instance, quite a safe assumption that nondemocratic rulers (for example, the former colonial rulers of Africa) only rarely yield to demands for democracy without being forced to do so by mounting people's power at the levels of production and daily social life. It is also a safe assumption, however, that people's power cannot survive for long without being institutionalized as democracy—after the defeat of undemocratic state power through the mobilization of people's power, as during the liberation struggles.

People's power—when translated into scientific language—turns out to be a wider, more sociological concept than democracy. It includes, in the longer run, democracy, without which it cannot survive. It is not defined institutionally and formally as democracy, however, but through its social contents, with regard to actual participation in the exercise of power in society, in production, and in daily social life as well as in political decisionmaking.

In terms of political structure, as conceptualized in our image, democracy can be conceived of under varying degrees of power inequality/equality because representative democracy is quite compatible with considerable hierarchy. People's power requires, however, more equal distribution of power.

The other major difference between the two concepts is that democracy is primarily political, whereas people's power is social, political, and economic, and is thus not limited to the level of political structure. One may think of people's power as emerging when or if people jointly assume control of their own life situations. The concrete beginnings are local. The extension of people's power beyond the more local levels is, however, inconceivable except in connection with democratization.

Orientation of Actual Policies

As we, in our image, finally regard the orientation of actual policies; that is, the actual measures resulting from the working out of interests confronting each other at the political level, this is conceptualized here in terms of the application of criteria of (world) market profitability versus politically defined criteria. Another possible way of putting this would be the degree of commoditization of government.

To what extent are policies formulated and implemented in terms of politically defined needs? To what extent do notions of market profitability and needs for hard currency put limits on political and administrative decisionmaking? How are, for instance, taxation and other ways of raising state revenue affected by the ways decisionmakers think and act in these regards? How are priorities set in actual practice?

In many Third World countries, narrow limits are set for national decisionmaking, as the goal of producing for the world market to gain hard currency is placed above all other societal goals. Because of the consequences of such policies for people's lives, they sometimes cannot be carried through without recourse to harsh political repression, in turn sometimes resulting in pressures for democratization.

At one end of the scale, the criterion of (world) market profitability dominates societal resource allocation and development measures (actually applied policies). At the opposite end, socially, politically, and administratively defined needs dominate.

Note that the process leading up to the definition of needs may, in the latter case, be either democratic or dictatorial in shifting combinations. There is no necessary correlation whatsoever between political and democratic decision-making.

Concrete policies are, of course, usually based on the application of combinations of market and political criteria located at various points in between the end points of the scale. Giving priority to market governed economic growth is often presented by national leaders (as well as by representatives of international credit and aid suppliers) as a way of satisfying socially and politically defined needs. This may be either true or untrue. The distinction made here, however, does not refer to the declared intentions of decisionmakers, but to the mechanisms of rule and the criteria of decision and allocation that are actually applied, in concrete action.

International Autonomy

International autonomy, can be most consistently viewed as a common factor which, initially, can be seen as one important aspect of the social basis of the state, and then works itself out independently at all the three levels simultaneously, and ultimately can be operationalized most easily at the level of actual policy implementation. Both theoretical and practical reasons would thus seem to favor its exclusion from the kind of simplified abstract image that is presented here.

Theoretically, the international autonomy of a society can be achieved in three different ways: by superior strength in relation to other societies, by equal mutual dependence, and by closing oneself off. Full analysis of the dimension of autonomy will thus have to distinguish between strength in relation to others and degree of integration in the surrounding world. One single dimension simply will not do, in this context, for such a variable, as seen from Figure 3. In the terms of this figure, international autonomy of various kinds may be found in blocks 1, 3, and 4, and possibly also in block 2.

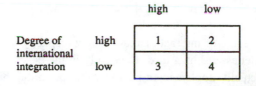

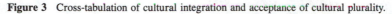

Figure 3 Cross-tabulation of cultural integration and acceptance of cultural plurality.

Autonomy by superior strength in relation to others is found primarily in block 1, but also in block 3, where the strength may be looked upon as a latent force or safeguard against imposed integration. The block 1 version of this is most clearly exemplified by the "superpower" position in the international system (the United States and, at least until the late 1980s, the Soviet Union). A good example of the block 3 version is China between the break with the Soviet Union in 1960 and the gradual international reintegration beginning during the 1970s. The China of that period is, at the same time, an example of "autonomy by closing oneself off" (see below). It combines those two types.

Autonomy by equal mutual dependence is found primarily in block 1, but can be conceived of also in 2. The latter case would be characterized by equal mutual dependence between low-strength countries, institutionalized for example as regional cooperation. The block 1 version of this is to various degrees represented by the typical "developed country"/nonsuperpower position, where the term "equal" should not be taken literally but only signifying the fact of belonging to the "in-group" of countries in the international system. The block 2 version hardly exists empirically. It is represented by the notion of regional cooperation between Third World countries or by the efforts during the 1970s to propagate a "new international economic order."

Autonomy by closing oneself off is found in block 4, but also in block 3 where it is underpinned with relative strength. As already mentioned, the block 3 version of this may be represented by the China of the 1960s and 1970s, while the block 4 version differs from 3 in not being based upon relatively high strength but solely upon various degrees of self-reliance. The most extreme examples are provided by Albania until recently, and the Kampuchea of the mid-1970s. The Tanzania of the Arusha Declaration (1967)—more goal or vision than reality—represents a milder version of autonomy by self-reliance as in block 4.

The most characteristic Third World position, however, is not any of the autonomy positions now discussed, but low autonomy (or even lack of autonomy), or low capacity for self-steering in the international system. This position is found in block 2. It combines high integration in the international economic system (and more variously also in the international political system) with low strength. Examples are numerous in today's Third World. As we shall see further on in the text, both Guinea-Bissau and Mozambique are among those examples.

In practice, the degree of international autonomy (capacity for self-steering) of Third World societies is shown most frequently in the degree of world market adaptation of actually implemented policies; that is, at the third level. The broader the internal popular base of the state, the greater the chances of mobilizing political support and material resources for policies that do not pay off directly on the world market, such as schools, health, basic nutrition, technology adapted to local customs and ecological conditions, and so forth. The size of imports from the world market, which, in any case, will have to be financed with export earnings of hard convertible cash, poses an objective limit to the space available for maneuvering, provided that the international system itself does not change, or at least provides breathing space in the form of new credits, suspension of debt payments, offers of aid, or possibilities of playing potential aid-givers off against each other. These, in turn, often create new ties of dependence that limit the space for maneuvering available to the regimes. Conceptually, these ties can be defined as components of the class basis of political power. In some cases they are absolutely vital to the regimes' chances of survival.

The Cultural Basis of the State

The cultural basis of the state shares with international autonomy the characteristic of working itself out simultaneously at all three of the levels included in our analytical image, while obviously having in addition also an international dimension. Nor can it fruitfully, for our purposes, be abstracted to unidimensionality.

Class and culture are complexly intertwined. Class divisions are rooted in social relations of production and reproduction. Classes emerge in history, when some are able to control and make use of the surplus produced by others, developing institutions and ideologies to safeguard and legitimize this kind of privilege. Culture is consciousness. "Ethnicity" is cultural. "Ethnic groups" are marked by common identity of culture and consciousness, of which language, religion, and art are some important expressions. Ethnic unity and disunity are cultural. National unity and national sentiment are cultural in the same sense. They are extensions of ethnic unity and sentiment, most often made possible through a measure of economic and political integration. Groups of people belonging to the same classes can still be opposed to each other for ethnic and national (thus cultural) reasons, because they belong to different communities.[7]

One crucial dimension of the cultural basis of the state is the degree of cultural integration of the society in question. Degree of cultural integration can be defined as the extent to which there exists in a given society a common consciousness of belonging to the same community.

Culturally integrated states are more frequent in Europe than in the Third World. But there are many multicultural (multiethnic) states also in Europe,

Degree of acceptance of
cultural plurality

		high	low
Degree of cultural	high	1	2
integration	low	3	4

Figure 4 Cross-tabulation of cultural integration and acceptance of cultural plurality.

such as Great Britain, Spain, Belgium, Switzerland, Finland, Czechoslovakia, Yugoslavia, and the Soviet Union, to mention just a few examples. As economic integration within the state has, on the average, proceeded much further in Europe than in the Third World, staying together is still usually less of a problem there than in many of the multicultural states of the Third World. Quite frequently in these states nothing but open state violence seems to remain, when ideological manipulation does not do the trick. The integrative legitimacy of the state is fragile, perhaps particularly so in Africa. Recent developments in the Soviet Union and Eastern Europe are also illustrative.

Several different languages spoken by different peoples and groups of peoples within the borders of the same state is a common indication of cultural plurality. Sometimes the same people with the same language are divided between different states. Differences of language sometimes coincide with and sometimes cut across differences of religion. From the point of view of high and centrally located wielders of power, cultural plurality is most often viewed as a problem. In a democratic perspective it would, on the contrary, be more consistent to view it as a source of spiritual and even material richness.

This brings us to the second dimension of the cultural basis of the state—crucial enough to cause us to abstain from operating with one single dimension of culture in our analytical image: that is, the degree of recognition and tolerance of cultural plurality. In culturally completely integrated societies, this obviously is not very relevant at a national (intrasocietal) level. In culturally pluralistic societies, it is a politically crucial variable in its own right, thus providing the following two-dimensional Figure 4 for the cultural basis of the state.

Everything else being equal, the chances for what in this text is called people's development would clearly seem to be greatest in the types of situations represented by blocks 1 and 3. If this observation is correct, it follows also that "degree of acceptance of cultural plurality" is of more overriding developmental importance than "degree of cultural integration."

Basic Reason for Parsimony

We see thus that neither international nor cultural factors are excluded from our analytical image as insignificant. Those two types of factors are, on the contrary, temporarily excluded only for the sake of such concentration upon fundamentals that will make it possible to bring them back in, in their full richness and in proper context.

It is possible that the international and cultural dimensions could well be visualized as circles around the simple three-level image. This is not attempted here, however.

Anticolonialism, Nationalism, National Liberation, and Nation-State in Africa

Those political movements that organized and led armed struggle against colonialism began generally during the 1960s to be called national liberation movements. The models were Algeria's *Front de Libération Nationale* (FLN) and Vietnam's *Front National de Libération* (FNL). The anticolonial liberation movements in Portugal's African colonies were also considered by themselves and others to be "national" liberation movements.

It is important, however, to note the limited relevance of nationhood in the European sense to the modern states emerging from the anticolonial struggles and movements of Sub-Saharan Africa. The decisive coupling of nation with state is basically (although not exclusively) a European contribution to world history—Central America and the Middle East are examples of other regions (beyond Africa) where it has not taken root.

It is well known that most colonial borders in and between the African societies of the nineteenth century were drawn, completely regardless of existing divisions, into peoples, cultures, economic regions, or, for that matter, into nations. Whatever coincidence there was in Sub-Saharan Africa between colony and "nation" appears to have been almost random. Still, the urge is today very strong among the leaders of Africa's independent states to follow the historical example of European nation-states. The principle of untouchability of colonial frontiers adopted by the Organisation of African Unity (OAU) is a symbolically paradoxical expression of this heritage of colonialism, functioning both at the levels of ideology and realpolitik.

In the colonies, the notion of community within the geographical borders of the colony was no more than embryonic and limited to the narrow "petty bourgeois" stratum of the population that had managed to get a measure of modern education and to climb a few rungs on the socioeconomic ladder of colonial society.[8] The attribute "national," in the concept of "national liberation movement," thus primarily expresses the leadership's ambition to create economically and culturally integrated (or at least viable) "nation-states" within the inherited territorial borders of the colonies.

The immediate interests of the power wielders within these entities are political and territorial control, cultural integration, benefits from credit and aid, economic "modernization" or "development." But the idea that people's development, as indicated in the introductory remarks of this chapter, would be indissolubly linked to the emergence of new nation-states in every former colony of Africa, is actually an ideological myth serving the interests of power wielders rather than a proposition founded on historical insight.

Actually it is quite difficult to see why the European experience of the development of capitalism (let along socialism) and the emergence of nation-states would be simply repeated in today's Africa on a general level. The kind of dialectic between economic and cultural integration on the one hand, and consolidation of state power on the other (characteristic of European development), was a product of very specific historical conditions. There are significant differences both between early and late capitalism and between the relationships of those capitalisms to, respectively, yesterday's Europe and today's Africa. Taking for granted that Africans today would have to, or indeed could, merely repeat the stages of European history to develop their forces of production and raise their levels of life is hardly well founded. Why bend abstractly and deterministically—whether in Marxist or mainstream social science fashion—to an assumed necessity of a "capitalist stage"?—as if periphery capitalism were not already a reality, and a harsh one at that.[9]

Cultural and national pluralism, weakly rooted states in terms of integrative legitimacy, periphery status on the world market—all this would rather seem to indicate different types of futures and different types of solutions to people's (and peoples') problems of state-building.

From Liberation Movement to State Power in Guinea-Bissau and Mozambique

Anticolonial movements everywhere have typically been under the leadership of politicians recruited from the intermediate strata of colonial society. Sub-Saharan Africa is no exception. In some African countries, and most characteristically in the former Portuguese colonies, colonial resistance against decolonization was so strong that armed struggle appeared to the liberation movements as the only conceivable alternative. This resulted in effective but not always easy political alliance between the more radical elements of the so-called petite bourgeoisie and large sections of the farming population, mostly peasants.

Characteristic examples of this historical process are provided by Guinea-Bissau and Mozambique, the two countries whose historical experiences will serve as illustrations in this essay. There, as elsewhere, the struggle for liberation from colonialism was fought basically by an alliance of petit bourgeois leaders from the intermediate strata of colonial society and the farming people of the countryside. The common goal of putting an end to colonialism united people and leaders, making them mutually dependent upon one another. This necessitated, among other things, a measure of democracy within the liberation movements as well as in the liberated areas of the countries. Through their common struggles, important elements of the petit bourgeois leadership and many among the more or less traditional peasants who had been mobilized for the struggle were radicalized politically. Peoples' power came to be wielded against colonialism. Democracy and even socialism were placed on the political agenda.

The external ideological influence exercised on the liberation movements by the Soviet Union and allied countries supporting the armed struggle is often emphasized in the debate. Although this certainly had its significance, it is still important not to overlook the basically internal dynamics of the radicalization brought about through the struggle. No slogans imported from Moscow could ever, by themselves, have caused the peasants to rise against colonialism. In a political sense there was thus a real link between "national" or anticolonial liberation and socialist goals of societal transformation (compare Rudebeck in Lopes and Rudebeck 1988:22). In the post-colonial situation, however, the constellation of class forces is different; the basis shattered for the political alliance sustaining this link. The colonial state is gone, although it has left a heavy legacy of institutions and attitudes.

The former leaders of the liberation movement are today the wielders of state power. They work for the accumulation and control of a surplus derived from a national economy that they are simultaneously seeking to create. In the case of Mozambique, the state's struggle for sheer survival in the face of South African aggression and destabilization has been added to all of this.

The coercive power of the colonial state is theoretically no longer available in the postcolonial situation. Until the changes of the 1990s, the official ideology and analysis asks for people's power in its place. But mutual dependence between the people and their leaders was not as self-evident as before. Class contradictions between rural producers and the wielders of state power surfaced, which exacerbated existing regional and cultural divisions. Cultural, ideological, and even personal contradictions were sharpened within the leading strata, as the societal base began to yield.

The democratic momentum of the liberation struggle was evident. It gave rise to demands and hopes for radical development policies. But history provides no guarantees in the new situation. People's power and democracy do not come from the sky, either in Guinea-Bissau or Mozambique or any other society, but only when those who have a real stake in more equal distribution of power are also strong enough to make their interests felt. The stake is still there in Guinea-Bissau and Mozambique, as strong as ever, but the balance of forces in society is shifting, a new historical conjuncture is taking shape. What kinds of questions relevant to "people's development" does this raise from the point of view of political theory and political economy?

The Two Examples

The historical cases of Guinea-Bissau and Mozambique differ from each other in important respects. One country is small, while the other is large. Internal differentiation with regard to culture and class differs significantly between the two. Internationally, Guinea-Bissau has been spared the kind of ruthless destabilization and cruel aggression to which Mozambique has been subjected by South Africa.

But there are also significant similarities: common Portuguese colonial heritage, anticolonial movements with common historical and ideological roots, armed struggle to achieve decolonization, successful political alliances for this purpose between petit bourgeois leaders and the peasantry, efforts to transform the liberation movements into "vanguard" parties on principles of "democratic centralism" after independence.

It is also significant that neither Guinea-Bissau nor Mozambique is a culturally and economically integrated nation. Rather, both are highly pluralistic societies that were arbitrarily carved out of their regional and historical contexts by colonialism.

In both of the countries official postcolonial ideology, born of the liberation struggle, posed people's power (poder popular) as a necessary goal and condition of development. Nevertheless, during the first decades of postcolonialism, the major part of the financing of the states of the two countries did not come from the productive work of their peoples. Neither state mobilized any net surplus from the peasant agriculture that represents most of their respective populations. Thus, the two states were not popularly based in this most fundamental sense.

Superficially seen this may appear surprising, given the historical background of popularly based and highly politicized liberation movements. But, as already pointed out, the balance of forces in society is shifting in both countries. Postcolonialism is very different from anticolonialism. One crucial question to be asked is for what goals the rural people were originally prepared to support the PAIGC and FRELIMO. A second question concerns the links between these same rural people and today's states. The processes of mobilization that brought the present regimes of Guinea-Bissau and Mozambique to power did involve large sections of the rural populations of those two countries. But what about today and tomorrow?

As already stated, there will be greater detail on Guinea-Bissau than on Mozambique, for the simple reason that my own studies of Guinea-Bissau are less limited.[10] But Mozambique will be drawn into the picture for comparative purposes.[11]

The social basis of anticolonial mobilization is discussed in some depth for Guinea-Bissau, while only indicated in the case of Mozambique. For both countries this is followed by reports on local case studies, one for each country, intended to shed some light on the second question; that is, on postcolonial relations of power between rural people and the state. The Mozambican case study is part of, and thus rests upon, more comprehensive field work for a larger area than the Guinean study, which has its strength, though, in its focus on one and the same village over a long period of time.

There is no intention in this essay to embark upon the much greater task of outlining the overall development of postcolonial Guinea and Mozambique with regard to the three levels of our image. Quite the contrary, a kind of bottom-up approach is attempted, where the postcolonial outcome of anticolonial mobilization is only spotlighted through two empirical examples rooted in local realities. Consideration of the existing general body of knowledge on both countries (including in the case Guinea-Bissau) will help set the examples in proper context and avoid their haphazard utilization for unwarranted generalizations (compare note 25:79).

Our task in the following sections will thus be to illustrate the interrelationships between the social basis of political power, its internal structuring, and the policies resulting from its exercise, with the aid of one example each from Guinea-Bissau and Mozambique, respectively. Some points on international dependence and on cultural integration will also be introduced.

GUINEA-BISSAU

Decolonization was the general historical trend in Africa during the 1950s and 1960s, but Portuguese colonialists absolutely refused to yield. In the colony of Portuguese Guinea (Fig. 5), this intransigence resulted in the clandestine founding of the PAI (later PAIGC)[12] in Bissau, the small capital city, on September 19, 1956. Two years later, there was a brutally suppressed strike by the Bissau dockworkers, followed by the until then urban-based movement's decision to

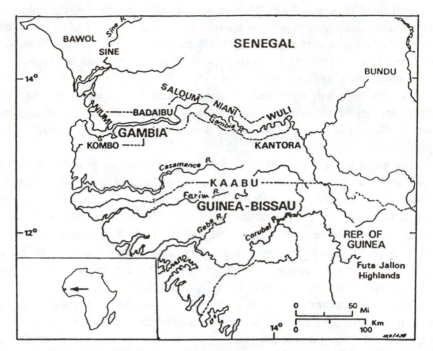

Figure 5 The location of the Kaabu empire within the area of Senegambia-Guinea. Map adapted from Joye Bowman Hawkins, *Conflict, Interaction, and Change in Guinea-Bissau: Fulbe Expansion and Its Impact, 1850–1900,* Ph.D. dissertation, University of California, Los Angeles, 1980, p. 195. Reprinted with permission.

embark upon a policy of peasant mobilization against the colonial power. The first armed attack on a Portuguese military camp came on January 23, 1963. There was then a combined political and military liberation struggle until the fall of fascism in Portugal in 1974, to which the Guinean struggle contributed significantly. A unilateral declaration of the state of Guinea-Bissau was announced on September 24, 1973, before the fall of the Portuguese regime. What was the class basis of all this? How was it all rooted in the structure of Guinean society?

The social basis of anticolonial mobilization in Guinea-Bissau. In earlier discussions on the class character of the mobilization initiated and organized by the PAIGC in Guinea, it has been argued that the mobilization was class based in the sense of being guided by Amilcar Cabral's clear understanding of the political potential for resistance of the various classes and strata which he distinguished in Guinean society. At the same time, it was not class-based in the sense of preparing for the assumption of political and economic power by the surplus-producing class, who in the Guinean context are basically the peasants. The PAIGC of the preindependence period was an anticolonial, potentially national, liberation movement, united behind a political goal transcending class divisions.[13]

Amilcar Cabral was not only a political leader of historical significance in Africa, but also made original contributions to the theoretical analysis of national liberation and development. His "Brief Analysis of the Social Structure in Guinea" is the most famous and most often quoted analysis of the social structure of colonial Guinea.[14] Although Cabral's text deals mainly with the small urban component of the class structure—that is, the superimposed capitalist-colonialist structure, the petite bourgeoisie, and the fairly small marginalized stratum of uprooted power—it also provides an important theoretical key to the understanding of differentiation within the peasantry:

> In the rural areas we have found it necessary to distinguish between two distinct groups: on the one hand, the group which we consider semi-feudal, represented by the Fulas, and, on the other hand, the group which we consider, so to speak, without any defined form of state organisation, represented by the Balantes. There are a number of intermediary positions between these two extreme ethnic groups [as regards the social situation] (Cabral 1969:46).

As we see, Cabral starts from the basic distinction between class society and more or less classless society, where political and economic power is organized along vertical and horizontal lines, respectively.[15] Within the Guinean context, the Fula (around 12% of the population) and the Balanta (around 30%) represent one pole each of this sociological dimension, while the approximately 20 remaining ethnic groups (as distinguished by anthropologists) are located at various points in between.

Fula society is characterized by a strong hierarchy of chiefs who exploit the labor of "their" peasants, and who were also prepared to cooperate with the Portuguese to retain their power and social positions. Another feature of Fula society is the subordinate position of women; polygamy is common. The latter institution, however, is by no means exclusively Fula.

Balanta society, on the other hand, is generally described as "stateless" and more egalitarian. There is no central authority, but only a horizontally recruited council of elders representing the extended families of the community. Each family works for its own gain on communally held lands, and the position of women is considered to be relatively free both socially and economically. Juridically, though, the Balanta woman is subject to male authority in the public realm (compare Handem 1986:68–72).

The two largest of the other ethnic groups are the Mandinga (about 10%), with a fairly vertical type of organization, and the Mandjack (about 17%), in historical transition toward the vertical type. Among the other major groups, the Pepel and Brame are generally regarded as evolving in the same direction as the Mandjack people with regard to the basic distinction now discussed. The people of the Bissagos islands have a vertical system with distinct groups related to the tasks of warfare. A few other smaller groups retain the horizontal type of organization represented by the Balanta.

Religion is naturally an important aspect of culture, and it is actually possible to discern a patterned relationship between the forms of social organization and the religious beliefs of the various ethnic groups. It is generally considered that about one-third of the population of Guinea-Bissau is Moslem and about two-thirds "animist," while the Christians constitute only a few percent. Islam is predominant in the more vertically organized Fula and Mandinga societies, whereas the Balanta maintain their traditional religion to a large extent. The correlation between hierarchy and Islam on the one side and communal egalitarianism and "animism" on the other is by no means perfect, however, and the lines of distinction appear quite fluid.

The vertical/horizontal distinction applied by Cabral is a powerful analytical tool. It helps us grasp a dynamic dimension of Guinean peasant society. Such empirical and theoretical work as that of Christian Sigrist on the resistance potential of what he calls acephalous societies ("without head," that is, without central power), of which the Balanta are considered an example, has contributed to advancing our thinking about the political potential and limitations of tribal peoples (demonstrating thereby the analytical power of the distinction) (Sigrist 1979a). The PAIGC's own use of the distinction in understanding successes and failures in their own political practice is another telling demonstration of its fruitfulness. The distinction is put to use also by the Guinean sociologist Carlos Lopes in his work on the historical transition from national liberation movements to state independence in Guinea-Bissau (Lopes 1982b:13–123).

It is quite possible, though, that the strong appeal of this kind of distinction has tended to overshadow other possible lines of distinction, not least the one opposing almost all peasants of Guinea (or other countries), be they vertically or horizontally organized, to almost all centralized state authority historically known so far, be it colonial or national. This is what Lopes talks about as two "logics" in conflict, that of "ethnic rationality" as opposed to "state rationality" (Lopes 1982a:15–80). Pacts between the colonial state and Fula chiefs or Mandjack *régulos* were only a limited way of bridging this conflict. National integration under colonialism could never have been brought about by such means—nor by any other, one may add quite safely. This was the dilemma, for instance, for governor Spinola's late-in-the-day "better Guinea" policy, which he tried in vain to apply in the early 1970s to counter the advances of the PAIGC (Rudebeck 1974:62–66).

In this perspective, an important reason that it became possible to reconcile "ethnic rationality" with the rationality of the PAIGC party/state of the liberated areas during the armed struggle was that the unity requested by the party, and gradually also offered by the people, did not appear to threaten ethnic or cultural integrity. The creation of a nationally integrated economy under the direction of a state is quite a different matter, however, as clearly indicated by today's crises of development and state power.

The most general point made by Cabral about mobilization for national liberation was that it had proved less difficult to mobilize the Balanta and similar groups than the Fula, as the Fula peasants were obedient to their chiefs, who had, in many cases, developed ties of mutual dependence with the Portuguese colonial authorities. The groups "without any defined organization," on the other hand, had ". . . put up much more resistance against the Portuguese than the others and they (had) maintained intact their tradition of resistance to colonial penetration. *This is the group that we found most ready to accept the idea of national liberation*" (Cabral 1969:50, my emphasis).

It is, of course, paradoxical that the least "modern" groups were found by Cabral to be the most receptive to "the idea of national liberation." It indicates, among other things, a need for further analysis. At least in hindsight, it is also clear that Cabral's analysis has inspired some partially misconceived interpretations—quite possibly precisely because of its persuasive and demonstrated far-reaching applicability.

It has been noted by Lopes, for instance, that some analysts refer to Cabral in pointing to the vertical organization of Fula society as the actual cause of weak participation in the struggle. In so doing, Lopes claims, they lose sight of the cultural autonomy of the Fula people, which prevented their assimilation by the colonial power (Lopes 1982a:15–16). This autonomy was protected by the very same vertical organization, rightly said (we must believe) to discourage them from nationalist militancy. Things are thus more complex than the quick and easy application of the vertical/horizontal distinction may indicate. It is true that the PAIGC found it less difficult to persuade the Balanta than the Fula to take arms against colonialism in the 1960s. But this fact says very little about the respective class positions of Fula and Balanta peasants vis-à-vis the state, whether colonial or postcolonial.

Adding significantly to the awareness of complexity, Rosemary Galli points out that Cabral analyzed the internal class structure of Guinea-Bissau's peasants' social relations without direct reference to the impact of colonialism, while charging the radical petit bourgeois party and state leadership with the actual task of national development. The question of specific power relations was left open, however, or only vaguely or idealistically dealt with, as it still is in independent Guinea-Bissau.[16]

Galli's point is crucial. In his 1964 "brief analysis," Cabral had maintained that the principal contradiction within Guinean society, after liberation, would be between what he named the semifeudal rulers of the vertically organized ethnic groups and "the members of the groups without any defined form of organization." (Cabral 1969:52.) The only chance, in this situation, to carry the Guinean revolution further would be for the petit bourgeois leaders to side with the people, in a joint effort to achieve national development. Cabral "down-played internal class dissension," says Galli, "because he concentrated his energies on the immediate national problem." (Galli 1986:60.) The official post-independence ideology of the PAIGC has consistently done the same. Top-heavy concentration of power thus seems to have ideological roots traceable far back in the history of the PAIGC.[17]

By focusing on the vertical/horizontal distinction, which refers to the socio-political organization of power within the peasantry but only indirectly to the relations of exploitation between the state and the peasants, those relations, for instance, that integrated efficient Balanta rice producers of the south into the colonial economy, Cabral also avoided bringing peasant conservatism—cultural, economic, social—into focus as a form of passive class struggle (Galli 1986:60). Thus he was able to define the Guinean peasantry as a whole, regardless of vertical/horizontal organization, as merely a "physical force" but not a "revolutionary force," although virtually the only surplus producers of the country.[18]

The class basis of the national liberation movement of Guinea-Bissau was set into political motion through a strategy based upon this kind of analysis. In 1964, Cabral consciously focused attention on that dimension of the social structure of Guinean society that was most relevant to the political task of mobilizing the peasants for anticolonial resistance. He was successful in this, as we know. But even at this early stage—the armed struggle had only begun—Cabral seems to have been aware of the ambiguity involved in defining the peasants as only a "physical force" in the revolution. This is indicated by his insistence upon the necessity of people's power for the future success of the Guinean revolution. In 1964, however, he mentioned no other way of bringing this about than by asking the leadership to make a conscious choice to "abandon power to the workers and the peasants." (Cabral 1969:57.) It is easy, today, to point out that this analysis was very far from complete, and in fact much more limited to the specific tasks of the anticolonial struggle than was generally thought at the time. This was becoming quite clear to Cabral himself, as the struggle went on.[19] But insight alone is not enough to change the balance of forces in society. One possible conclusion is, of course, that decolonization and people's development are historically related, but still different tasks, requiring the support of partly different class forces as well as different kinds of transformations.

Class and "Ethnicity"

A few additional comments may be needed on the complex intertwining of class and cultural "ethnic" divisions underlying the processes of mobilization in Guinea-Bissau.

The Balanta, Fula, Mandinga, Mandjack, and others of Guinea-Bissau belong to different cultural communities. They have both separate and common identities and histories. They speak different languages and they formulate their existential beliefs differently. But they farm the same land and they were subjected to the same colonialism. To liberate themselves from that colonialism, they had to join forces. In so doing, they also began to develop a sense of community transcending the old ethnic divisions such as extended ethnicity and potential nationality. Such a sense of community had existed only embryonically under colonialism. As a result, class struggle is now beginning to unfold on a national level in Guinea. This had not been possible so as long as each ethnic (even village) community lived and produced separated from the others, or only confronted each other a few at a time—Fula versus Mandinga, for instance, often in wars of conquest.

Surely, the contradiction opposing the peasant producers of Guinea and the Portuguese colonial-capitalist class was a class contradiction. But to most Guineans it appeared as a contradiction between an alien political power and their own ethnic community, which it *also* was. This was the basis upon which they were first prepared to be mobilized, and it was cultural community rather than class.

The horizontally organized Balanta probably fought originally for the freedom to live without a state. Most of them probably did not fight consciously to support the creation of a new state, be it "progressive" or even "their own." There cannot have been much in their historical experience indicating that a strong state would be useful to them either politically or in a straight material/ economic sense. The Fula community, however, already had its own state that existed in a kind of reluctant symbiosis with the colonial state. In a sense it was even protected by colonialism through the cooperation established between the colonial state and some chiefs. Thus, the Fula peasants were probably generally less conscious than the Balanta of being opposed to colonialism. Still, they may well have been subjected to even harsher exploitation than their Balanta class brothers and sisters.

This brings us back to our main point: that is, the people of Guinea were not mobilized for liberation from colonialism primarily on a class basis, but on a political basis. The role of culture in this process was, by the way, forcefully emphasized by Cabral in 1970: "Whatever the conditions under which a people have been subjected to foreign domination, it is generally in the cultural realm that the germ of contest is found that leads to the structuring and development of the liberation movement" (Cabral 1970:5). The point holds true also—perhaps even in particular—for the petite bourgeoisie of Guinea, of which many but far from all were of Cape Verdean parentage. In their case, though, the two types of mobilization basis—that is, class and cultural/ethnic/potentially national/political, were combined and confounded in a very intricate way. Those people were provoked into vaguely nationalist consciousness on cultural grounds, a sense of humiliation and frustration in the colonial system. But national liberation was also in perfect agreement with their class interest, narrowly conceived, as they were predetermined to occupy the political and economic posts of command in an independent Guinea-Bissau.

In purely class terms, the petite bourgeoisie of Portuguese Guinea, as of any similar colonial society, was a subordinate stratum of the colonial capitalist class. But for cultural, emerging nationalist, and political reasons, they were opposed to colonialism. The only possible way of securing a social and political basis for this anticolonialism was to join forces with the peasantry to organize what was conceived as national liberation. The decision to do exactly this was taken by the PAIGC in September 1959, after the massacre of the striking Pidjiguiti dock workers. Six principles were adopted. The first of these was: "Without delay mobilize and organize the peasant masses who will be, as experience shows, the main force in the struggle for national liberation." The third principle was: "Develop and reinforce unity around the Party of the Africans of all ethnic groups, origins, and social strata."[20]

It should not be surprising to anyone that the application of such a strategy, however politically correct at the time, would later bring new contradictions to the fore. Rather than fortifying the previous political alliance, the successful completion of the anticolonial struggle has even shattered its very basis—limited as it was in reality to the task of decolonization.

Postcolonialism in One Guinean Village 1976–1986

In my own studies of postcolonial developments in Guinea-Bissau, I have tried to add to the overall picture by focusing also upon the experience of one particular village (*tabanca*) in the northern part of the country, in an effort to concretize the contradiction between the postcolonial state and the peasantry. The village I have had the privilege to learn something about, however limited, is Kandjadja, central village of a section that also includes twelve smaller villages with an approximately total of 8000 inhabitants, located a few kilometers south of the river Farim (Fig. 6), in the sector of Mansaba, region of Oio.[21] This is ancient West African peasant land, where Mandinga people of Muslim faith lived long before Portuguese sailors first set foot on the Guinean coast around the middle of the fifteenth century, and where they still live.[22]

In February 1976, the party-appointed political commissar for the section of Kandjadja spoke at one of the weekly citizens' meetings regularly held in the village during the early years of independence. Most inhabitants had by then already returned from their wartime lives as refugees in the Casamance of southern Senegal. The commissar spoke boldly:

> We have no state here. We ourselves are the state. What can the political commissar do without the base committee? What can the committee do without the people? Here in Kandjadja, if we really want to, all of us together, all men and all women, are the committee.

The commissar may not have intended that his words be taken literally in the theoretical sense of the state having become superfluous. But he certainly wished to state that political authority in newly liberated Guinea-Bissau was exercised under popular control, and that the country could not be governed against the people's will and interests. Even this may have been idealistic,

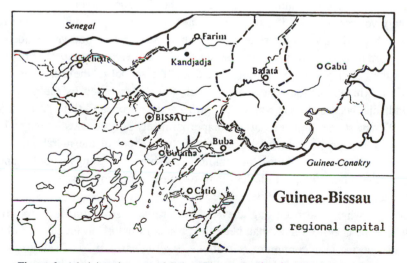

Figure 6 Administrative map of Guinea-Bissau, showing the village of Kandjadja.

although it reflected commonly held beliefs and aspirations at the time which were, in turn, reflected in an active and busy political atmosphere with high levels of political participation at many places all over Guinea-Bissau, including Kandjadja.

In Kandjadja in early 1976, the nationally inspired activities of the PAIGC thus were not negligible. They also aroused a fairly strong local response. But nationally inspired politics remained basically at an ideological and organizational level. There were no visible signs of any innovative activities in the sphere of production. People worked hard, and they did much for their own material and social recuperation after all the hardships of the war. Beyond the school and a nurse sent by the state to live in the village, however, most of this was still done within the preexisting social framework, although it was sometimes dressed up in modern, nationalist, revolutionary rhetoric. Nothing new was introduced by the party/state in the sense of restructuring agricultural production in ways that would put a surplus at the disposal of the state or the national economy yet to be constructed. The People's Store (*armazen do povo*) picked up where the colonial state had left off in buying the annual groundnut production from the peasants for export, thus linking the village to the world market, as before.

It was characteristic of the situation in 1976, that the modernistic and ideological message ambitiously conveyed by the three young schoolteachers of Kandjadja seemed somewhat out of touch with the cultural aspirations of the community and with the type of actual transformation the local community was undergoing. There was also a different type of school, however, besides the one set up by the national authorities. This was the Koranic school, run on a completely voluntary basis. The teacher was a young man of around 20—the same age as his colleagues at the state school, where he was a second-year student in the mornings. But every evening at sunset, he gathered a number of boys to read the holy texts that were not studied in "the school of the Europeans" or "of the whites," as the state school is still sometimes called by the people of Kandjadja, because that is where "modern" and "European" things are taught. In 1976 the state school still attracted approximately 200 students—close to half of the young people of school age—while "the school of the marabout (local saint)" only drew a few tens. In coming years, however, things would change.

In November 1977, a little less than two years after my first stay, the most spectacular change was that the entire village had been moved to the site of the old well, which had been dug anew after wartime destruction. This return to "where the ancestors live" had been the project foremost on the agenda of the locally elected base committee (*comité de base*) in early 1976. Twenty months later it had been fully implemented. The huts of the earlier provisional site had been replaced with houses of sun-dried bricks, set along straight lanes, and surrounded by vegetable gardens, where the village had always been before the wartime upheaval, all done with local resources, without any material support from the state. The political commissar and the members of the base committee were justifiably proud of the work carried out "by the people of Kandjadja." Thus, the evolution underway in early 1976 remained firmly on its course in late 1977.

On November 14, 1980, Prime Minister João Bernardo ("Nino") Vieira, legendary guerillero of the liberation movement, was brought to the presidency through an armed coup d'état carried through with a minimum of direct violence. The constitutional president of the republic, Luis Cabral, was imprisoned for a year and then permitted to leave the country. The coup was an expression of the structural crisis into which the country had been sinking ever more deeply since the first years of independence. The crisis was marked by a growing economic and political gap between on the one hand state power resting on aid and credits and wielded by the petit bourgeois leadership and on the other hand the peasant producers left largely on their own. The new regime promised more rural-oriented policies, an end to wasteful investment projects out of touch with local realities, and a freer political climate. It is generally agreed also that president Nino is "closer to the hearts of the people" than Luis Cabral ever was.

Real changes were small, however, as they were bound to be, given that the objective structural conditions of development in Guinea-Bissau could not be changed by a mere reshuffling within the existing leadership in Bissau. In March 1984 elections were held for a new National assembly. Two months later the country returned formally to civilian government with Nino Vieira as the constitutional president of the republic.

Was the political drama staged at the central level of Guinea-Bissau reflected at the local level of Kandjadja? If so, how? In November 1981, one year after the coup, I returned to the village. It was still there, on the site of the ancestors. Outwardly very little had changed since 1977. Some material improvements could be noted, foremost of these was the presence of cattle. Other signs of relative progress were the whitewashed walls of the new people's store and, most strikingly, the almost completed construction in locally produced bricks of an impressive mosque.

Politically, however, important changes had occurred. The political commissar was gone: "We asked him to take a rest. He has returned to his native village." This had actually happened several years ago, I was told.

The old base committee had been dissolved. An assembly of the people had elected a new committee that never met formally. Whatever needed to be done at the local level was done anyway, on the authority of the new chairman/chief, who was the leading representative of the most respected family of Kandjadja. In fact, the formal political structure set up by the party and the state had, by the end of 1981, been dismantled for all practical purposes at this most local level.

The number of students of the state school had dwindled to approximately 50. There were only two teachers—none of the original ambitious three. The new school building was much smaller than the earlier provisional ones. It had only two small rooms, one of which, furthermore, was used by the Koranic school, which was thus symbolically placed on a par with the state school.

With regard to official health care, the regression was total. The nurse had left long ago; no one had replaced her. The roof of the small dispensary had fallen in, and empty medicine bottles were thrown in a corner.

The deterioration with regard to official social services was, however, balanced by visible advances within the established framework of peasant agriculture. There were even four ploughs available in the village—three private and one provided by "the state." Thanks to the rains, there would probably be enough to eat in 1982. But . . . (the chairman tells me)

> . . . the rest of the country shows no interest in Kandjadja. Our people live so far away. Many are born here and reach the age of fifty without ever seeing Mansaba [at twenty kilometers' distance] and much less Bissau. All they know is here and Farim. They don't belong to the party, don't take part in politics.

By the end of 1981, thus, a contradictory image emerged. On the one hand, there was a striking demobilization both of the political structures and the official services born of the struggle for independence. On the other hand, there was a certain autonomous regeneration and dynamism of the locally rooted culture and economy.

At visits toward the end of 1984 and in early 1986, the image and tendencies of 1981 were strongly confirmed in the village of Kandjadja. The gap seemed to be widening between central state authority and local society. The formal political structure remained in place. Everything indicates, though, that it derived most of its authority from the local standing of the family whose members occupied the key posts rather than from the PAIGC and the state of Guinea-Bissau. The following theme, struck both by an activist of the youth organization and by an old hunter, kept recurring in interviews and conversations:

> All we have is the people's own strength and our fields. During the war we worked for the party. We collected money where we lived in Senegal. We carried food and ammunition on our heads to the frontier. But now the state and the party

have forgotten us. They have left us in a hole. All we have is the people's own strength. We need some support from the state too.

Still Kandjadja of 1986 was not a stagnant community. People were politically organized, the youth organization had conducted a detailed census. People produced, consumed, traded, communicated over long distances, studied, organized cultural activities—over the 10-year period from 1976 to 1986 they had improved their material level of life. But the limits were narrow, restrictions strongly felt and resented, inputs from outside close to none. The school was run down, the health post abandoned. The people's store had been closed as a result of state "liberalization" policies, but no private trader had yet taken over. Thus there was not even a retail store any longer. Whatever dynamism there was, was not "national," Guinean, but rooted in the local economy, inserted in its own regional context cutting straight across the colonial/postcolonial state frontier with Senegal, nourished by age-old Mandinga cultural consciousness, but not linked to creative innovations supported from outside.

The people themselves had expected much more in 1976. In 1986 they were disappointed—"tired" was the word used more often. After liberation from colonialism, they had supported the PAIGC goal of creating a people's state, based on people's power,—that is, a state that would help them achieve "development" in the sense of material security and human dignity—people's development as the term was used in our introduction. According to their own analysis, "the people's strength" alone, although essential, was not sufficient for this. "Some support" from a more broadly based authority, a "state," was also necessary. Under what conditions can such support be expected from the wielders of state power? This is a question of high relevance both for the people of Kandjadja and within political economy research.

The question can be turned around, too, and posed in the perspective of national policymakers in Bissau. Why is it that whatever "development" there was in Kandjadja and thousands of other villages up to the mid 1980s seemed to have been moving in directions contrary to those foreseen in the heads of planners and in official documents?[23] There were no producers' cooperatives, except the communal fields organized to finance the mosque. There was ever increasing interest in the Koranic school, at the expense of the state's "modern" education. There was isolation of the Balanta teacher in a Mandinga community, instead of breakdown of "tribalism." The state retail store was so completely "lacking in strength," that its final closing appeared quite logical. The old power structure flourished inside the new shell. There was dependence on trade ("smuggling" in a state perspective) across the Guinea-Senegal border for such simple things as notebooks and pencils to be used in the school.

Regardless of whether the question is posed from a local or central view-point, the answer is political, as well as economic, necessity. The villagers did not get the "support" they deemed necessary, because they did not influence, let alone control, state power—or for that matter any other power outside their own community. The Bissau policymakers, however, did not reach the villagers with their plans and wishes because the social basis of their power was else-where. Thus, they did not formulate their plans and actions in concrete cooper-ation with any of the social strata among the villagers.[24]

MOZAMBIQUE

Until the overthrow of the old regime in Portugal with the coup on April 25, 1974, the Portuguese had been just as adamant about maintaining colonial rule in Mozambique (Fig. 7) as in Guinea-Bissau.[25] FRELIMO had been founded on June 25, 1962, as a joint front organization, in an attempt to unite previously existing resistance organizations of Mozambicans in Rhodesia (today Zim-babwe), Tanganyika (today Tanzania) and Kenya, and in Nyasaland (today Ma-lawi).[26] Armed struggle for liberation from colonialism was initiated by FRE-LIMO in September 1964, over a year and a half after the first shots were fired in Guinea-Bissau. The first attacks were carried out in the two northern prov-inces of Cabo Delgado and Niassa as well as farther south in the provinces of Tete and Zambezia. Soon afterward, the FRELIMO forces were concentrated in the north, where "liberated zones" were consolidated from 1965 onward. (See clarification in note 26.)

As an anticolonial organization and liberation movement, FRELIMO ini-tially followed the general pattern of petit bourgeois leadership trying to mobi-lize broad popular support—necessarily the more peasant the more popular, given the social structure of the country. What gradually came to distinguish FRELIMO was the fairly consistent ideological radicalism it developed as an organization, both in theory and practice, after the second congress, held at Machedje in the province of Niassa from June 20–25, 1968.

In the official, popularized version of FRELIMO history, this process of ideological consolidation is simply described as the struggle between the "reac-tionary" and the "revolutionary" lines: settled to the advantage of the revolu-tionaries at the 1968 congress, still marked by a serious setback for the revolu-tionaries with the murder of the organization's founding leader Eduardo Mondlane by letter bomb reaching him in Dar es Salaam on February 3, 1969, but culminating in revolutionary victory with the election by the central com-mittee of Samora Machel as president and Marcelino dos Santos as vice presi-dent of FRELIMO in May 1970.

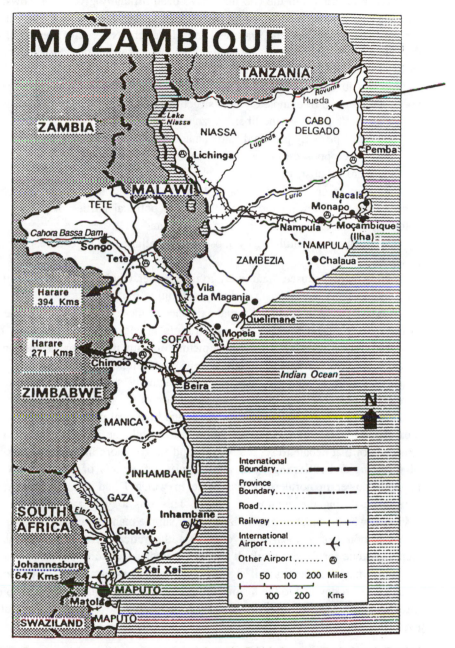

Figure 7   Map of Mozambique. Map adapted from the British Overseas Trade Board, Tropical Africa Advisory Group, Trade Mission to Mozambique, October 15–29, 1980.

The characteristics of the two lines have been officially given as follows:

There were those who proposed [for the administration and government of the liberated zones] that the system of traditional chiefs, régulos, be used, or that the system set up by the Portuguese be used, substituting Mozambicans (blacks) for the Portuguese (whites).

Opposed to these people were the more revolutionary elements who proposed the creation of completely new structures that would permit the creation of real people's power in the liberated zones.

The lack of properly prepared cadres made it necessary to use many individuals who were opposed to people's power.

They were tribalist, racist, and ambitious.

They tried to enrich themselves through the struggle and through independence. Closely following the examples of the political parties of the British colonies, they took on the designation "chairman."

This situation was utilized by those who continued to defend reactionary positions.

Their ambition caused them to try to take power within FRELIMO, so that they could enrich themselves rapidly by exploiting the people.[27]

Without placing in doubt the actual existence of these two lines or tendencies in the history of anticolonial/national struggle in Mozambique, historical research is gradually giving us a credible picture of many more nuances and much greater complexity, bringing to light serious contradictions within the "revolutionary" camp, as well as "reactionaries" actually supporting FRELIMO's struggle in practice, even after the consolidation of the more radical line.[28]

This is not the place to enter into the actual historical debate over the complex class character of national liberation in Mozambique, but only to note the existence of that debate to set the background for the more limited undertaking of reporting and reflecting upon some significant aspects of a field study of people's power in northern Mozambique in which I had the opportunity to participate during the autumn of 1983.[29] This was a typical case study, the results of which cannot be generalized in any simple manner but can, of course, be used both for comparisons, continued theoretical reflection, and as a stepping-stone for further work. It should be emphasized too, that this particular study only assumes its full significance when viewed as part of the total research effort devoted to the history of national liberation in Cabo Delgado by the Center of African Studies at the Eduardo Mondlane University, Maputo, ever since the early 1980s.[30]

A case study of people's power in Mueda. The People's Republic of Mozambique, established on June 25, 1975, is divided into 10 provinces. The northernmost one of these is Cabo Delgado, bordering eastward on the Indian Ocean and northward on Tanzania. Until September 1986, Cabo Delgado was, in turn, divided into 12 administrative districts, the northwesternmost one of which was Mueda, the historic cradle in the early 1960s of the struggle for liberation from colonialism led by FRELIMO. Mueda has since been divided into two districts (Mueda and Muidumbe), with the southwestern part being transferred to the district of Montepuez. What still remains as the administrative district of Mueda is the actual "high plain of the Makondes" and the northwestern forest land just south of the river Rovuma, which marks the international frontier with Tanzania. The former district of Mueda had about 130,000 inhabitants of the approximately 14 million people living in Mozambique, while the new district formed in 1986 has about 90,000. The geographical distance from Mueda to the capital city of Maputo in the south is about 2000 kilometers.

The people of Mueda are basically peasant farmers. From the middle of the 1920s onward, they were reached by the colonial-capitalist economy mainly through the mechanisms of forced cotton cultivation on their own land and through forced labor on sisal plantations along the coast. The first arrival of Christian missionaries around 1920 also opened up an important form of contact with the colonizers. "The most important link of the high plain of Mueda with the colonial state seems to us to have been the missionary activities beginning in the twenties." (*Não Vamos Esquecer* 1, 1983:7.)

Besides being the district where FRELIMO's first mobilization for anticolonial struggle took place, Mueda is also one of the few districts where almost all peasants were, in the early 1980s, reported to live in communal villages (*aldeias comunais*). The communal village was the organizational and political framework of the intended transformation of Mozambique's countryside, as this was officially visualized before the disarray of the mid-1980s caused by the South African-directed war of destabilization. In the early 1980s, 16% of all of Mozambique's peasants were reported to be living in such villages.

Mueda is, thus, highly exceptional in Mozambique, both with regard to its historical significance and with regard to villagization. But precisely for those reasons, it also constitutes an instructive borderline case of the history and functioning of people's power as a political mechanism for linking peasant people and national leadership to each other.

The focus of the field work was on the functioning of the structures and institutions of people's power in the district of Mueda. The bulk of our work was done in the form of interviews and close study of various Frelimo (party) and state documents. The interviews were conducted with party and state officials and elected representatives at the levels of the district, subdistrict (*locali-*

dade), communal village, and local agricultural cooperatives. This included Frelimo branches ("cells") and the Executive Councils of the Popular Assemblies as well as representatives of the women's organization (OMM, *Organização da Mulher Moçambicana*) and the People's Tribunals. At the most local levels, our work came to be focused upon two places: on the one hand the *localidade* of Ngapa in the northwesternmost part of Mueda district, with its communal village and outlying settlements, and on the other hand the village of Nandimba, only ten kilometers from the district center, with the neighbor settlement of Nambavala, illegally established by part of the population of Nandimba.

Communal Villages

The conception of communal villages in Mozambique was presented as being based on the experiences of the armed struggle and the organization of life in the liberated territories of those years. The third congress of Frelimo (1977) formulated the key role intended for the communal villages in the continued transformation of rural life as follows:

> [It is a main task of the party in the economic field . . .] to promote and develop the communal villages, an invaluable instrument of the Mozambican Revolution. They provide the model of collective life based on collective production that we aim to install in our country. They contribute decisively to the implementation of *the power of the worker-peasant alliance in the rural areas* (*Programa e Estatutos* 1977:16 and following, my emphasis).

Despite slow and difficult progress in the following years in extending communal villages over the country, the program adopted in 1983 by the fourth congress employs an identical formulation (*Statutes and Programme of the Frelimo Party* 1983:12).

In practice, the Mozambican communal village had by the early 1980s developed into a general organizational frame, the actual content of which differed widely from place to place, region to region, and time to time. With regard to historical origin, four main types may be distinguished: origin in the preindependence liberated territories, in colonial strategic settlements (*aldeamentos*), in resettlements after the floods of the rivers Limpopo, Incomati, and Zambezi in 1977 and 1978, and, finally, in a minority of villages created directly as *aldeias comunais* after independence.

Although those communal villages that had their historical roots in FRELIMO-controlled settlements within the liberated territories are all found in the north, only Nandimba of the two Mueda communal villages within which our field work was done had that kind of origin. It was formed during the transitional 1974–1975 government, in an effort by FRELIMO to bring together people who during the struggle had lived dispersed in the forest in small settlements, although politically integrated through the structures of *poder popular*. Ngapa, however, is a mixture of former colonial aldeamento and settlements of refugees returning from Tanzania after liberation, but including also people who had been living with FRELIMO in the forest during the war years.

Approximately 1.8 million people were reported to be living in communal villages in 1982, but only 37,000 of them were also members of agricultural producers' cooperatives (*Relatório do Comité Central ao IV Congresso* 1983:31). Thus, the overwhelming majority of Mozambican peasants, who have not seen their lives disrupted through South Africa-directed or inspired destabilization, live and produce within the ordinary family cultivation sector. This is certainly true of the people of Ngapa and Nandimba.

Besides being intended to facilitate the organization of the rural people for various forms of collective production, which actually materialized only to a very limited extent, it was also the original task of the communal villages to provide the basis for organizing health, trade, educational, and other cultural services, as well as for developing democracy—that is, people's power, at the local level. In 1982, there were reportedly around 1350 communal villages throughout the country. Of these, 460 were reported to have elected their Assemblies of the People and 156 to have elected their People's Tribunals, while the remaining had not yet held elections. Functioning party branches were reported to exist in 516 communal villages (*Relatório* . . . 1983:21). The localidade of Ngapa and the communal villages of Ngapa and Nandimba were, in 1983, provided both with assemblies, tribunals, and party branches.

Assemblies of the People

Until the pluralistic constitutional reforms first proposed in early 1990, the Assemblies of the People were "the supreme organs of power of the Popular Democratic state" (Article 1 of the electoral law, *Lei Eleitoral* 1980:7), in turn oriented and directed by Frelimo, which is "the leading force of the state and of society." (Articles 2 and 3 of the constitution.) There were six types of assemblies, elected at four different administrative levels: nation, provinces, districts, and at the most local administrative level, cites, localidades (subdistricts), and communal villages or other newly formed concentrations of people. The national and provincial assembles were, according to the electoral law, elected for five years, the others for two and a half (Articles 2 and 3, *Lei Eleitoral* 1980:8 and following).

The first national elections of assemblies were organized in 1977, at which time a district assembly for Mueda was elected for the first time. In 1980, elections were organized all over the country below the provincial level, thus including Mueda. The elections planned to be held in 1983 were postponed but eventually were held in 1986 with considerable difficulties owing to the generally very difficult situation in the country.

In the 1980 elections, Assemblies of the People were elected for the first time in the localidade of Ngapa and in the communal village of Nandimba. Formally, at least, assemblies were also elected in the ten communal villages of Ngapa. The communal village investigated by us was located close to the administrative center of the localidade, and carried the same name. In accordance with the electoral law, elections at the grassroots level were done at general meetings of the citizens. District level elections were run by "electoral conferences"—that is sessions of delegates elected locally at general meeting of the citizens. Candidates were proposed by the party (Article 15, *Lei Eleitoral* 1980:16 and following).

The hierarchy of assemblies which were, until 1990, the institutional cornerstones of people's power in Mozambique were supposed to function in close cooperation with the organs of the party and of the mass organizations (women, youth, labor) at the various levels.

"Disaggregation" of Communal Villages

As an initial general observation, our investigation clearly indicated that the party and the state in Mueda functioned in such symbiosis that the official formula, often repeated in our interviews, according to which "the party directs and the state executes," rang very abstract.

The extreme weakness, in a straight material sense, of the party/state structure, particularly in the outlying area of Ngapa, was also striking. The young secretary, who in 1983 was the highest representative of the state in this large and faraway border zone with about 23,000 inhabitants had, for instance, no means of transportation either for moving around in the localidade or for visiting the district center of Mueda over 60 kilometers away. His only available options were to walk or to catch a ride with some rare visitor. He did not even have a communication radio and lacked most other material resources as well. The party could be said to be organizationally somewhat stronger than the state outside the center town of Ngapa, but equally weak in the material sense.

At the time of our field work in the autumn of 1983, the Assemblies of the People had not met for over a year either at the district level or in Ngapa. The assembly of the village of Nandimba had been formed in 1980, in a top-down party steered process, and did not seem ever to have functioned since. The same was true of the ten separate communal village assemblies of the Ngapa localidade.

The functioning of the structures and institutions of people's power in Mueda was thus in a precarious situation in 1983. A year later there was no fundamental change within sight (Adam and others 1986:59).

The clearest indication of the political problems involved was the co-called disaggregation of many of the communal villages (*desagregação das aldeias comunais*). The issue of disaggregation became an important focus of our study, as it directly concerns both people's power and a key problem of Mozambican development in general: that is, the failure so far of the Frelimo regime to mobilize the peasants of the country into producing a national economic surplus.

As already indicated, there had been a movement away from the communal village of Nandimba by a number of dissatisfied peasants, who in early March 1983 had established themselves at a site called Nambavala, half way between Nandimba and the center town of Mueda. Despite being openly resisted by the authorities—in February 1983, for instance, the supply of piped water was cut, forcing the inhabitants of Nambavala to walk four kilometers for water—the new settlement flourished and the people were determined to stay on.

The problem of disaggregation had left its mark also on the entire localidade of Ngapa, where we were able to visit and study three so-called cooperatives—Chitope, Nambungale, and Muimbua. These were actually autonomous villages established in the forest by peasants who had abandoned the center village of Ngapa, but used the designation cooperatives in an effort to legitimize their undertaking in the eyes of the authorities. The most distant of the three villages, Muimbua, was located about 25 kilometers northwest of the center of Ngapa, close to the river Rovuma and, thus, to Tanzania.

With regard to the background conditions of the process of disaggregation, there are some striking similarities with conditions in faraway Kandjadja, in Guinea-Bissau, on the opposite side of the continent—particularly in the case of Ngapa.

Considering for example the feeble presence of the state and the lively unofficial trade across the nearby northern frontier, it does not appear exaggerated to say that the social and economic life of the Ngapa subdistrict was, at the end of 1983, out of the control of the Mozambican state. The situation was serious too with regard to the satisfaction of basic material and social needs. People lacked clothing and other fundamental necessities. The schools did not function well, not only for material reasons but also because the parents distrusted them and did not always send their children there. Health services were totally insufficient. Transportation, except by foot, was virtually nonexistent. There was much resentment among the local population for these reasons, which was expressed through political cynicism and distrust of party and state authority. In all of those respects, the Ngapa situation was reminiscent of Kandjadja, although generally more loaded with a feeling of acute crisis.

The disaggregation of the communal villages in Mueda was explained to us in opposite ways by the peasants on the one side and most party and state officials on the other. The most basic general reason given by the peasants was that they wanted to live close to their best lands to avoid long and tiring daily walks, sometimes as much as three, four or even five hours on foot from their permanent homes. Reference was also made to various kinds of conflicts between groups, making life difficult in the concentrated settlements favored by the authorities. In the perspective of most party and state officials, on the other hand, the problem resulted fundamentally from a resurgence of reactionary and tribal political power, historically rooted in collaboration with the colonialists and in backward traditions—in short, the old "reactionary line" discussed above—tendencies to be fought with all means available, including, if necessary, open force.

In the autonomous villages of Ngapa, we were able to note a tendency of merging between the customary power of the elders with the formal structure of cooperatives adopted to legitimize the breakaway settlements. But neither in Ngapa nor in Nandimba were we able to find anything substantial to support the accusations of "tribalism" and "reactionary" opposition against the regime.

In the eyes of party and state authorities, the case of the Nambavala breakaway from Nandimba, close to the district center, was more immediately threatening than the autonomous "cooperatives" of Ngapa. It was perceived as an open challenge of the authority of the state. The real background, however, was highly complex, involving dissatisfaction with the top-down way the village had originally been formed, personal and family rivalries, the fact of some leaders having local authority without being trusted by Frelimo, and also general disillusionment with the incapacity of the Frelimo regime to help people resolve their elementary problems of "life and development." As far as our research team could discover, however, there was nothing in all this to substantiate the accusations of active resistance against the new state. Still, after considerable hesitation and wavering, the governor of the province of Cabo Delgado finally, in early 1984, gave the order to finish once and for all with the settlement of Nambavala. The houses were destroyed and its 260 inhabitants forced to move—some to the district center five kilometers away and others to the low-land area below the high plain (*Noticias,* Feb. 10, 1984; Adam and others 1986:35).

In Ngapa, events evolved with less open confrontation. Even there, some burnings by the army of dwellings in one of the outlying villages (Nambungale) were reported to have occurred before our field work. But the houses had been quickly rebuilt and ordinary day-to-day activities resumed by the population. Toward the end of 1984, the localidade of Ngapa was touched by the activities of the MNR (*Movimento Nacional de Resistência*) bands operating from Malawi. This caused the new administrative chief installed in Ngapa in 1984 to decide that Chitope, Nambungale, and Muimbua be administratively joined together into one single cooperative. Military security was given as a reason. Thus the inhabitants of those three autonomous villages were told to live in the center village of Ngapa and to coordinate their productive work, while they were allowed to visit, only in order to work, the three sites where they wanted to live. What this meant in actual practice, during the following years, is not clear to me at the moment of writing and revising this text. The MNR do not seem to have gained any real foothold in Ngapa, and it has not been possible to establish any connection between their activities and the various movements of the peasants away from the communal villages. Still, it can, of course, be said that the disaggregation does indicate the existence of such contradictions and reasons for dissatisfaction that the MNR could have exploited, had they been interested in working politically at the local level, which they were not.

Our conclusion, as researchers, was that the process of disaggregation arose fundamentally from the inability of the state to give adequate support to the people. With only minor inputs from outside in combination with readiness on the part of state and party officials to take the views of the local farmers seriously, the three sites in Ngapa that we studied could all have been transformed into units of production contributing constructively to the economic development of the district of Mueda. But this did not happen. Instead, party and state were seen by the people as sources of promises never fulfilled. In moving away from the communal villages of the state, the farmers were simply trying to solve their problems of life and development as best they could.

All this is not to say that we found the attitude of the party/state to be simply rigid or dogmatic. It was, on the contrary, marked by considerable pragmatism and the officials often admitted that the peasants may well have had good, concrete reasons for moving away. The dilemma, from the state's point of view, was the politically independent character of the new settlements. In the face of this, the representatives of the party/state tried to establish compromises with the people, keeping the threat of force as a final resort. What seemed to be lacking, though, was the active search for a dynamic third way, marked neither by simple short-term pragmatism nor by "revolutionary" violence.

Underlying this entire situation was the Mueda version of Mozambique's general crisis. The farmers of Mueda produced enough food for their own bare survival. Drought had not destroyed their livelihood, and there was no real famine, but, in all other material respects, they were, at the time of our study, left almost without resources. The state had very little to offer them to meet their primary needs in return for whatever surpluses they were able to produce. The lack of clothing and other sheer necessities was grave.

At the national level, the crisis resulted from a combination of historical and present factors, all supporting each other in a vicious downward spiral. Among the most important of those factors were: the continued structural dependence on the South African economy combined since independence with the breakdown of the colonial network of distribution, and the heavy reduction of migrant labor as a source of income; South African economic and military warfare, strategically supported by U.S. policies vis-à-vis South Africa; ecological disasters (floods and drought); all this and more in combination with the dangerous neglect by the Frelimo regime of the crucial peasant sector of the economy to the advantage of large-scale state farms, at least until the 1983 party congress when this line was belatedly criticized officially.

In Mueda the historical legitimacy of Frelimo can be assumed to be particularly strong, owing to the historical origin of the anticolonial liberation struggle and the early establishment of liberated territories in this part of the country. Despite this, the indications of political demobilization were clear, including a certain recrudescence of ethnic loyalties and disillusionment with the hardships of postcolonial life.

Within a people's power perspective, however, there is no other solution to this than policies that correspond to the interests experienced and expressed by those very people who will have to pay with their own labor for improving the situation. Such policies require functioning structures, organs, and institutions of people's power. "The people need some support" was a recurring formulation in interview answers from peasants in the disaggregated settlements.

At Least Some Support . . .

In concluding our report on the field study, we emphasized that building people's power, in FRELIMO's sense, depends most critically upon the type of relationship established between the people and their leaders. Wherever people's power became a reality during the armed struggle for liberation, it resulted from a social process in which the people participated actively in discussing and resolving their own problems. Such social relations of power do not fall from the sky; they arise from common goals and interests. They require concrete efforts on the part of the leadership to listen and act together with the people to resolve the manifold development problems. The real difficulty, we wrote, comes at the moment when party and state officials no longer share these problems with the people or when they find ways of resolving them only for themselves (Adam and others 1986:60–61).

Whatever the differences between the situations of the people of Kandjadja on one side of Africa and the people of Ngapa and Nandimba on the other—and there are, of course, many differences—it is hardly a coincidence that they express themselves almost identically when demanding at least "some support" from the states whose power they have been instrumental in establishing through the struggle for liberation from colonialism.

COMPARATIVE DISCUSSION

The Analytical Image

Returning for a moment to our earlier analytical image, let us try to use it to sum up comparatively some essentials of what has been shown thus far.

Our illustrations from Guinea-Bissau and Mozambique can be fruitfully interpreted by starting from the insight that the liberation movements of those two countries were based primarily on anticolonial political alliances between petit bourgeois leaders and peasant producers. They were not based on any class interest of the peasants in supporting centralized states appropriating their surpluses for purposes beyond their control. The socialist-oriented radicalization— including elements of people's power—that developed in both countries during the struggle (ideologically more strongly formulated in Mozambique than in Guinea-Bissau) was real enough insofar as it was rooted in the requirements of political mobilization for the struggle and in the liberated zones. But in the postcolonial situation, there was not much concrete substance left to sustain it.

During the periods of armed struggle against the Portuguese colonial regimes in Guinea-Bissau and Mozambique, there was thus within the liberation movements and in the liberated areas a tendency toward harmonization between the three societal levels of social base, power structure, and goal orientation, represented in our image. Although not based on long-term common class interests, both PAIGC and FRELIMO united broad groups of people and leadership behind common goals, which could, in turn, only be realized through a power structure taking the views and interests of the broad base into account.

The thorny question of the class character of the postcolonial state to be constructed was, of course, debated within the liberation movements. In Mozambique, as we have seen, it even developed into a hot political issue forcing a showdown between opposed tendencies and leading up to a turning point in the ideological development of FRELIMO. Even so, the real test could not and would not come until after independence had been achieved.

The growing political gap between peasant producers and the state indicated by our illustrations from Kandjadja and Mueda can reasonably be interpreted as a consequence of the class character of the postcolonial states of Guinea-Bissau and Mozambique. The wielders of state power and the peasant producers no longer experienced the community of interests that had brought them together for anticolonial struggle. The basis for structures of people's power narrowed. The making of actual policies no longer involved the broad majorities of people in any credible manner, as it had at times within the liberation movements. The orientation of actual policies consequently came to be guided by a combination of short-term pragmatism and the ideology of the leadership, marked in Guinea-Bissau principally by very weak policies until the IMF and World Bank instigated market liberalization of the 1980s, and in Mozambique by sometimes harshly attempted socialist policies, until liberalization forced its way even there after 1983.

In both countries, the fact that policy was often weakly rooted politically in the first place, naturally contributed to further narrowing the social basis of state power, in turn making it even more difficult (or not necessary from the power point of view of power wielders) to uphold democratic practices.

The International Dimension

With regard to international autonomy or capacity for self-steering in the international environment, the remarks made earlier in this text are quite applicable to our two examples, although the emphasis of our concrete illustrations has not been on the international aspects of development. Using the terms of the Figure 3, and without extending the scope of our empirical analysis to the international field, let it just be noted that the measure of "strength in relation to others" which Guinea-Bissau and Mozambique actually had at their moments of independence was based on the popular mobilization achieved through successful anticolonial struggle, underpinned with military support from the Soviet Union and allied countries as well as with other forms of international support from other countries and organizations. The roots of that strength were internal, but it clearly did have an international dimension.

In the new situations of independence and thereby of changing tasks, broad popular mobilization as before could be sustained only through development policies meeting "concrete and fundamental interests of the people as experienced by them." (Above, compare also Hermele 1989.) But with the defeat of the colonial regime, military support from outside became largely irrelevant to the successful implementation of such policies, although in the case of Mozambique, military support did continue to be crucial to the very survival of the new state. Nor was any large-scale support for development policies meeting the needs of the people as experienced by themselves forthcoming from the forces of the world market. In practice this meant that the state, both in Guinea-Bissau and in Mozambique, was left with popular mobilization as the only conceivable source of firm support for such development policies that had to be implemented precisely to sustain that very mobilization. Breaking though that kind of deadlock would, in turn, have required the institutionalization and broadening of those very elements of radical democracy or people's power that had evolved from the liberation struggle. As we know, the predominant tendency at the level of political structure in the analytical image was, however, in the opposite direction, caught as this level was in the negative dynamics just described.

If the initial situations of independent Guinea-Bissau and Mozambique can be generally characterized as fairly similar with regard to the factor of "strength" in terms of the Figure 3, the same can hardly be said about the factor of "international integration." Neither one of the countries existed in autarchy, but Mozambique was more deeply and conflictually integrated in, and also more important in strategic and economic terms to, the surrounding world than was Guinea-Bissau. As the internally based strength of the two newborn states was being sapped in the manner already analyzed, Mozambique was thus becoming an ever more clear case of block 2 in the Figure 3 (high integration/ low strength). The case of Guinea-Bissau was superficially less clear, with neither the financial and labor market dependence on a powerful enemy neighbor (South Africa) nor the kind of imposed warfare (first with Southern Rhodesia and then more and more openly with South Africa, after Zimbabwe's independence) that faced Mozambique. But Guinea-Bissau was and remains a peripheral country in the capitalist world market. In that sense it is—as Mozambique, although in a very different way—also a case of high integration/low strength (block 2) in the Figure 3.

Both Mozambique and Guinea-Bissau thus find themselves in the characteristic situation of low autonomy or low capacity for self-steering in the international system. But Mozambique is subjected to a harsher and more extreme version of this situation, combining international aggression and the inequitable pressures of the world market in a deadly way, while Guinea-Bissau provides a more "normal" illustration of what periphery status on the world market is about.

The most important conclusion from all this for our present discussion is that, whatever the differences between them, the respective international situations of Guinea-Bissau and Mozambique have, in both cases, served to reinforce the negative dynamics—from the point of view of people's development as defined in the introduction—between the three levels of societal reality included in our analytical image. Let me emphasize the notion of reinforcement, thus emphasizing also that those dynamics are seen as having an internal autonomy of their own.

The Cultural Dimension

The question of the cultural basis of the state will be raised even more briefly than that of international autonomy—and only to demonstrate its relevance to the kind of analysis developed in this text.

It was stated earlier that the extent to which cultural differences are respected and cultural pluralism accepted (in particular by the wielders of state power) is a factor of more overriding significance than cultural integration for that society's chances of maintaining legitimate political unity. If cultural diversity is mutually accepted, cultural integration will not stand out as a necessary condition of political integration. This is, however, as we know, a very big "if."

Without developing the empirical analysis here, let me just advance the hypothesis that in the cases of the culturally diverse societies of Guinea-Bissau and Mozambique, cultural acceptance of diversity on equal terms would be facilitated through equalization of the power structure. The argument is that the more rooted in people's self-experienced and self-expressed interests the political structure is, the less likely that policies of forced cultural integration will be imposed. This may appear as too simple an argument, in view of historical examples of democratization and ethnic conflict developing side by side, and also in view of colonial policies of (ethnic) divide and rule. As a general hypothesis it is still plausible, however, serving at the same time logically to indicate a way of linking the cultural level of analysis to our analytical image.

With regard more specifically both to Guinea-Bissau and to Mozambique, there is much to support the notion that policies of accepting diversity on equal terms, as a simple human right, would be more likely to foster both unity and people's development than would state enforced cultural integration.

A Note on Implications for Development and Democracy

Our introductory section on the nation-state was concluded with the suggestion that the cultural, political, and economic conditions of postcolonial Africa in general might offer solutions to the problems of state-building that have not yet been entirely formulated and perhaps not even foreseen. It cannot be excluded that the combination of everyday hardship and political repression will create strong pressures for new kinds of power structures, simultaneously more democratic and pluralistic, and more in the direction of a supra-state.

Under such institutional conditions, the people themselves would be able to build and extend elements of people's power as discussed above. However disconnected from today's political practices, the idea of people's power is, nevertheless, rooted in historical realities of the independence struggles and in the internal processes of transformation then set in motion in countries such as Guinea-Bissau and Mozambique. The seeds of hope for a life of dignity that are sown in people's minds all over Africa may appear irrelevant, at the level of state power, in today's contexts of IMF and World Bank austerity programs, but it would still be rash to conclude that they have lost all of their long-term significance.

As already indicated, people's power and democracy do not emerge from nowhere—whether in Guinea-Bissau, Mozambique, or anywhere else. The chances that they will gain some foothold are, on the contrary, strongest whenever the people involved who are most in need of more equally distributed power manage to gather enough strength of resistance to make their interests seen, heard, and felt in society.

Notes

1. Compare, for instance, books and articles (alphabetically ordered here) as different from each other as Amin in Anyang' Nyongo'o 1987, pp. 1–13; Baumann and others 1983; Beckman 1985, 1988:II; Egerö 1987; Eteki-Otabela 1987; Galli & Jones 1987; Huntington 1986; Hydén 1983, 1988; Lazreg 1976; Mamdani in Anyang Nyongo'o 1987, pp. 78–95; Martinussen 1980; Mouzelis 1986; Myrdal 1968; Nuscheler and Ziemer 1980; Rudebeck 1970:I, 1970:II, 1987:II; Sandbrook 1986; Schiefer 1986; Sklar 1987; Terray 1987; Törnquist 1989. There are, of course, many others. My purpose here is only to give an indication of the range and variety of writings on and around the theme of weakness of Third World states (particularly in Africa) with regard to economic development.

2. Almond 1960 and Apter 1965 and 1968 offer prominent examples. Almond and Powell 1966 is also (perhaps because of its textbook character) exceptionally straightforward with regard to what the modernization approach or school is all about. In Rude-

beck 1970:II and 1970:III, I dealt critically with this. I still regard my 1970 critique as basically valid and not untopical even today.

3. Examples are almost too numerous to cite. Sklar 1987 on "developmental democracy" is an interesting example on a subject close to that of the present essay. The major four-volume work edited by Diamond, Linz, and Lipset 1988 draws heavily on this approach, although attempting to broaden it into a "comprehensive theory." Even Apter 1987, moving along somewhat "postmodern" lines of his own in trying to synthesize modernization and dependency thinking, does not really seem to break out of his earlier paradigm.

4. My purpose here is not to review the vast literature fitting more or less roughly or neatly into my four-field diagram, but only to give a small number of relevant indications. Alavi 1972 is mentioned in the text for its seminal importance in the neo-Marxist debate over the state in the Third World. In analogous manner the two issues that have appeared so far of the *African Journal of Political Economy*—no. 1, 1986, on the theme of the "Labour process in Africa" and no. 2, 1987, on "Southern Africa in crisis"—are cited for marking so clearly a significant current trend of Third World political economy. Another important political economy journal is the *Review of African Political Economy,* established in 1974. Beckman's "Critique of a Kenyan Debate," published in 1980 in that journal, added fire to the discussion on how to transcend dependency theory without throwing out the baby with the bath water. Werker 1985 is another highly interesting contribution to that discussion. Compare also *Labour and Democracy* 1986, which is an attempted outline of a research program in political economy, and the report on achievements and plans given in *Report of the AKUT Group 1987–1990 and Plans for 1990–1993,* 1990.

5. Martinussen 1980, pp. 1506–1507, and 1982, p. 12, goes further than most political scientists with regard to conceptual specification and clarification of political structure in his analyses of the states in India and Pakistan. Still, he settles for two complex types of "form" of "state," "regime," or "order" (in 1982 he settles for the term *"form of regime"*): parliamentary-democratic versus bureaucratic-authoritarian. Nevertheless, those two "forms" combine two variables (parliamentary/bureaucratic and democratic/authoritarian) that do not necessarily vary together.

6. Compare Clastres 1980 (in particular pp. 103–145) for a provocative statement of the position that power may actually have been completely nonexistent in certain "primitive" societies of precolonial South America. Sigrist 1979:II investigates the mechanisms of "regulated anarchy" in "segmentary" African societies.

7. The Cape Verdean writer and political scientist Onésimo Silveira sums up his discussion of this issue in a similar vein (Silveira 1976, p. 57): "The nation, like the ethnic and tribal groups, is an existential structure and as such contains aspects of active differentiation and identification which are profoundly rooted in history."

8. From studying historical data on Italian colonialism in Eritrea not previously used for such purposes, Negash 1987, pp. 161–164, concludes, perhaps surprisingly, that 50 years of Italian domination over that country did not result in the emergence of any Eritrean nationalism worth the name. In Portugal's African colonies, however, limited petit bourgeois strata did emerge, members of which would later, as also in Eritrea, come to lead movements with "national" and "nationalist" appeals. Comparing the impacts of Italian and Portuguese colonialism in Africa would, perhaps, be a worthwhile project of historical research.

On the terminological question of how to label those "modern" social strata, to the emergence of which colonialism certainly contributed in a decisive manner, I have argued earlier (Rudebeck in Egerö and Rudebeck, 1982, p. 13) in favor of the term "intermediate strata" rather than "petty/petite bourgeoisie" (1) to rid our analytical language of the derogatory connotation of "petty", and (2) to avoid the theoretical confusion involved in lumping together in one category small commodity producers (the original Marxian meaning of petit-bourgeois) with all others who are neither capitalists, proletarians, nor real peasants, i.e. with various kinds of salaried employees, merchants, and intellectuals. Here, however, I will nevertheless use "petty bourgeois(ie)" with quotation marks, both because it is the term found in the English language version of Amilcar Cabral's texts to be quoted, but also because the term is so widely used in the third world context to refer to the intermediate strata of colonial and postcolonial societies, that it is hard to avoid using it.

9. As far as bending to an assumed necessity of a capitalist stage is concerned, there is, in fact, an interesting similarity between the arguments for such a position by Lopes in Lopes/Rudebeck 1988 and the arguments of Hydén 1980, 1983, 1986, as I point out in my comment on Lopes' text (pp. 22 and following). Compare, for instance, Amin 1986, where an entirely different and less deterministic perspective is outlined, as well as Amin's contribution to Anyang' Nyongo'o 1987, pp. 1–13. Compare also Sardan in Terray 1987, pp. 175–186, on "national and collective identities," who offers a fresh perspective on the question of national consciousness.

10. See Rudebeck 1972, 1974, 1977, 1978, 1979:I, 1979:II, 1982:I, 1982:II, 1983:I, 1983:II, 1984, 1986, 1987:II, 1987:III, 1989, on Guinea-Bissau.

11. My own work on Mozambique is limited to Rudebeck 1985; Adam, Bragança, Depelchin, Egerö, Littlejohn, Rudebeck 1986.

12. The original initials PAI stood for *Partido Africano da Independência.* According to Lopes 1987, pp. 29 and 38 (note 2), the initials PAIGC (*Partido Africano da Independência da Guiné e Cabo Verde*) did not come into use until October 1960.

13. The following up to p. 55 is basically a condensed and revised version of the analysis found in Rudebeck 1983:II, incorporating also my readings of Achinger in Meyns 1988, pp. 178–198; Cardoso 1986; Dowbor 1983; Galli 1986; Galli and Jones 1987; Handem 1986; Lepri 1986:I and 1986:II; Lopes 1986 and 1987; Ribeiro 1986; Ribeiro and Cardoso in Meyns 1988, pp. 155–157; Santos 1986; Schiefer 1986; *Soronda* 1986–1989.

14. This was first presented at a seminar held at the Frantz Fanon Center at Treviglio, Milan, in early May 1964. I am using here the English language version published in Cabral 1969, pp. 46–61, which I have checked against an early but incomplete official PAIGC version, Cabral 1966.

15. The distinction between vertically and horizontally organized societies is not found in "Brief analysis . . ." But it was introduced by Cabral in his speech at the first Tricontinental Conference of the Peoples of Asia, Africa, and Latin America, held in Havana in January 1966. This speech is included in Cabral 1969 under the title "The weapon of theory," pp. 73–90. The distinction vertical/horizontal is found on p. 78.

16. Galli 1982, pp. 11–12. Compare also Galli 1986, pp. 58 and following.

17. Rudebeck 1974, pp. 116 and following, 144–147, 151 and following; Galli and Jones, pp. 55–108. Compare also note 21.

18. Cabral 1969, p. 50. Interestingly enough, Schiefer 1986 (pp. 156–160), al-

though critical, falls into the same trap as Cabral of viewing the peasant producers as somehow innately conservative, and for the same reason: acceptance of the dualist theoretical assumption of a culture-bound inclination of Guinean and other peasants to cling no matter what to traditional use-value oriented production, an assumption of the primacy of cultural variables that blurs the contradiction between producers and the state striving to appropriate the value they produce.

19. On May 10, 1972, just over eight months before he was murdered, I had a long talk with Amilcar Cabral in Conakry. He described to me the system of government he wanted to see at work in his country after liberation. This was a system whose political and economic power would be firmly anchored in decentralized assemblies of the people, which, in turn, would elect a national assembly. The functions of the state were to be strictly limited. The freely elected assemblies of the people were to be the only sovereign organs of people's power. In his discussion with me, Cabral called this system "cooperative democracy," In a revolutionary perspective, such a system obviously rests on the assumption that the people are a "revolutionary force" and not a mere "physical force," as Cabral had called the Guinean peasants in 1964. We see thus how two different modes of thinking were ambivalently posed against each other within Cabral's own analysis of the class basis of the liberation movement, one marked by classical Leninist party theory combined with conventional modernization thinking, the other revolutionary-democratic.

20. Davidson 1981, pp. 16 and following; Andrade 1980, pp. 80–82. This is quoted and analyzed from a colonial perspective by Correia da Cruz 1968 (p. 60 of transcript): "In fact, the reaction on the part of the authorities and of the population to the upheavals [the strike of the dock workers] that occurred and the consequent neutralization of various clandestine networks convinced the native leaders that the struggle in urban centers could not be developed in such a way as to achieve their objectives."

21. I have reported on Kandjadja in Rudebeck 1977, pp. 34–42 and 104–135, 1982:II, pp. 36–42, 1987, and 1989.

22. In these parts of West Africa, the Kaabu empire gradually developed out of the Mali empire, the decline of which set in at the end of the fourteenth century. From the sixteenth century onward, Kaabu provided the dominant state structure of the region stretching from the Atlantic coast to the Futa Jallon highlands of present-day Guinea-Conakry and bordered in the north by the river Gambia. Kaabu was not decisively broken up and superseded by colonial state structures until the end of the nineteenth century. It is still likely to be alive in the minds of many people. On the Kaabu empire see "Actes du Colloque . . . ," *Ethiopiques* 1981; Hawkins 1980, pp. 52–106; Lopes 1989; and Mané 1989.

23. According to *Introdução à geografia económica da Guiné-Bissau* 1980, p. 140, there are about 3600 villages in Guinea-Bissau with an average population of slightly more than 200 inhabitants.

24. The analysis performed in this text ends around the mid-1980s. Thus, it does not bring into focus the structural adjustment policies implemented since then in Guinea-Bissau and Mozambique, in agreement with the World Bank and the International Momentary Fund. In a separate publication (Rudebeck 1989, in Portuguese in 1990), I have, however, reported on developments in the village of Kandjadja up to early 1989, telling among other things about the closing down of the state school, the reopening of the former People's Store under private ownership, the existence in 1988 of 12 ploughs

among the villagers, and the political tensions traceable to disillusionment with the state and a kind of return to ethnic culture and local solutions.

25. The bibliography given at the end contains a number of titles on Mozambique not explicitly referred to in the following text. They are, however, all in some way or other, and to a greater or lesser extent, relevant to my presentation of our Mozambican example. Compare also my argument on p. 47, on the function of the two examples in our analysis.

26. Until its third congress (1977), FRELIMO (*Frente de Libertação de Moçambique*, Liberation Front of Mozambique) was held to be a front organization. At the third congress, it was changed into the Frelimo Party, "vanguard party of the worker-peasant alliance," changed again in 1989 by the fifth congress into "the party of the entire people." In this text, I use capital letters when referring to the pre-1977 front and small letters when referring to the party, in accordance with the most frequent Mozambican usage.

27. *História da Frelimo* 1983, pp. 11–12 (my translation from original in Portuguese).

28. See Adam 1988; Adam, Bragança, Depelchin, Egerö, Littlejohn, Rudebeck 1986, Alpers 1983; Bragança and Depelchin 1986; Ernst and Hutschenreuter 1981; Hermele 1986, 1987; Issacman 1982; Kruks 1983; *Não Vamos Esquecer* 4, 1987; Negrão 1981, 1984; *Towards a History of the National Liberation Struggle in Mozambique: Problematics, Methodologies, Analyses*, 1982; Vieira 1979.

29. Adam and others 1986. See also Rudebeck 1984; Littlejohn 1984; Egerö 1987.

30. See Adam 1986, 1988; Bragança and Depelchin 1986; Littlejohn 1984; *Mozambican Studies* 1980, 1981; *Não Vamos Esquecer* 1983, 1987; *Towards a history . . .* 1982, as well as other contributions not listed in our bibliography.

References

Achinger, Gertrud. 1988. "Ergebnisse empirischer Untersuchungen zum Entwicklungspotential der bäuerlichen Landwirtschaft in Guinea-Bissau," in Meyns (ed) pp. 178–198.

"Actes du Colloque international sur les traditions orales du Gabu," Dakar, May 19–24, 1980, special issue of *Ethiopiques* (Dakar), 28 October, 1981.

A construção da nação em África. Os exemplos de Angola, Cabo Verde, Guiné-Bissau, Moçambique e S. Tomé e Principe. 1989. With an introduction by Lars Rudebeck, Instituto Nacional de Estudos e Pesquisa (INEP), Bissau.

Adam, Yussuf. 1986. *Cooperativização agrícola e modificação das relações de produção no período colonial em Moçambique* (*licenciatura* thesis), Centro de Estudos Africanos, Eduardo Mondlane University, Maputo.

———. 1986. "Kollektive ländliche Entwicklung und Genossenschaften in Mozambique. Die Lage in den alten 'befreiten Gebieten' von Cabo Delgado," in Meyns (ed) 1988 pp. 60–110. Revised version of larger version in Portuguese, "Desenvolvimento rural collectivo em Moçambique: a situação nas antigas 'zonas libertadas' de Cabo Delgado," Maputo, (mimeo).

———. 1987. "Dreams and Revolution. Toward an Understanding of the Mozambique Situation," review of Egerö 1987. *Southern Africa Political and Ecomonic Monthly* (2): 27–30.

Adam, Yussuf; Bragança, Aquino de; Depelchin, Jacques; Egerö, Bertil; Littlejohn, Gary; Rudebeck, Lars. 1986. *Poder popular e desagregação nas aldeias comunais do planalto de Mueda,* Centro de Estudos Africanos, Report 1, 1986, Eduardo Mondlane University, Maputo.

African Journal of Political Economy/Revue Africaine d'Economie Politique. 1986. (1).

Alavi, Hamza. 1972. "The State in Post-Colonial Societies: Pakistan and Bangladesh." *New Left Review* (74): 59–81.

Almond, Gabriel A. 1960. "Introduction: A Functional Approach to Comparative Politics," in Almond, Gabriel A., and Goleman, James S. (eds), *The Politics of the Developing Areas.* Princeton: Princeton University Press.

Almond, Gabriel A. and Powell, G. Bingham. 1966. *Comparative Politics: a Developmental Approach.* Boston: Little, Brown & Co.

Alpers, Edward A. 1983. *"To seek a better life": The implications of migration from northern Mozambique to colonial and independent Tanzania for class formation and political behavior in the struggle to liberate Mozambique,* paper for workshop on "The class basis of nationalist movements in Angola, Guinea-Bissau and Mozambique." Department of Afro-American and African Studies, University of Minnesota, Minneapolis (mimeo).

Amin, Samir. 1986. "Etat, nation, ethnie et minorités dans la crise. Quelques aspects de la critique de l'idéologie de la nation et de l' ethnie," paper presented at conference on "The formation of the nation in 'the five' (Angola, Cape Verde, Guinea-Bissau, Mozambique, S. Tomé e Principe)," Instituto Nacional de Estudos e Pesquisa (INEP), Bissau, (mimeo).

———. 1987. "Preface: the state and the question of development," in Anyang' Nyongo'o (ed) pp. 1–13.

Anacleti, A. Odhiambo. 1983. *Research on Africa and African Societies. A Need for New Approach.* Turku: University of Turku, Publications in Political History E:2.

Andrade, Mario de. 1980. *Amilcar Cabral. Essai de biographie politique,* Paris: Maspero.

Anyang' Nyongo'o, Peter (ed). 1987. *Popular Struggles for Democracy in Africa,* Studies in African Political Economy, United Nations University and London: Zed Books.

Apter, David E. 1965. *The Politics of Modernization.* Chicago and London: University of Chicago Press.

———. "Political systems and developmental change." 1968. In Apter, David E., *Some Conceptual Approaches to the Study of Modernization,* Englewood Cliffs: Prentice-Hall.

———. *Rethinking Development. Modernization, Dependency, and Postmodern Politics,* 1989. Newbury Park, Beverly Hills, London, New Delhi: SAGE Publications.

Arnfred, Signe 1985–1986. "Bønder og statsmagt i Moçambique." *Den ny verden* (Copenhagen) 19 (1): 62–69.

Baumann, Herbert; Fredmann, Bernd; Friedländer, Stephan, Rosenfeldt, Rüdiger 1987. "Einige Grundzüge der Entwicklung bürgerlicher Demokratie in befreiten Ländern Asiens, Afrikas und Lateinamerikas." *Asien, Afrika, Lateinamerika. Zeitschrift des Zentralen Rates für Asien-, Afrika- und Lateinamerikawissenschaften in der DDR* (Berlin) 15 (6): 949–962.

Beckman, Björn, 1980. "Imperialism and capitalist transformation: critique of a Kenyan debate." *Review of African Political Economy* (Sheffield) (19), 48–62.

——. 1985. "Bakolori: peasants versus state and capital," *Nigerian Journal of Political Science* (Zaria) 4 (1-2): 76–104.

——. 1988. "The post-colonial state: crisis and reconstruction," paper presented to the African Futures Conference, Centre of African Studies, University of Edinburgh, 9-11 December 1987, revised for publication, May 1988, Department of Political Science, University of Stockholm, (mimeo).

——. 1988, "Comments" on contribution by Göran Hydén, in *Recovery in Africa. A Challenge for Development Cooperation in the 90s*. Stockholm Ministry for Foreign Affairs.

Bowen, Merle Luanne. 1986. "Let's build agricultural producer cooperatives": Socialist Agricultural Development Strategy in Mozambique, 1975-1983 (Ph.D. thesis). Toronto: University of Toronto.

Bragança, Aquino de. 1986. "Independência sem descolonização: a transferência do poder em Moçambique," *Estudos Moçambicanos* (Maputo) (5-6): 7–28.

Bragança, Aquino de and Depelchin, Jacques. 1986. "Da idealização da Frelimo à compreensão da história de Moçambique," *Estudos Moçambicanos* (Maputo) (5-6): 29–52. Also as "From the idealization of Frelimo to the understanding of the recent history of Mozambique," *African Journal of Political Economy* (Harare), 1, 1986, pp. 162–180, and "Una storia del Frelimo fuori del mito," *Politica Internazionale* (Rome), 6–7, pp. 111–121.

Cabral, Amilcar. 1966. *Fondements et objectifs de la libération nationale.* I—Sur la domination impérialiste. Conakry: PAIGC (mimeo).

——. 1969. *Revolution in Guinea. An African people's struggle.* London: Stage 1.

——. 1970. "Libération nationale et culture," Eduardo Mondlane memorial lecture, delivered at the University of Syracuse, February 20, 1970. Conakry: PAIGC, Conakry, (mimeo).

Cahen, Michel. 1987. *Mozambique. La Révolution implosée.* Paris: L'Harmattan.

Cardoso, Carlos. 1989. "A historicidade da construção nacional na Guiné-Bissau, 4: a problemática da construção nacional na fase pós-independência, dificuldades e perspectivas," in *A construção da nação em Africa*, 281–297.

——. 1989. "Conflitos interétnicos. Dissolução e reconstrução de unidades políticas nos rios da Guiné e de Cabo Verde (1840-1899)." *Soronda. Revista de Estudos Guineenses* (Bissau), (7): 31–62.

Clastres, Pierre. 1980. *Recherches d'anthropologie politique*, Paris: Editions du Seuil.

Constituição da República Popular de Moçambique. 1982. Maputo: Edição do Instituto Nacional do Livro e do Disco.

Correia da Cruz, Luis Fernando Dias. 1968. "Some aspects of subversion in Portuguese Guinea," *Ultramar* (Lisbon), pp. 125–147 (in *Translations on Africa*, 767, pp. 58-66, partial transcript).

Davidson, Basil. 1981. *No Fist is Big Enough to Hide the Sky.* London: Zed Press, (reprint of *The liberation of Guiné*, Penguin, London, 1969, plus four new chapters).

Depelchin, Jacques. 1987. "Anti-communism and the re-writing of the histories of national liberation in southern Africa," Brussels: UCB, (mimeo).

Diamond, Larry, Linz, Juan J., and Lipset, Seymour Martin. 1988 and after.

Democracy in Developing Countries, (1–4). Boulder and London: Lynne
Rienner.

Dowbor, Ladislau. 1983. *Guiné-Bissau. A busca da independência económica.* São
Paulo: Brasiliense.

Egerö, Bertil. 1987. *Mozambique: a dream undone. The political economy of democracy.* 1975–84. Uppsala: Scandinavian Institute of African Studies.

Egerö, Bertil and Rudebeck, Lars. 1982. "Socialist development. Problems of class
analysis: contradictions and social movements in the third world," AKUT 22. Uppsala: Department of Development Studies, University of Uppsala.

Elsenhans, Hartmut. 1988. "Suggestions pour une analyse comparative de l'Etat en
Afrique noire . . . ," Unpublished paper.

Ernst, Klaus and Hutschenreuter, Klaus. 1981. "Die Herausbildung und Entwicklung
von Gemeinschaftsdörfern auf der Grundlage landwirtschaftlicher Genossenschaften
im Distrikt Mocuba/Provinz Zambésia." Centro de Estudos Africanos, Eduardo
Mondlane University, Maputo and Centre of African and Near East Studies, Karl
Marx University, Leipzig.

Eteki-Otabela, Marie-Louise. 1987. *Misère et grandeur de la démocratie au Cameroun.*
Paris: L'Harmattan.

Galli, Rosemary E. 1982. *Amilcar Cabral and rural transformation in Guinea-Bissau: a
preliminary critique.* University of Calabar, Nigeria. (mimeo).

———. 1986. Amilcar Cabral and rural transformation in Guinea-Bissau: a preliminary
critique. *Rural Africana* (East Lansing) (25–26): 55–73.

Galli, Rosemary E. and Jones, Jocelyn. 1987. *Guinea-Bissau. Politics, economics and
society.* London: Francis Pinter, and Boulder: Lynne Rienner.

Handem, Diana Lima. 1986. "Nature et fonctionnement du pouvoir chez les Balanta
Brassa," Collection "Kacu Martel" (1) Bissau: Instituto Nacional de Estudos e Pesquisa (INEP).

———. 1989. "A historicidade da construção nacional na Guiné-Bissau, 3: a luta de
libertação guineense," in *A construção da nação em Africa,* 267–280.

Hawkins, Joye Bowman. 1980. "Conflict, interaction, and change in Guinea-Bissau:
Fulbe expansion and its impact," 1850–1900. (Doctoral dissertation), Los Angeles:
University of California.

Hermele, Kenneth. 1984. *Migration and starvation. As essay on southern Mozambique.*
(AKUT 32) University of Uppsala: Department of Development Studies.

———. 1986. *Contemporary land struggles on the Limpopo. A case study of Chokwe,
Mozambique, 1950–1985.* (AKUT 34) Department of Development Studies, Univer-
sity of Uppsala, Also as "Lutas contemporâneas pela terra no vale do Limpopo.
Estudo do caso do Chokwe, Moçambique, 1950–1985," *Estudos Moçambicanos*
(Maputo) 1986 (5–6): 53–81.

———. 1988. "Land struggles and social differentiation in southern Mozambique. A
case study of Chokwe, Limpopo 1950–1987." Research Report 82. Uppsala: Scandinavian Institute of African Studies.

———. 1989. "Structural adjustment and political alliances in Angola, Guinea-Bissau,
and Mozambique," in Hermele and Rudebeck. (AKUT 41): 5–16 University of Uppsala: Department of Development Studies.

Hermele, Kenneth and Rudebeck, Lars. 1989. *At the crossroads: Political alliances and
structural adjustment. Two essays on Angola, Guinea-Bissau, and Mozambique,*
(AKUT 41): University of Uppsala: Department of Development Studies. In Portu-

guese as *Nas encruzilhadas: Alianças políticas e ajustamento estrutural. Dois ensaios sobre Angola, Guiné-Bissau e Moçambique.* (AKUT 41) 1990.

História da Frelimo. 1983. Maputo: Department of Ideological Work, Frelimo.

História de Moçambique, Volume 2. *Agressão imperialista* (1886/1930). 1983. Department of History, Eduardo Mondlane University, and Maputo: Tempo.

Huntington, Samuel P. 1968. *Political order in changing societies.* New Haven and London: Yale University Press.

Hutschenreuter, Klaus. 1985. "Der soziale Charakter der politischen Macht im Prozess sozialisticher Orientierung—das Beispiel der Volksrepublik Moçambique." *Leipziger Beiträge zur Revolutionsforschung.* Leipzig: Karl Marx University. (11): 44–61.

Hydén, Göran. 1980. *Beyond ujamaa in Tanzania. Underdevelopment and an uncaptured peasantry.* London: Heinemann, Nairobi: Ibadan.

———. 1983. *No shortcuts to progress. African development management in perspective.* London: Heinemann, Nairobi: Ibadan.

———. 1986. "The anomaly of the African peasantry," *Development and Change* (London: Sage) (17): 677–705.

———. 1988. "State and nation under stress," in *Recovery in Africa. A challenge for development cooperation in the 90s.* (Stockholm: Ministry for Foreign Affairs), pp. 145–157.

Introdução à geografía economica da Guiné-Bissau, 1980. State Commissariat of Economic Coordination and Planning, Bissau.

Isaacman, Allen. 1982. "The Mozambique cotton cooperative: the creation of a grassroots alternative to forced commodity production." *African Studies Review* 25 (2–3): 5–25.

———. 1988. "Mozambique." *Survival* London: International Institute for Strategic Studies. 30 (1): 14–38.

Justiça Popular, 1984. Journal of the Ministry of Justice, 8–9 Maputo.

Kruks, Sonia. 1983. "From nationalism to Marxism: the ideological history of FRELIMO," Paper for workshop on "The class basis of nationalist movements in Angola, Guinea-Bissau and Mozambique." Department of Afro-American and African Studies, University of Minnesota, Minneapolis (mimeo).

———. 1984. "The state, the party and the female peasantry in Mozambique," *Journal of Southern African Studies* (London) 11 (1): 106–127.

Lazreg, Marnia. 1976. *The emergence of classes in Algeria. A study of colonialism and socio-political change.* Boulder: Westview Press.

Lei Eleitoral. 1980. Imprensa Nacional, Maputo.

Lepri, Jean-Pierre. 1986. *"La formation de la nation Bissao-guinéenne: contribution à l'analyse de sa problematique."* Paper presented at conference on "The formation of the nation in 'the five' (Angola, Cape Verde, Guinea-Bissau, Mozambique, S. Tomé e Principe)." Bissau: INEP. (mimeo).

———. 1986. "Sobre as causas do insucesso escolar." *Soronda* (Bissau), 2): 21–27.

Littlejohn, Gary. 1984. "Rural development in Mueda district, Mozambique," Postgraduate School of Studies in Social Analysis, University of Bradford, (mimeo).

———. 1987. "Central planning and market relations in socialist societies." Postgraduate School of Studies in Social Analysis, University of Bradford, (mimeo).

Lipset, Seymour M. 1960. *Political man. The social bases of politics.* London, Melbourne, Toronto: Heinemann.

Lopes, Carlos. 1982. "Ethnie, état et rapports de pouvoir en Guiné-Bissau," Itinéraires. Notes et Travaux (22) Geneva: University Institute of Development Studies.

——. 1982. "A transição histórica na Guiné-Bissau. Do movimento de libertação nacional ao estado." Theses in development studies (16) Geneva: University Institute of Development Studies.

——. 1986. "A historicidade da construção nacional, 2: a questão nacional e a Guiné dita 'portuguesa' ." in *A construção da nação em Africa*, 243–266.

——. 1987. Guinea-Bissau. *From Liberation Struggle to Independent Statehood*. Boulder: Westview Press and London: Zed Books.

——. 1989. "Resistências africanas ao controle do território. Alguns casos da Costa da Guiné no século XIX." *Soronda* (Bissau) (7): 5–16.

Lopes, Carlos and Rudebeck, Lars. 1988. "The socialist ideal in Africa: a debate." Research Report 81. Uppsala: Scandinavian Institute of African Studies. 1988.

Mamdani, Mahmood. 1987. "Contradictory class perspectives on the question of democracy: the case of Uganda," in Anyang' Nyongo'o, *Popular Struggles for Democracy*, pp. 78–95.

Mané, Mamadú. 1989. "O Kaabú. Uma das grandes entidades do património histórico senegambiano." *Soronda* (Bissau) (7): 17–30.

Martinussen, John. 1980. *Staten i perifere samfund: Indien og Pakistan. En histoisk-konkret analyse med teorigenererende sigte* (four volumes). Politica, Århus.

——. 1982. *Social classes and forms of state and regime in peripheral societies*, AKUT 24, Department of Development Studies, University of Uppsala.

Meyns, Peter (ed). 1988. *Agrargesellschaften im portugiesisch-sprachigen Afrika*, Social Science Studies on International Problems 129. Breitenbach, Saarbrücken and Fort Lauderdale.

Moore, Jr., Barrington. 1966. *Social Origins of Dictatorship and Democracy*. Boston: Beacon Press.

Mouzelis, Nicos. 1986. "On the rise of postwar military dictatorships: Argentina, Chile, Greece." *Comparative Studies in Society and History* (London), 28, (1): 55–80.

Mozambican Studies. 1981. Centro de Estudos Africanos, Eduardo Mondlane University, Maputo, 1, 1980: 2, 1981.

Myrdal, Gunnar. 1968. *Asian drama. An inquiry into the poverty of nations*. (3 Vol.), New York: Pantheon.

Não Vamos Esquecer. 1987. Centro de Estudes Africanos, Eduardo Mondane University; Maputo, 1, 2–3, 4.

Negash, Tekeste. 1987. *Italian colonialism in Eritrea, 1882–1941. Policies, praxis and impact*. Acta Universitatis Upsaliensis, Studia Historica Upsaliensia, 148. Stockholm: Almqvist & Wiksell.

Negrão, José Guilherme. 1981. *Sobre a política da produção da FRELIMO*. Maputo: Centro de Estudos Africanos, Eduardo Mondlane University. (Mimeo).

——. 1984. *A produção e o comercio nas zonas libertadas*. Arquivo Histórico de Moçambique. Maputo: Centro de Estudos Africanos, Eduardo Mondlane University.

Noticias (Maputo), daily newspaper.

Nuscheler, Franz and Ziemer, Klaus. 1980. *Politische Herrschaft in Schwarzafrika. Geschichte und Gegenwart*. Munich: C. H. Beck.

Olivier de Sardan, Jean-Pierre. 1987. "Identité nationale et identités collectives," in Terray. *L'état contemporain en Afrique* pp. 175–185.

Relatório do Comité Central ao IV Congresso. 1983. Maputo.

"Programa e Estatutos." 1977. Documentos do III Congresso da FRELIMO, Maputo.

"Report of the AKUT Group 1987–1990 and Plans for 1990–1993." 1990. (AKUT 42) Uppsala: Department of Development Studies, University of Uppsala.

Review of African Political Economy. 1974. (Sheffield).

Ribeiro, Carlos Rui. 1989. "A historicidade da construção nacional, 1: a articulação histórica dos povos da Senegâmbia pré-colonial (os crioulos como embrião da nação guineense)," in *A construção da nação em Africa,* 219–242.

Ribeiro, Carlos Rui and Cardoso, Carlos. 1988. "Bemerkungen zu den sozialökonomischen Strukturen der Agrargesellschaften in Guinea-Bissau und ihrem historischen Wandel." In Meyns. pp. 155–177.

Rudebeck, Lars. 1970. "Developmental pressure and political limits: a Tunisian example." *The Journal of Modern African Studies.* (Cambridge), 8, 2: 173–198.

———. 1970. "*Utveckling och politik. En samhällsvetenskaplig teoristudie med anknytning till konkret politisk verklighet.*" Stockholm: Wahlström & Widstrand.

———. 1970. "Political development. Towards a coherent and relevant theoretical formulation." *Scandinavian Political Studies* (Oslo), 5: 21–63.

———. 1972. "Political mobilisation for development in Guinea-Bissau." *The Journal of Modern African Studies.* (Cambridge) 10 (1): 1–18.

———. 1974. *Guinea-Bissau. A study of political mobilization.* Uppsala: Scandinavian Institute of African Studies.

———. 1977. *Guinea-Bissau. Folket, partiet och staten.* Uppsala: Scandinavian Institute of African Studies.

———. 1978. "Conditions of development and actual development strategy in Guinea-Bissau." In Palmberg, Mai (ed), *Problems of socialist orientation in Africa.* Uppsala: Scandinavian Institute of African Studies, pp. 164–183.

———. 1979. "Development and class struggle in Guinea-Bissau." *Monthly Review* (New York), 30, 48: 14–32.

———. 1979. "Socialist-oriented development in Guinea-Bissau." In Rosberg, Carl G. and Callaghy, Thomas M. (eds), *Socialism in sub-Saharan Africa. A new assessment.* Institute of International Studies, University of California, Berkeley: 322–344.

———. 1982. "The social basis of state power and developmental options—some notes for discussion." In Egerö & Rudebeck *Socialist Development,* pp. 12–18.

———. 1982. "Transition difficile en Guinée-Bissau. Problèmes de pouvoir populaire et du développement," Research Report 63. Uppsala: Scandinavian Institute of African Studies.

———. 1983. "Problems of transition from struggle for national liberation struggle for social and economic liberation through state action." In Melasuo, Tuomo (ed), *Liberation and Development.* Tampere: Finnish Peace Research Association, pp. 197–207.

———. 1983. *On the class basis of the national liberation movement of Guinea-Bissau.* Paper for workshop on "The class basis of nationalist movements in Angola, Guinea-Bissau and Mozambique," Department of Afro-American and African Studies, University of Minnesota, Minneapolis, 1983:II (mimeo). Also as "Über die Klassenbasis der nationalen Befreiungsbewegung von Guinea-Bissau," *Leipziger Beiträge zur Revolutionsforschung,* Karl Marx University, Leipzig, 11, 1985, pp. 62–81.

———. 1984. *"Sur la transition de mouvement de libération nationale au pouvoir d'état."* Contribution to international conference on "The political personality of Amilcar Cabral," Bissau, (mimeo).

———. 1984. *"Development and democracy. Notes related to a study of people's power in Mozambique,"* AKUT and Department of Political Science, University of Uppsala, 1984, revised in 1985 (mimeo).

———. 1986. "Some facts and observations on relations between the Nordic countries and the officially Portuguese-speaking countries of Africa," In Weimer, Bernhard (ed), *Die afrikanischen Staaten portugiesischer Sprache: interne Entwicklungsdynamik und internationale Beziehungen,* SWP-K, Stiftung Wissenschaft und Politik, Ebenhousen, pp. 119–133.

———. 1987. "Utveckling och demokrati. Från nationell befrielserörelse till statsmakt." in Lewin, Leif (ed.), *Festskrift till Carl Arvid Hessler,* Acta Universitatis Upsaliensis, Publications of the Political Science Association in Uppsala 103, Stockholm: Almquist & Wiksell, pp. 292–305.

———. 1987. "Guinea-Bissau between world market and subsistence." *Soronda. Revista de Estudos Guineenses* (Bissau) 2 (4): 174–184. In Portuguese as "Guiné-Bissau: Que desenvolvimento?" 1, 251–265. in *Revista Internacional de Estudos Africanos* (Lisbon), 6–7, 1987. Shortened German version in *Peripherie* (Münster), 27, 1987, pp. 82–84, 1987.

———. "Kandjadja, Guiné-Bissau, 1976–1986. Observações sobre a economia política de uma aldeia africana," *Soronda* (Bissau), 5, 1988, pp. 61–82. In English as "Kandjadja, Guinea-Bissau, 1976–1986. Observations on the political economy of one African village," *Review of African Political Economy* (Sheffield), 41, 1988, pp. 17–29. In German in Meyns 1988 (see under that heading), pp. 199–233.

———. "Structural adjustment in a West-African village," in Hermele and Rudebeck, AKUT 41, Department of Development Studies, University of Uppsala, 1989, pp. 17–71. In Portuguese as "Ajustamento estrutural numa aldeia oeste-africana," in AKUT 41, 1990, pp. 21–93.

———. 1990. "The effect of structural adjustment in Kandjadja, Guinea-Bissau," *Review of African Political Economy* (Sheffield), 41:34–51.

Sandbrook, Richard. 1986. "The state and economic stagnation in tropical Africa," *World Development* (Oxford) 14 (3): 319–332.

Santos, Manuel dos. 1986. "Guiné-Bissau: a formação da nação."

Saul, John S. 1979. *The State and Revolution in Eastern Africa.* New York: Monthly Review Press.

Schiefer, Ulrich. 1986. *Guiné-Bissau zwischen Weltwirtschaft und Subsistenz. Transatlantisch orientierte Strukturen an der oberen Guinéküste,* ISSA-wissenschaftliche Reihe 20, Bonn.

Schröer, Herbert. 1980. "Thesen zum 'Nizer-Kapitalismus' in Moçambique." *Peripherie* (Münster) (3): 53–64.

Serra, Carlos, *Como a penetração estrangeira transformou o modo de produção dos camponeses moçambicanos.* Vols. 1 and 2. Colecção Moçambique e a sua história. Maputo: Núcleo editorial da Universidade Eduardo Mondlane.

Sigrist, Christian. 1979. *Traditional societies and western colonialism. The case of*

Guinea-Bissau and the Cape Verde islands. Berlin Institute of Comparative Social Research. Also in German in von Grevemeyer (ed.), *Traditionale Gesellschaften und europäischer Kolonialismus,* Syndikat, Frankfurt am Main, 1981, and in Portuguese in *Economia e Socialismo* (Lisbon), 1980.

——. 1979. *Regulierte Anarchie. Untersuchungen zum Fehlen und zur Entstehung politischer Herrschaft in segmentären Gesellschaften Afrikas,* Syndikat, Frankfurt am Main, (first edition by Walter Verlag AG Olten, 1967).

Silva, Artur Augusto da. 1980. *Usos e costumes jurídicos dos Fulas da Guiné-Bissau,* 3rd ed. Bissau: DEDILO.

Silveira, Onésimo. 1976. *Africa south of the Sahara: party systems and ideologies of socialism* Publications of the Political Science Association in Uppsala 71, Stockholm: Rabén & Sjögren.

Sklar, Richard L. 1987. "Developmental democracy." *Comparative Studies in Society and History.* (London) 29 (4): 686–714.

Skocpol, Theda. 1979. *States and social revolutions: a comparative analysis of France, Russia, and China.* Cambridge: Cambridge University Press.

Skocpol, Theda and Amenta, Edwin. 1986. "States and social policies." *Annual Review of Sociology.* (Palo Alto), pp. 131–157.

Soronda. Revista de Estudos Guineenses 1986. (Bissau) (1).

"Statutes and Programme of the Frelimo Party." 1983. (Official English language version) Maputo.

Terray, Emmanuel (ed). 1987. *L'état contemporain en Afrique.* Paris: L'Harmattan.

Towards a history of the national liberation struggle in Mozambique: problematics, methodologies, analyses. 1982. Paper presented by The History Workshop, Centro de Estudos Africanos, Eduardo Mondlane University, to meeting on problems and priorities in social science training in southern Africa, organized by the Mozambican National UNESCO Commission, Maputo (mimeo).

Törnquist, Olle. 1989. *What is wrong with Marxism? On capitalists and state in India and Indonesia.* New Delhi: Manohar Publications.

Vail, Leroy & White, Landeg. 1980. *Capitalism and colonialism in Mozambique: a study of the Quelimane district.* London: Heinemann and Nairobi, Ibadan.

Vieira, Sergio. 1979. "Law in the liberated zones." *Principles of revolutionary justice.* State papers and party proceedings, Series 2, (2): 11–16. (Published by Mozambique, Angola and Guiné Information Centre, London).

Werker, Scott. 1985. "Beyond the dependency paradigm." *Journal of Contemporary Asia.* (Stockholm and Adelaide) 5 (1): 79–95.

White, Gordon, Murray, Robin, and White, Christine (eds). 1983. *Revolutionary socialist development in the third world.* Brighton: Wheatsheaf Books. 1983.

Wield, David. 1983. "Mozambique—late colonialism and early problems of transition," In White and others, *Revolutionary Socialist Development,* pp. 75–113.

Wuyts, Marc. 1978. *Peasants and rural economy in Mozambique.* Centro de Estudos Africanos, Eduardo Mondlane University, Maputo.

Chapter 3

In Defense of the Primitive

K. P. Moseley

. . . as soon as a need is satisfied . . . new needs are made; and this production of new needs is the first historical act.

Karl Marx and Friedrich Engels

The philosophers, who have inquired into the foundations of society, have all felt the necessity of going back to a state of nature; but not one of them has got there. . . . Every one . . . constantly dwelling on wants, avidity, oppression, desires and pride, has transferred to the state of nature ideas which were acquired in society; so that, in speaking of the savage, they described the social man.

Jean-Jacques Rousseau

As Stanley Diamond* did in his "Search for the Primitive" (1974b:117), I will try to state my arguments here "as simply and strongly, indeed as naively," as I can. This essay will follow in his footsteps in certain respects, especially in its insistence on the contemporary "Uses of the Primitive" (1974c) for purposes of comparison, inspiration, and critique. In contrast to the predominantly cultural thrust of Diamond's work, however, I will embark upon more economic terrain, where not only the desirability but the practical feasibility of the "primitive" will be of prime concern. In the process, connections will be made to certain intellectual routes and strategic branch lines not explicitly developed in his work.

This trajectory reflects the peculiar vantage point of the author, which is located intellectually in the nether regions between anthropology and the other social sciences, and between orthodox Marxism and its more critical wings; spatially, it is located in a West African semiperiphery where the dialectics of very different social formations are still very much in view. In these border-

---

*This chapter was originally an essay designed for a *festschrift* for the late Stanley Diamond [*Dialectical Anthropology*, Vol. I, C. Gailey and S. Gregory, eds., Florida State University Press, forthcoming.]

lands, communal systems hang on in various stages of resistance or decline, while the hegemony of capitalist industrialism—or the rival world views it has spawned—remains partial and insecure.

From this cluttered, untidy field of vision, a clear problematic can nonetheless be posed. This concerns the mutual implications of our theories of history and development, on the one hand, and the status of the "primitive," both in principle and in fact, on the other. We might begin with a simple observation: it is the development imperative that lies behind the ongoing elimination of the "real, existing primitive" today; it is the idealization of "development" that provides the justification and rationale. Conversely, the very idea of the primitive "weighs like a nightmare" on the modern mind, informing, yet challenging, our ideologies of progress and economic growth. The subversive implications of the communal regime are reflected in the extraordinary ambivalence with which it has been treated in modern thought, and the peculiar evasions that mark the resulting theories. And, if it turns our that communal systems or patterns are still with us, not entirely relegated to the Museum of Antiquities after all, our cognitive anxieties are compounded by more practical and moral issues.

The defense of the primitive thus emerges as a key intellectual and strategic task, on a number of grounds. Communal systems, first of all, provide an acid test for the universality of our theories—particularly for our theories of history and the implicit or explicit teleologies they entail. More specifically, the adaptive success of such systems over the very long term provides a telling corrective to our conventional models of development, models based on indefinite processes of accumulation, resource exploitation, and growth that are already proving difficult to sustain. If the positive significance of communal modes can be defended in these domains, one can take a further step, reincorporating the primitive, in new ways, to our wider, emancipatory projects of systemic change and reform. At the same time, it would become imperative to defend the primitive in practical terms: the defense of the right of less powerful cultures to exist, survive, and even revive, if they will.

The *longue durée* of communal forms—still more their persistence in the here and now—has implications of two different but hopefully complementary kinds. On the one hand, it constitutes a mute but radical transgression of the hegemonic orders of the present, which, once understood, can be linked to other elements of resistance, autonomy, and critique. On the other hand, it is a source of practical economic lessons that may help modern civilization to survive in some recognizable form. In both cases, sacrifices would have to be made in the areas of self-image and ideology and in forms of production and of growth. The fabled process of "creative destruction" would be slowed, and would finally cease to be an exclusively one-way affair; it may be here, rather than at the end of the process, that new kinds of emancipation can begin.

THEORETICAL AMBIVALENCE: THE PRIMITIVE AS THREAT

So far as I know, we are the only people who think themselves risen from savages; everyone else believes they descend from Gods.

Marshall Sahlins

The mapping of the social structure and ecology of small-scale, egalitarian groups, based on hunting/gathering, horticulture, or other specialized subsistence modes, has been an area of significant intellectual advance in recent decades (see, for example, Diamond 1974b; Moseley and Wallerstein 1978). Increasing appreciation and understanding—accompanied by extensive interchange between Marxist and other scholars—have created strains, however, for our larger frameworks of epistemology and historical interpretation. As we will see in the next section, these problems have been intensified by social and economic trends that are also casting doubt upon contemporary models of development.

As Diamond has noted (1974c:203), our mental relationship to primitive peoples is asymmetrical: we theorize about them, culling their worlds for good and bad, while they take themselves for granted and remain indifferent, insofar as possible, to us. This contrast is magnified by modern social science, which claims a privileged cognitive status vis-à-vis the self-understanding of "everyday" actors, in general, and of precapitalist cultures, in particular (see, for example, Lukacs 1968; Scholte 1979). At the same time, there has been continuing ambivalence between universal schemas of explanation and the recognition of the specificity of different social systems and their particular "laws of motion." The longstanding debate between "formalist" and "substantivist" interpretations of precapitalist economies provides a case in point.

These two analytic modes have been most successfully combined, I feel, in materialistic theories, whether of ecological, technological, or Marxist bent. The tension between them continues, however, all too often resolved by the projection backward of factors extrapolated from the particular experience and self-image of the capitalist-industrial West. Most commonly, this involves imputing one or another abstracted model of individualistic, rational, economic man to societies dominated by quite different concerns. This tendency is characteristic of bourgeois economic thought, as Marx so brilliantly pointed out.

There is reason to believe, however, that Marxism itself has erred in this sense, though with greater subtlety and mixed feelings, taking the capitalist preoccupation with the constant expansion of production and needs to be the ultimate motor of the historical process as a whole (Sahlins 1976; Dumont 1977; Abdel-Malek 1981: Ch. 2, 6; compare Krader 1979).

Even more explicitly Eurocentric are the unilinear evolutionary models that have shaped Western thought since the time of Condorcet and Comte. The details of the later versions may vary—consider the stages adumbrated by Stalin (and Amin 1980), Rostow, or Leslie White—but the overall process is the same: expanding production and resource mobilization, increasing rationality and control, culminating in advanced industrial systems whether of the capitalist or socialist type (Compare Wallerstein 1984a; Diamond 1974b). Such sequences, of course, may well occur. The problem is the claim to the intrinsic necessity, superiority, and finality of the technologically advanced. Historical materialism can strengthen its explanatory framework in this respect by shifting from (largely tacit) assumptions about needs to more explicit reference to ecology, culture, or volition; all these tendencies can be found in Marxism today. Its particular doctrine of progress, however, in which human emancipation is deferred to the achievement of abundance on an advanced industrial base, is more difficult to relinquish.

As one might suspect, the analytic incorporation of communal (not to speak of "Asiatic") modes is often accompanied by marked ambivalence of moral and evaluative kinds. Again, we might note the asymmetry in outlook to which Diamond has been so sensitive: the small community tends to treat the cultural peculiarities of the stranger with tolerant indulgence or indifference; the "civilized," however, are obsessed with invidious categorizations and establishing cultural hierarchies that obviously buttress real inequalities in power and resource control. And justification was required, of course, for the conquest, enslavement, assimilation, or extermination with which complex systems have so often extended their control.

At the level of the Western intelligentsia, things have taken a curious turn. Along with the theories of progress and cultural and racial superiority that accompanied capitalist expansion, countercurrents appeared: nostalgic appreciations of simpler cultures, and admiring contrasts of at least certain of their traits with those of European societies. From Rousseau through the German romanticists to Morgan, Marx, and modern anthropology, the discovery of lost virtues has been more or less joined to critiques of the modern and to the refashioning of its future along alternative lines (Horton 1970, Diamond 1974c). Indeed, were it not for extensive borrowing from communal cultures, the moral content, even the conceptual possibility, of radical, anticapitalist critique would be seriously eroded. As Morgan put it, to what more can we aspire than "a revival, in a higher form, of the liberty, equality and fraternity of the ancient Gentes" (cited in Engels 1948:175). And as Diamond adds: "The search for the primitive . . . is the search for the utopia of the past, projected into the future, with civilization being the middle term" (1974c:208).

What is also striking here is the qualification—the need for a "middle term" and an eventual "higher form" (see also Diamond 1974b:174–75; Stein 1964:207–8). Marxism is particularly explicit in this respect—each advance of civilization is accompanied by increasing exploitation and impoverishment; each advance is nonetheless progressive and necessary, and a final recovery of communal social relations will only be possible on a still more advanced industrial-socialist base (Engels 1948:170 and following). But as P.M. (1985:5) bluntly asks, "Why the big detour?"

It is amazing how few scholars actually address this point. In a retrospective vein, Rousseau did, of course, while P.M. has answered the question with his extraordinary utopia, *bolo'bolo* (1985), a systematic defense of a return to communal forms. Of the more conventionally progressive authors, it is only Marx and Engels who seem to have much to say. First of all, they do not mince words about the characteristics of precapitalist modes, which they would like to eliminate—ranging from oriental stagnation and the "idiocy of rural life" to the "sheeplike consciousness" and lack of historic dynamic of the communal stage. And they do suggest a reason for the "long detour"—to free the individual from artificial and unnatural constraints, not only those imposed by property, classes, and the commodity form, but, in communal systems, by the bondage to nature and to the "primordial community" itself (Engels 1948:98, 111; Dumont 1977: esp. 178–180; compare Wallerstein 1984b:148–50). But does this not take us back to enlightenment and bourgeois notions of the essential character of man? And are these notions—to say nothing of a society based on large-scale industry and mass consumption—compatible with even the more desirable features of communal modes?

I would suggest that, to evade these issues, two major strategies are employed. First, we extract the positive characteristics of the primitive as mere abstractions—without the real, whole, working systems from which they are derived being taken seriously on their own terms. This also allows us to ignore silently the fact that the few surviving examples of such real systems are now under mortal threat. Indeed, to remove all vestige of anomaly, we may even deny that "real" communal modes any longer exist at all. This is apparently the position of Soviet anthropology—that we have today no more than "degenerate" relics, incorporated to (superior) systems of larger scale (see Diamond 1979a:5 and following; compare Amin 1980: Ch. 1). The incorporation thesis of dependency and world-system theory can yield a similar result (for example, Wallerstein 1984b:164–65).

Second, and more specifically, we tend to embrace the principles governing social relations in communal modes, while deemphasizing or even rejecting those prevalent at the level of the economic base. But we know very well the mutual implications of these two levels, and should by now suspect that there is something about the modern accumulation process or productive system that stands in the way of communally derived ideals. But to come to terms with "primitive" economic principles is extremely threatening, putting in doubt the one area of uncontested superiority of modern civilization—the economy—and the ideologies of growth and development to which both capitalism and state socialism subscribe.

CONTEMPORARY CRISIS: THE PRIMITIVE AS HOPE

> Not even the Second World War could convince the gullible inhabitants of this planet that the nineteenth century was over.
>
> Fernando Henrique Cardoso

It is since World War II, in fact, that capitalist industrialism has enjoyed its greatest success. It has been intensified in the advanced countries to support "Fordist" regimes of mass consumption (Lipietz 1986), spreading out to transform some of the old tropical estates in its own image, creating new ones yet farther afield. Socialism itself, through its association with state power and its defensive-competitive stance vis-à-vis the capitalist core, has proved another great engine of commoditization and accumulation on a global scale. Classical visions of progress, meanwhile, have narrowed in an ever more economic sense, and have given way to a "productivist" ideology of indefinite growth now propounded by virtually "every politically active person in every regime" (Lefebvre 1976:100, 118) throughout the world.

Yet, like a shadow, myriad contradictions follow in industrialism's wake, many of which were hardly discernible when industry was confined to a tiny segment of the globe. On the one hand, we now have a great extended family of what Wallerstein has called the "anti-systemic" movements, which for present purposes might be divided into three major movements or strands. There is the traditional struggle of the working class, of which Marxism remains the most advanced expression. This has been partly displaced, partly encapsulated, by the national struggles—South versus North, East versus West, and the resistence to more particular hegemonisms within the different blocs. Finally, and especially with the advent of "the era of a thousand Marxisms" (Wallerstein 1984a) approximately 20 to 30 years ago, there are the other diverse movements thrown up by the development process from the interstices of the dominant structures—including peasant, ethnic, and community movements; environmental, cultural, and gender issues; and demands for self-management and the "humanization" of work within the enterprise. What is in question is often not more growth or redistribution, but qualitative change; according to Lefebvre (1976:81), we have here an emergent "world proletariat" with "the mission which Marx attributed to the working class as such: to negate the existing . . . in order to reconstruct it, radically transformed."

Antisystematic prospects have been conventionally linked to one or another scenario of revolution, evolution, or structural collapse. The dominant systems, however (and still more the world system as a whole), have proved remarkably capable of weathering storms and recuperating from such breakthroughs that occur. This impasse might continue indefinitely, were it not for the appearance of another great fault line, along with the radical critiques—pointing to crisis, not of the economy as such, but of its physical, ecological base (for example, Brown 1974; Meadows and others 1972; Woodhouse 1972; Schumacher 1973).

Now the particular problem announced by Malthus can in principle be resolved. Population can be limited, and food supplies can be expanded or redistributed, and there are signs that both are being accomplished. But the contemporary industrial system, predicated on mass production using labor-saving rather than resource-saving technologies, and mass consumption at ever-increasing levels and on an ever-increasing geographic scale, presents contradictions of a much more fundamental kind. It depletes resources, many of them nonrenewable, at higher levels than can be sustained; this, together with environmental pollution, now seems to be altering the entire ecosystem in ways that directly threatens life itself. Given the destructiveness of this system, its very success, each new per capita progression of the GNP, may hasten its eventual demise.

Facing this contingency is extraordinarily difficult for everyone—haves and hope-to-haves, advanced countries and those that are developing. At the same time, awareness is growing—especially among scientists and development practitioners—sparked by the onset of one or another crisis in particular parts of the world (see, for example, *Development Forum, IFDA Dossier,* and the Worldwatch and Earthscan reports). Increasingly, concern for specific reforms (such as "appropriate technology") is being integrated into more inclusive development models, based on such principles as self-reliance, community participation, and basic needs (see Cardoso 1982). These ideas, in turn, are being linked back to the global critiques of competitive accumulation, in general, and capitalism, in particular, including the "modes of consumption" that these productive modes entail. In various European countries, one should add, ecology-oriented "Green Parties" now account for small but persistent proportions of the vote.

In this world-historical conjuncture, the practical significance of the "primitive" could finally be appreciated. Coincidentally, perhaps, during past decades, the scholarly reevaluation of subsistence-centered modes was also underway (see, for example, Lee and Devore 1968; Netting 1971; Sahlins 1974). The result was the delineation of "original affluent societies," accounting for 99% of human history, and distinguished, inter alia, by systematic limits on consumption, resource-exploitation, and growth. The inference was inescapable—such limits were key to an unparalleled adaptive viability and success, veritably dwarfing the more complex formations that have arisen over the past 5000, and particularly the last 500, years. The (variable) demise of such systems, moreover, has been linked less to built-in tendencies to innovation or growing needs than to external pressures—first, because of population growth in areas that were geographically circumscribed (see Cohen 1977; Wilkinson 1973); second, because of sheer differences in power once larger polities had emerged.

If this picture is correct; indeed, if it is even possible, it points to a rather radical resolution of some of the theoretical issues discussed earlier. First and most broadly, we see the inevitability of history giving way to contingency, immanent causes to historically specific ones. Progress, moreover, gives way to difference, and the contingent and relative character of contemporary systems stands exposed. This is particularly true regarding the maximizing imperatives by which they are most distinguished from precapitalist modes. Expanded reproduction, in turn, is not a natural process, but, as Lefebvre reminds us (1976:27–28, 78–80), demands continuous, deliberate intervention; chronic tendencies for over-accumulation and stagnation occur nonetheless, in both socialist and capitalist regimes. The production process itself becomes ever more complex and demanding, and, as we have seen, is extremely maladaptive in ecological terms. The "illusion of unlimited powers" (Schumacher 1973:14) afforded by modern technology thus figures as another shibboleth to be relinquished. As Schumacher notes, modern man "talks of a battle with nature, forgetting that, if he won the battle, he would find himself on the losing side." ✓

If contemporary productivist modes are not to be the unhappy end-point of history, how shall we proceed? One key philosophical and scientific task will be the critical reanalysis of "needs" and consumption "standards"; communal formations inform at least the lower end of possibilities in this respect. Drawing from another precapitalist case, Schumacher (1973:57) has proposed a "Buddhist economics" in which "the maximum of well-being with the minimum of consumption" would be a cardinal aim. An emphasis on social as opposed to individual needs would also act to limit growth, while neither "breaking with it crudely or prolonging it indefinitely" (Lefebvre 1976:11). As this implies, a second step would be to subordinate production to the "logic of consumption" (Cardoso 1982:161–62) so defined, and a third, to reorganize production to minimize resource use.

It is at the interface of economy and environment that subsistence regimes will have the most to teach us, not only at the level of principle but with respect to concrete adaptive techniques. Here we may broadly envision an "economics of permanence" (Schumacher 1973:33) or a "steady-state" situation, in which the basic elements of population, technology, and "basic needs" are gradually tailored to what the global ecosystem can support. Work on such models of "sustainable development" has begun, but we should emphasize the urgency of the problem; a time frame of even a few hundred, to say nothing of a thousand, years would be an enormous advance in this respect. In any case, we are approaching the first stage of wisdom, which is to realize the depths of our ignorance as far as long-term adaptation is concerned. If modern civilization is to be even a "detour" to the future, moreover, we must not only clear our minds, but also begin to act to achieve it.

IMMEDIATE PROSPECTS FOR REFORM

What would the world be, once bereft
Of wet and wilderness? Let them be left,
O let them be left. . . .

                                                            Gerard Manley Hopkins

Let us assume, for purposes of argument, that human survival is the first priority. It will take time to work out a sustainable vision of the good life, and still more to evolve one that will be acceptable in political and economic terms (compare Harman 1987:4). We must be prepared for a long and uncertain interval, during which there will certainly be no agreement on any "one best way." Emphasis, rather, should be on abstention from what is obviously destructive or even risky, while devising strategies to obtain agreement on what is possible and desirable at any point in time. Conditioning both action and inaction is what Castells (1983:310) has termed the "three-dimensional" character of our world: "relationships of production are integrated at the worldwide level, while experience is culturally specific and power is still concentrated in the nation states. . . ." Given the ignorance and confusion that still prevail in the development domain, this fragmentation may be a blessing in disguise. In any case, we must allow for balance and diversity between levels of organization and ways of life for a considerable time to come.

In terms of this modest prospective, the "defense of the primitive"—the real, existing primitive, in this case—should be of paramount concern. There are numerous reasons for this, to which the remainder of this paper will be devoted. Confining ourselves for the moment to the ecological rationale, it is clear that the preservation of subsistence regimes—as a source of adaptive principles and techniques and as custodians of precious resources and ecosystems—is almost surely in the long-term interest of us all. If we know that "species-diversity," for instance, should be defended against processes of "ecocide," this should now be matched with a vigorous critique of the "ethnocide" that threatens to eliminate what little cultural diversity remains. This is particularly important, as Bodley (1978:204) notes, "now that cultures which specifically reject many of the values resulting in our present world-wide environmental problems are themselves to disappear."

And disappearing they are. The process, of course, began long ago. Bodley (1975:39–40), in his unique survey of the modern period, estimates that tribal populations declined by 30 to 50 million, circa 1780–1930, when the most massive displacement and extermination occurred. Given the small size and low densities typical of such groups, one wonders how many now are left. In any case, the devastation continues. While there is mounting concern to save the tropical forests and other still-marginal ecological zones, the peoples and their cultures are disappearing almost as fast as the trees. Because it occurs in remote areas, which are often undetected or concealed, the overall scale of the phenomenon is not clear. Particular cases range from the 250,000 victims (one-third of the total population) claimed by the Indonesian conquest of East Timor since 1975 (George 1985:66); the hundreds killed by soldiers and thousands displaced in the Chittagong Hills of Bangladesh over the past few years (*Survival International* 1985:1–2); to the murder of the sole Jesuit protector of the Guarani Indians of the Matto Grosso, an area under threat from logging firms.

In these and other cases where displacement is violent, what is almost always at stake is the land—the foundation of the entire economic and cultural complex of subsistence regimes, but now desired by more powerful interests and groups for timber, ranches, or farms (compare Bodley 1975:82 and following). But even more widespread are subtler forms of coercion and persuasion in favor of cultural and technological change which, however well-intended, is often ultimately equally destructive. Here, subsistence practices and orientations themselves:

. . . are considered "obstacles to progress" . . . slated for drastic modification. When these and other stabilizing factors are weakened, the way is opened for perpetual relative deprivation (i.e. "poverty") and rapid environmental deterioration. As wants and population increase . . . people discover that the new goals . . . remain just out of reach. . . . They are then told they must abandon even more of their culture and that they have "no choice but to go forward with technology" as Redfield told the (Maya - KPM) people of Chan Kom (Bodley 1978:197).

How is the situation perceived by the major parties involved? As the above would suggest, the targets of the displacement/modification process, who are committed to the security and other satisfactions provided by their own cultures, are invariably opposed. Rousseau noted long ago "the invincible repugnance they have of adopting our morals and living in our way" (cited in Diamond 1974a:24–25). Whether through avoidance of contact, withdrawal, overt resistance, or rejection of innovations (see Bodley 1975:16–21, Ch. 3; Alvares 1983), the evidence remains overwhelming on this point; they may be "conscripts of civilization" but "not volunteers" (Diamond 1974c:204). This resistence is typical of all precapitalist peoples, of course, but seems to vary inversely with their scale of organization, extent of sedentarization, and previous incorporation to market or state.

"Modern" culture, on the other hand, displays its characteristic ambivalence. It has enshrined the concept of "human rights," including the principle of the equal worth of peoples and cultures, and the right to cultural retention and choice. Specific reference to the rights of minority cultures was added to the U.N. Declaration of Human Rights in 1966 (Bodley 1975:108). But who speaks for the primitive in this regard? I may be ill-informed, but the voices, growing in number, still seem plaintive and weak. The depredations underway are occasionally reported in the mass media (e.g., films such as *Emerald Forest, Dances with Wolves*). Many anthropologists, of course, are concerned, as reflected in a steady stream of monographs and ethnographic films, as well as a new edition of Bodley's classic exposé, *Victims of Progress*. The problematic impact of development on indigenous peoples is also the theme of a collection edited by Bodley (1988), and has been acknowledged even by that archdeveloper itself, the World Bank (1982). There are, finally, the publications of such organizations as the Rainforest Action Network, Minority Rights, the International Work Group for Indigenous Affairs (IWGIA), Cultural Survival, and Survival International, the latter two specifically devoted to the rights of threatened "tribal peoples." But on the whole, the problem is still treated with considerable reserve. This remains evident on the left—despite breaches by Zed

Press, for instance (ICIHI 1987; Trainer 1985)—where one would expect greater enthusiasm for this new category of the exploited and oppressed. The silence is most noticeable in the developing countries, where most incidents involving tribal peoples now occur.

One need not look far for the reasons. There is a genuine lack of information and publicity, which we all share, partly reflecting the fact that only recently anywhere, and still less in progressive circles, has it been thought that there might be good reason for "resistance to change." Rather, as Eduard Bernstein (cited in Davis 1967:95) wrote a century ago, support for "savages and barbarians who resist the penetration of capitalistic civilization" has been considered romantic—and this heritage lives on, reorganized around the mystique of "development" (see Bazin 1986; Alvares 1983), the dual struggle against imperialism and "backwardness," and intensified, in poorer countries, by enormous internal and international pressures for rapid growth. Although these pressures may be transmitted through the state, the first mover remains the world system of capitalism, which forces countries to behave like competitive firms, subjecting ever greater areas of their own internal space to intensive exploitation, and reconverting their emancipatory initiatives—independence, socialism, self-reliance—to the logic of growth. The "defense of the primitive," in these circumstances, may seem a reactionary diversion; at best a luxury that few can afford.

Yet, it is unlikely to be an issue that will disappear, particularly considering its link to the ecological crisis and the new development strategies that seem to be gaining ground. Nor, on moral grounds, should it be forgotten. Thinking along minimalist lines for the moment, what, during the "uncertain interval" noted at the beginning of this section, might be done? Apart from further scientific work on subsistence economies, we should think about more direct ways of redefining them in normative terms. One aspect of this redefinition might be terminological reform, replacing such diffuse, invidious concepts as backward/advanced, primitive/civilized, progress/development with words of more precise empirical reference. It is not enough to say that one does not intend the connotations (compare Diamond 1974b:123 and following); they have already shaped the popular consciousness of all the world, subverting, in the process, any notion of equal cultural worth.

An equally challenging task would be to extend the concepts of human and cultural rights explicitly to respect the desire of communal peoples not to be interfered with culturally, not to develop, and to be generally left alone. This must also include reference to rights in land, without which such cultures cannot survive. In practice, of course, this would be a matter of degree. Bodley's (1978:200 and following) proposal for "cultural autonomy" includes not only land rights but the option of complete independence and rejection of contact. This seems unlikely and unnecessary. As he notes (1975:125; 1978:202), formal political incorporation and the occasional outside visitor have little impact per se, and even after intervention or disruption has occurred, traditional patterns have often been restored. One might suggest instead some form of indirect rule, an arrangement which, historically, has allowed subordinate societies to preserve their identities over long periods of time.

At a general level, this line of argument finds precedent and support from an unexpected direction: urban political economy, where recent work by Lefebvre (1976) and Castells (1983, 1984) has incorporated a defense of cultural specificity and community autonomy to the broader Marxian critique. It is interesting that Lefebvre (1976:34–35) also poses the problem in terms of rights: the "right to the town," versus spatial displacement and marginalization (this could be rephrased, for present purposes, as the "right to (free) space"); and the "right to be different," versus the tendencies to cultural homogenization that advanced capitalism promotes. At this point, we can begin to shift the question of the "primitive" from the terrain of survival and reform, and consider its possible significance in antisystemic terms.

EMANCIPATORY PROSPECTS: THE FUTURE AND THE PAST

Every theoretical system has another system inside it struggling to get out.

Alvin Gouldner

Despite its urban bias, the framework Lefebvre and Castells propose is designed to embrace a wide array of peripheral and peripheralized groups that are located outside the cities and outside the industrial enterprise and working class. For as capitalism extends outward from these centers, disrupting and reorganizing local spatial and social relations, space itself becomes "the terrain for a vast confrontation which creates its center now here, now there, and which cannot be either localised or diffused" (Lefebvre 1976:85). What is being proposed, moreover, is linkage, perhaps, but certainly not cooptation, to the old official program and parties of the Left, themselves converted to one or another version of the "ideology of growth." Rather, the principles of diversity and autonomy should be developed, against the "superior logic of the totality" (Ibid.:249) and the "enlightened despotism of the state" (Castells 1984:247–248). Greater self-management at various levels of organization, in fact, would be both a means and an end of the transformation in view.

In this perspective, the emancipatory function of difference itself, along with diverse, more or less spontaneous transgressions of the dominant order, stands sharply revealed:

> . . . capitalism is changing and, as such, disintegrating, even in the process of realising its own concept. Transgressions serve as geiger-counters, causing the process to appear in all its contradictory and dialectical totality (Lefebvre 1976:14).

What greater transgression, in this context, than the primitive, not only the idea but the real-existing primitive, refusing incorporation, occupying the last bastions of free space, and providing a coherent, living example of self-reliance, equality, and the subjection of the economic to an autonomous conception of needs? It is Diamond, again, the anthropologist, who has been most aware of this. For politics, he notes, is most basically, concerned with choices about ways of life:

> Civilized peoples . . . have, therefore, been particularly sensitive to political action on the part of "backward" peoples which created the possibility of autonomous societies and alternative cultures. In the mind of the imperialist, the world is small, and loss of control in one area threatens the whole (1974a:2).

Protests at the grassroots, however, and above all those of remote communal groups, are fragmented and have little voice. Here, the critical intelligentsia has an essential role to play, articulating diverse oppositions, suggesting an alternative vision of what men and women really want, and "tearing aside the veil of ideologies" (Lefebvre 1976:119) that sustains the system in force. "Transgressions can sustain such a project, but they cannot realise it" (Ibid.:34), and extensive, preparatory theoretical work is one of the things required. A key task will be the "decentralization" of Marxism, preserving its emancipatory potential from a too narrow focus on production relations and the enterprise, and from economistic, officially imposed, interpretations of human needs (Ibid.:98–99; Castells 1984:247–248). This, in turn, demands the "delegitimization" of the ideologies of progress, development, and growth for growth's sake, which, as Wallerstein (1982:6) notes, are no better for being "clothed in Marxist or *Marxisant* garb." Even more broadly, our lingering assumptions of historical inevitability must be both brought to light and finally put away, to be replaced by a sharper awareness of the reality and inevitability of choice (Diamond 1974a:24, 24, 240; Wallerstein 1984a:16–18).

To this poststructuralist problematic, I would add an additional point. Gouldner (1980:346 and following), working from an internal analysis of

Marxist theory, has noted its tendency to "surrender" social structure to the economic (and thus, in the end, to the state). Capitalism, particularly, appears as a self-moved mover, with the structures of civil society reduced to mere forms in which the economic is expressed. Particular versions of this reduction have appeared in urban political economy—where, thanks, in large part, to Lefebvre, they are now beating a retreat. They still wax strongly in the dependency and world-system schools, in which it is the elimination or subordination of precapitalist elements that is especially stressed. In my view, the most critical theoretical work lies here, in demonstrating both the analytic autonomy and, in many cases, the real anteriority and substantive independence of such structures vis-à-vis the dominant mode.

Outside the West, there are two major repositories of these forms: the great civilizations (along with the nations that are their heirs) (compare Abdel-Malek 1981), and the surviving communal formations (with the "primitive" constituting the least dominant and least penetrated of them all). They act on the present, not only as historic memories, but as living sources of difference, transgression, and critique. And, as both Gouldner (1980) and Diamond (1979a:10) suggest, it is in coming to terms with such autonomy and difference that an emancipatory socialism can be constructed and sustained. At this complex juncture of traditions, structures, and projects, we—the sociologists, the anthropologists, the Marxists—will find our work cut out for us. As Lefebvre (1976:91) writes:

> The *transition* has not followed the political revolution, as it did in Marx's outline. It precedes it. The situation demands a global, concrete *project* for a new and qualitatively different society. . . . It cannot be elaborated unless we call upon all the resources of learning and the imagination. It is, in its essence, revisable. Its chances of failure are many, for it has at its tactical disposal no social efficacy and no political force. The new values are not imposed: they are proposed.

My case for the primitive, for now, rests here.

References

Abdel-Malek. Anouar 1981. *Social Dialectics,* Vol. I: *Civilizations and Social Theory.* Albany: State University of New York Press.

Alvares, Claude. 1983. "Deadly Development," *Development Forum* (October) 3–4.

Amin, Samir. 1980. *Class and Nation.* New York: Monthly Review Press.

Bazin, Maurice. 1986. "The Technological Mystique and Third World Options." *Monthly Review* (July–Aug.) 98–109.

Bodley, John H. 1975. *Victims of Progress*. Menlo Park, Calif: Cummings.

———. "Alternatives to Ethnocide: Human Zoos, Living Museums, and Real People." In Ahamed Idris-Soven and others., eds. *The World as a Company Town: Multinational Corporations and Social Change*. The Hague: Mouton, pp. 189–207.

———. ed. *Tribal Peoples and Development Issues*. Mt. View, Calif.; Mayfield Publishing Co.

Brown, Lester R. 1974. *By Bread Alone*. New York: Praeger.

Cardoso, Fernando Henrique. 1982. "Development Under Fire." In Harry Makler and others., eds., *The New International Economy*. Beverly Hills: Sage, 1982, pp. 141–65.

Castells, Manuel. 1983. *The City and the Grassroots*. Berkeley: University of California Press.

———. 1984. "Space and Society: Managing the New Historical Relationships." In Michael Peter Smith, ed., *Cities in Transformation*. Beverly Hills: Sage, 235–260.

Cole, Mark Nathan. 1977. *The Food Crisis in Pre-history: Overpopulation and the Origins of Agriculture*. New Haven: Yale University Press.

Davis, H.B. 1967. *Nationalism and Socialism*. New York: Monthly Review Press.

Diamond, Stanley. 1974a. *In Search of the Primitive: A Critique of Civilization*. New Brunswick: Transaction Books.

———. 1974b. "The Search for the Primitive." In Diamond, 1974a: 116–175.

———. 1974c. "The Uses of the Primitive." In Diamond 1974a: 203–226.

———. 1979a. "Introduction: Critical Versus Ideological Marxism." In Diamond 1979b: 1–10.

———. (ed.) 1979b. *Towards a Marxist Anthropology*. The Hague: Mouton.

Dumont, Louis. 1977. *From Mandeville to Marx: The Genesis and Triumph of Economic Ideology*. Chicago: University of Chicago Press.

Engels, Friedrich. 1948. *The Origin of the Family, Private Property and the State*. Moscow: Progress Publishers.

George, Susan. 1985. "East Timor: Forgotten Genocide." *AfricAsia* (June) 66.

Gouldner, Alvin W. 1980. *The Two Marxisms*. New York: Oxford University Press.

Harman, Willis W. 1987. "For a New Society, a New Economics." *Development Forum* (April) 3–4.

Horton, Robin 1970. "The Romantic Illusion: Roger Bastide on Africa and the West." *Odu* n.s. No. 3 (April) 87–115.

Independent Commission on International Humanitarian Issues (ICIHI) 1987. *Indigenous Peoples: A Global Quest for Justice*. London: Zed Books.

Krader, Lawrence. 1979. "The Ethnological Notebooks of Karl Marx: A Commentary." In Diamond 1979b: 153–171.

Lee, Richard and Irwin DeVore, eds. 1968. *Man and Hunter*. Chicago: Aldine.

Lefebvre, Henri. 1976. *The Survival of Capitalism*. London: Allison and Busby.

Lipietz, Alain. 1986. "New Tendencies in the International Division of Labour: Regimes of Accumulation and Modes of Reproduction." In Allen J. Scott and Michael Storper, eds., *Production, Work, Territory*. Boston: Allen and Unwin, pp. 16–40.

Lukacs, George. 1968. "Class Consciousness." In his *History and Class Consciousness*. London: Merlin Press.

Meadows, Donella H. and others. 1972. *The Limits to Growth*. New York: Signet.

Moseley, K. P. and Immanuel Wallerstein. 1978. "Precapitalist Social Structures." *Annual Review of Sociology* IV: 259–290.

Netting, Robert McC. 1971. "The Ecological Approach in Cultural Study." Reading, Mass: Addison Wesley Modular Publications.

P. M. 1985. *bolo'bolo.* New York: Semiotext(e).

Sahlins, Marshall. 1974. *Stone Age Economics.* London: Tavistock.

———. 1976. *Cultural and Practical Reason.* Chicago: University of Chicago Press.

Scholte, Bob. 1979. "From Discourse to Silence: The Structuralist Impasse." In Diamond 1979b: 31–67.

Schumacher, E. F. 1973. *Small is Beautiful: Economics as if People Mattered.* New York: Harper and Row.

Stein, Maurice. 1964. "Anthropological Perspectives on the Modern Community." In Stanley Diamond, ed., *Primitive Views of the World.* New York: Columbia University Press, pp. 194–210.

Survival International. 1985. *Survival International News,* No. 10.

Trainer, P. E. 1985. *Abandon Affluence!* London: Zed Books.

Wallerstein, Immanuel. 1982. "Who Wants Still More Development?" Paper presented at Annual Meetings of the American Sociological Association, San Francisco, Sept. 6–10.

———. 1984a. "Marxism at Utopias: Evolving Ideologies." Paper presented at Annual Meetings of the American Sociological Association, San Antonio, 29 August.

———. 1984b. *The Politics of the World-Economy.* Cambridge: Cambridge University Press.

Wilkinson, Richard G. 1973. *Poverty and Progress: An Ecological Perspective on Economic Development.* New York: Praeger.

Woodhouse, Edward J. 1972. "Revisioning the Future of the Third World: An Ecological Perspective on Development." *World Politics* XXV, I (1972): 1–33.

World Bank 1982. *Tribal Peoples and Economic Development: Human Ecologic Considerations.* Washington, D.C.: World Bank.

Chapter 4

Toward an Historical Understanding of Industrial Development

Frederick Stirton Weaver

This chapter presents a particular historical approach to capitalist industralization—an approach that emphasizes changing technical and social relations of capitalist industrial production over time.[1] As I will argue throughout, this approach offers a unified analytical framework capable of explaining differential patterns of industrial development as well as the lack of industrial development.

All analyses of industrial development draw on a reading of historical experience, whether or not that reading is made explicit. Among the variety of possible historical interpretations that could be embodied in studies of industrialization, however, there is a strong, pervasive tendency to treat industrialization as an essentially uniform process whenever it occurred. I will discuss several approaches in the last section of the chapter, but for the purposes of illustration it is worth noting that this tendency is apparent among the works of scholars with widely different political convictions (for example, Lerner [1964], Rostow [1971], North and Thomas [1973], and Warren [1980]). These works are similar in that they use static and essentially ahistorical conceptions of industrial development, thus resembling functionalism and conventional economic theory in the way abstraction is used to stress similarities among different nations' experiences with industrial growth.

My approach emphasizes historically cumulative differences, and this chapter summarizes and reframes analyses that I have been developing over the years. (Earlier versions can be seen in Weaver [1970, 1974, and 1980]). In some very general sense, my work can be seen to be in the same tradition as Gerschenkron (1952; 1966), Hewlett and Weinert (1982). Hirschman (1968), Kurth (1979), Moore (1966), and Trotsky (1932). Even many of these writers, however, who do give pride of place to national and historical differences, still regard industrial development as an essentially unchanging process, and attribute observed differences principally to national particularities (for example, "degrees of backwardness," or the organization of rural production).

This is not to deny that there definitely are some basic similarities in capitalist industrialization (for example, formation of a wage working class, urbanization, and so forth), and preindustrial social formations do significantly affect the process. But what I argue is that technical and social conditions of capitalist industrial production have changed significantly over time and that these changes have meant that the political and ideological conditions required for sustained industrial growth have varied over time. Moreover, the changes in the social dynamics of industrialization have been of a regular, discernible nature. Thus, by looking at the evolving character of preindustrial societies in light of the changing requirements and pressures that industrialization implies at different times (two sets of moving targets, as it were), we can more systematically comprehend the sources for the variety of nineteenth century industrial growth and use historical experiences more fruitfully for studying current efforts in the Third World to promote economic growth.

Central to this chapter, I see three general phases in capitalist industrial production: the first runs through the 1860's or 1870's; the second until World War I; and the third from the 1920s to the present.

In line with a long tradition of scholarship on capitalist development within already industrialized nations, I call these phases Competitive, Finance, and Monopoly Capitalism, respectively.

While this periodization and set of labels are consistent with those of Hilferding, Lenin, and more recent works by Steindl (1952), Baran and Sweezy (1966), and Levine (1975), the content of my categories is somewhat different. For those five scholars, both competitive and monopoly capitalism refer primarily to the organization of product markets and finance capitalism to the role of banks in the circulation sphere. In contrast, I consider that the most important distinction among the phases reside in the technical and social conditions of industrial production and in the industrial product mix that underlie them.

The degree to which firms control markets in which they buy and sell commodities and the institutional arrangements for financing production and distributing equity income are definitely components of each phase, but I do not consider these elements to be the major defining characteristics as have most scholars who have used the same three labels. The second major difference in my use of these terms is that scholars have used these phases of capitalist industrialization to identity the evolution of industrialized economies, and while my argument depends on these phases developing within industrialized nations, my principal interest in these phases is the manner in which they conditioned the paths by which nations became (or may become) industrialized.

After such emphasis, it may seem odd that the first section shows how the United States economy developed and changed through successive phases. I do this to identify and define the three phases of capitalist industrial production before applying them to the comparative study of becoming industrialized. U.S. history is very effective for highlighting the technical and sectoral features of these phases, because as a "newly settled region,"—the northern and western sections of the United States—the United States has had unusually flexible social and political institutions, and these regions were virtually a pure example of capitalist industrialization. As a result of this status, however, only very limited generalizations from U.S. economic history are warranted, and this section, therefore, merely describes the changing social and technical conditions of capitalist industrial production.

The next three sections briefly sketch the industrial developments of England, Germany, and Brazil as respective examples of competitive, finance, and monopoly capitalist industrialization processes. Table 1 indicates the time spans appropriate in each case. Although these sections contain some general observations, I summarize and present my conclusions in the fifth and final section.

These national studies are extremely selective and abbreviated and, thus, are more models than historical interpretations, but they are models based on the historical record. Nonetheless, their compactness lends a severely mechanical character to the exposition, and as I will repeat at the end of the essay, my principal argument is to show the value of an approach that incorporates a fuller range of historical change into our thinking about industrial development than do conventional uses of history. It is not to present a different but equally rigid and linear conception of industrial growth and development.

Finally, an important consequence of these studies' high degree of selectivity is that to make my argument clearer and more focused, I strongly emphasize processes internal to the nation (social formation). Weaver (1976) applies this general approach to questions of international economic expansion and imperialism.

UNITED STATES: THE PERIODIZATION OF INDUSTRIAL GROWTH

In the first half of the nineteenth century, wage goods (that is, consumer goods for working class families) were the predominant articles produced in U.S. factories. Such commodities as cotton and wool textiles, shoes and other leather goods, processed foods and beverages, cast iron stoves and utensils, and furniture were increasingly produced in factories that employed wage workers who were organized in interdependent divisions of labor that utilized power-assisted

Table 1
Industrial Growth in England, Germany, and Brazil

	England			Germany		
	1761/71	1815/24	1845/54	1850/54	1875/84	1905/13
Index of Ind. Output (*a*)	100	396	1146	100	282	855
Ind. Production as % of Total Production (*b*)	24	32	34	20	30	40

	Brazil			
	1939	1947	1960	1976
Index of Ind. Output		100	161	545	1878
Ind. Production as % of Total Production		17	22	25	29

(*a*) for United Kingdom
(*b*) 1761/71 for England and Wales; other dates for Great Britain.
Sources: B. R. Mitchell, "Statistical Appendix, 1700–1914," in *The Fontana Economic History of Europe*, v. 4, *The Emergence of Industrial Societies*, Part 2, ed. C. Cipolla (London: Collins/Fontana Books, 1973), p. 768; W. G. Hoffman, *Das Wachstum Der Deutschen Wirtschaft Seit Der Mitte Des 19. Jahrhunderts* (Berlin: Springer-Verlag, 1965), p. 33, P. Deane and W. A. Cole, *British Economic Growth*, 1688–1959 (Cambridge: University Press, 1969), pp. 143, 156, 295, W. Bagr, *Industrialization and Economic Development in Brazil* (Homewood, Ill.: Irwin, 1965), pp. 27, 28, 71; Inter-American Development Bank, *Economic and Social Progress in Latin America, 1977 Report* (Washington, D.C.: IDB), pp. 395, 400.

machinery. A few factories produced capital goods and some consumer goods firms were large (for example, breweries). By the standards of even 50 years later, however, mid-nineteenth century manufacturing was predominantly wage goods produced in many small firms that bought and sold in competitive markets, used rudimentary technologies and simple organizational forms, and made rather low-quality products. These are defining characteristics of competitive industrial capitalism. Most products for well-to-do consumers continued to be made under artisanal conditions (whether located in the United States or abroad) in which machinery and specialization of labor tasks were relatively unimportant.

Significant structural changes in manufacturing occurred in the fifty years after the Civil War. Table 2 indicates that the growth of consumer goods production lagged far behind that of such intermediate and capital goods as steel (replacing iron), rubber, chemicals, glass, and machinery. In 1869 manufactured food, textiles, lumber and wood articles, and leather products (including shoes) constituted almost half of total manufacturing output, but 30 years later, the output of these goods was only a little more than one-fourth of total manufacturing value added. Intermediate and capital goods were not only displacing consumer goods as the quantitively most important industrial commodities, they were undisputedly the leaders in technological and organizational innovation. Compared with consumer goods, intermediate and capital goods production occurred in large, highly capitalized plants where, by the beginning of the twentieth century, work tasks were carefully organized, specialized, and assisted by machinery. The figures in Table 2 show that primary power-producing capacity and capitalization among industrial product groups changed considerably more than the composition of output, which indicates the substantial differences in the way production was organized in intermediate and capital goods firms.[2]

These changes in the technical and social conditions of industrial production help to explain some key features of the late nineteenth and early twentieth centuries. The magnitude of the financial investment needed for establishing and operating a modern steel mill on an economically feasible scale encouraged the growth of large investment banks and the use of corporate forms of business organization, thus making finance capitalism an appropriate designation for this phase.

The increased scale and complexity of production and marketing led to greater divisions of labor and the growth of bureaucratic hierarchies to manage and coordinate production and marketing. Emergence of large intermediate and capital goods firms directly increased the centralization of capital, but the indirect centralizing effects were probably at least as important. The shift in the composition of industrial production stimulated large-scale mining and refining enterprises, the development of nationwide transportation and financial systems, and the formation of business bureaucracies that were capable of managing many diverse operations—all of which also encouraged mergers and centralization.

The gathering of large numbers of industrial, mining, and transport workers together at one working site contributed to the formation of coherent and aggressive labor organizations that, together with some unions in crafts and in

Table 2
Changes in the Composition of U.S. Manufacturing (% Distributions)

	Value Added in Manufacturing		Total Primary-Power Capacity in Manufacturing (incl. purchases of electricity)		Total Capital Invested in Manufacturing	
	1859	1899	1869	1919	1880	1919
Food, Textiles, Wood, Leather, and assoc. products (excl. furniture)	46.9	28.6	73.3	34.2	52.4	33.7
Tobacco, Apparel, and Furniture	11.7	17.6	2.0	1.9	11.1	7.0
Sub-Total	58.6	46.2	75.3	36.1	63.5	40.7
Paper, Printing and Publishing, Chemicals, Rubber, Petroleum, Stone-Clay, Glass, and Primary Metals	21.1	28.3	16.0	44.9	21.1	32.7
Fabricated Metals, Machinery, Transport Equipment, and Instruments	16.6	21.5	7.6	18.4	13.5	24.6
Miscellaneous	3.7	3.9	(a)	(a)	1.7	1.7
Sub-Total	41.4	53.7	23.6(b)	63.3(b)	36.3	59.0
TOTAL	100.0	100.0	100.0	100.0	100.0	100.0

(a) Included in "Fabricated Metals, etc."

(b) The proportion of total power which was water power in the two years were 48.2% and 6.0% respectively.

Sources:

Value Added: Albert W. Niemi, "Structural and Labor Productivity Patterns in United States Manufacturing, 1838–1919," *Business History Review,* v. 46 (Spring, 1972), p. 71.

Power: Allen H. Fenichel, "Growth and Diffusion of Power in Manufacturing, 1838–1919," in Conference on Research in Income and Wealth, *Output, Employment, and Productivity in United States after 1800* (New York: National Bureau of Economic Research, 1966), pp. 472, 477–478.

Capital: Daniel Creamer, *Capital and Output Trends in Manufacturing Industries, 1880–1948,* NBER Occasional Paper #4 (New York: National Bureau of Economic Research, 1954, 1954, pp. 36–39.

geographically concentrated activities (for example, apparel), helped to offset, even if only slightly and for a narrow stratum of workers, the tendency for the distribution of income to become skewed toward capital. In addition, the significant proportion of total industrial output in intermediate and capital goods that, relative to consumer goods, are subject to more volatile changes in demand, heightened the vulnerability of the industrial sector and the economy as a whole to cyclical fluctuations. The exercise of centralized economic power in key areas of the economy led to the demand by business groups and others for political intervention and regulation, the economic instability and capital-labor conflicts also paved the way for the central state's growth in size and authority. (Kolko, 1967; Weinstein, 1968; US, DOC, 1975: 1102–1108)

It was through these mechanisms, then, that the change in the composition of industrial production in the late nineteenth century contributed to (and was necessary for) significant new arrangements in social, political, and economic life. By the 1920s, however, a new phase of capitalist industrial growth was emerging, a phase that in the context of the United States development appeared to be merely extending the technical and social conditions characteristic of intermediate and capital goods' production into consumer goods' production. As such, the new phase—monopoly capitalism—was a matter of degree in U.S. history, but as I will demonstrate later in this chapter, it has considerable importance for comparative history of capitalist industrialization in other parts of the world.

Machine tool and chemical firms were the sources of innovation that radically altered the technical conditions of production in such consumer goods as processed foods (including milling and meat packing), cigarettes, shoes, pharmaceuticals, and cosmetics, and large, machine-using firms became predominant in these lines. Even more striking examples of the changes in the character of consumer goods production, however, was in new consumer goods such as rayon, nylon, and plastic products, the whole range of electrical appliances, and, of course, that symbol of U.S. consumer civilization—the automobile. For convenience and for the lack of a better name, I will categorize as "modern consumer goods" both the new consumer goods and the older ones in which production processes were transformed.

These modern consumer goods would become the most dynamic product lines of the mid-twentieth century, and in their production, plant scale, organization of work, and market organization resemble more closely that of intermediate and capital goods firms in 1900 than of the leading consumer goods of the mid-nineteenth century. My argument here, therefore, goes beyond that of the conventional "consumer durables revolution" (as criticized by Vatter, 1967); my emphasis on the manner in which goods are produced means

that they include complementary goods such as tires and fuels as well as
the entire range of previously mentioned articles produced in similar
ways.

Table 3 shows these changes in the composition of consumer goods production. The first group of commodities is, roughly, technologically "untrans-
formed" consumer goods, and the second group is modern consumer goods, as
defined above. Table 3 understates the extent to which the production mix has
changed, because such items as nylon textiles, cigarettes, and plastic toys are
included in the "traditional" consumer goods category even though the manner
by which they are produced means that they should be in the second category.
Added to the 1967 consumer goods totals are figures for governmental purchases broken down by the same categories to recognize more fully the changed
composition of production.

Table 3
Industrial Consumer-Type Goods (% Value of Final Goods)

| | | | 1967 | | | |
| | | | | Government Purchases | | |
	1899	1929	Consumer Purchases	Federal	State & Local	Total
Group I goods (*a*)	68.2	53.2	42.6	0.6	0.4	43.6
Group II goods (*b*)	6.3	19.3	19.9	13.2	1.0	34.1

(*a*) Manufactured food, tobacco, dry goods, clothing, footwear, household furnishings
(including crockery, cutlery, draperies, etc.), jewelry, clocks and watches: these are
Shaw's commodity categories numbers 320, 322, 329–331, 335, 339, 340, and 342;
input-output commodity categories numbers 14–19, 22, 23, 34–42, and 64.

(*b*) Heating and cooking apparatuses, passenger and recreational vehicles (including
accessories, tires, and manufactured fuel), electrical household appliances (including
radios, phonographs, and televisions), pharmaceuticals, recreational and photographic
equipment: Shaw's commodity categories numbers 323, 325, 332, 333, 336–338, 345,
346, 348, and 349; input-output commodity categories numbers 13, 27–29, 31, 32, 40,
53–56, 59, 60–63.

Sources: 1899 and 1929 from William H. Shaw, *Value of Commodity Output Since
1869* (New York: NBER, 1947), pp. 13–27, 30, 66, 213–234, 290, and U.S. Bureau of
the Census, *Historical Statistics of the United States, Colonial Times to 1970*, Part 2
(Washington, D.C.: Government Printing Office, 1975), pp. 699–702; 1967 from "The
Input-Output Structure of the U.S. Economy: 1967," *Survey of Current Business*, v. 54,
#2 (February 1947), pp. 34–43.

The centrality of modern consumer goods to the economy as a whole is further underscored by looking more closely at the 1967 input-output table. For one important example, firms producing modern consumer goods (Table 3) accounted for two-thirds of the demand for primary metals and metal products ("direct and indirect requirements" of categories 37, 38, and 39) in that year, and even a casual perusal of the input-output table will show the significant proportions of virtually all sectors' production that are derivative from consumers' and governments' demand for these types of goods. (*Survey,* 1974: 38–43, 50–55)

Modern consumer goods are the leading branches of twentieth century industrial production, and together with the capital and intermediate goods that are closely linked to them, they constitute the most progressive and prosperous areas of industrial production. Transportation, communications, mining, and finance are other economic sectors in which prosperity is directly correlated with the similarity of their productive organization to that of modern consumer goods and with the closeness of their market ties. Some government employment and professions are also high-income occupations, and their fortunes, too, depend on the leading industrial branches, whether through tax revenues or derived demand linkages.

In contrast, there are large portions of economic activity in which both employers and workers are considerably less well off, and older types of consumer goods in which production processes have not been transformed (for example, cotton textiles), some agricultural output, and many services are produced by small firms earning low rates of return on capital and employing (relative to value added) large numbers of low-paid workers. The capital intensity and technological progressiveness of the leading industrial firms sharply reduce their capacity to create new jobs, and the state and the passive low-wage private sectors are the major sources of new employment opportunities.

The state actively promotes leading firms' profitability through providing a range of services and subsidies to encourage general economical growth, and it engages in widespread welfare-type programs for those whom work does not adequately support. This second type of activity both expands market demand for modern consumer goods and contributes to social peace, although repression is vigorously applied when legitimizing mechanisms break down. (Averitt, 1962; Baumol, 1967; Braverman, 1974; Gordon, 1972; O'Connor, 1973).

From U.S. history, then, these are the characteristics and chronology of three major phases of capitalist industrial growth that crucially affect the process by which some nations have become industrialized and help explain the reason that others have not done so. The next three sections will apply and elaborate the argument.

ENGLAND: COMPETITIVE
CAPITALIST INDUSTRIALIZATION

In late eighteenth and early nineteenth century England, the technical conditions of cotton textile production and iron-working were such that small production units were economically viable, and a large number of small units characterized the organization of these wage-goods firms that, as Table 4 shows, constituted the dynamic core of early industrial growth. The fixed capital requirements for establishing such factories were modest, and the most serious financing needs were for inventories and wages. These short-term credit needs were met through informal borrowing and lending networks and through credit instruments (for example, letters of credit) that were developed for mercantile purposes, and once a firm was operating, the reinvestment of profits was the major source of financing expansion.

The most important qualities for successful entrepreneurship were the ability to deal competently with the vagaries of competitive input and product markets and, perhaps most important, to organize and control a work force in a factory setting. The low financial barriers to entry into factory production and the lack of formal education or even of craft experience for successful industrial entrepreneurship meant that industrial entrepreneurs could be drawn from various backgrounds. Although most of industrial entrepreneurs were from the middle and lower-middle strata of English society, there are numerous examples of successful factories being established and operated by people of humble origins. At this time, industrial entrepreneurship was a vehicle for significant social mobility.[3]

Table 4
The Structure of Early British Industrial Growth

	Index Numbers		% National Income	% Manufacturing, Mining, Building,	
Year	National Income	Manufacturing, Mining, Building	Manufacturing, Mining, Building	Textile Industry	Iron Industry
1770	100	100	24.0	37.5	n.a.
1821	285	380	34.3	43.9	10.6

Sources: B. R. Mitchell, "Statistical Appendix, 1700–1914," in *The Fontana Economic History of Europe,* v. 4, The Emergence of Industrial Societies, Part 2, ed. C. Cipolla, p. 768; P. Deane and W. A. Cole, *British Economic Growth, 1688–1959,* pp. 156, 166, 212, 225.

For understanding the development of domestic markets for factory produced wage goods and the sources of the large factory labor force required for producing them in the late eighteenth and early nineteenth centuries, we have to look at the English countryside and recognize the importance of "balanced" growth in English industrial expansion. Eighteenth century agricultural growth increased agricultural employment, and, as a result of enclosures, this was typically employment for wage workers. This organizational change discouraged extensive household production, which forced agricultural workers into the market as purchasers, and, with increased agricultural employment, the countryside became a substantial market for the cheap consumer goods flowing from the factories.

It is extremely important to stress this point, because there seems to be considerable confusion about it. Domestic markets were always quantitively important for English industry, and they were absolutely central to industrial growth throughout the second half of the eighteenth century before producers had the confidence to rely on exporting, as especially cotton textile firms did after the turn of the nineteenth century. (Deane and Cole, 1967: 31,59,185,196,225) The prosperity of English agriculture, therefore, remained essential to industrial growth. Agricultural exports were also important for cotton textile producers, for those exports earned much of the foreign exchange necessary to import raw cotton.

Agricultural growth also supported a population growth greater than the sector's own labor requirements. The development of the wage labor system in the countryside both allowed and encouraged these people to migrate to the cities where firms were increasingly located after the steam engine freed factories from dependence on water power. In the cities, the migrants joined the Irish and ruined artisans to supply the voracious labor needs of this form of industrial growth without raising wages. Urban workers, of course, also purchased cheap consumer goods.

The English agricultural-industrial dynamic was a crucial element in English industrial development. But it must be remembered that, unlike the depiction of agriculture in the so-called dual model of economic development (for example, Lewis, 1954 and Kelley, and others, 1972; but also see Luxemburg, 1913: 395–418), English agriculture was not backward. On the contrary, its productivity and progressiveness was vital from the mid-eighteenth century to supporting industrial growth by supplying food, labor, markets, foreign exchange, and some capital.

The relative openness and prosperity of eighteenth century English society was a necessary condition for the competitive capitalist form of English industrial growth that required freedom for the entrepreneurs and freedom for workers. These freedoms, defined negatively in the tradition of liberal political theory, were not parallel: the freedoms of the former were a lack of effective restrictions on their activities and accumulation; the freedoms of the latter were the lack of access to property and, within these constrained alternatives, freedom from restrictions on geographical mobility and choice of employer. (Marx, 1857–1858: 503–504) These freedoms were but tendencies in the eighteenth century, however, and large-scale industrial growth required the sure establishment of the preëminence of contractual relationships over other forms of obligation, the mobility of labor, and access to domestic and foreign markets, as well as mechanisms of social control to contain the newly formed industrial proletariat.

The diffusion of the new source of economic power among a large number of industrial entrepreneurs, the diverse background of that group, and their financial independence from preindustrial elites enabled the industrial bourgeoisie (frequently with help from the working class) to wield formidable political power and to elevate their aggressive individualism and materialism into the national ideology. That is, competitive capitalist industrialism, through creation of powerful new classes with only weak links to preindustrial elites and culture, was a potent social force that helped to fashion the political and cultural conditions necessary for its continuing development.

The industrial bourgeoisie's influence on the national state was thus effective in removing restrictions on commodity markets and in changing official attitudes, but the English state had only a minor role in actively promoting industrial growth. Even in the domain of social control, the Factory Acts and poor law legislation in the early nineteenth century were limited and largely ineffective efforts to regulate employers and ameliorate the misery of working-class life; the industrial bourgeoisie assumed major responsibility, exercised at the site of production, for containing worker unrest. The small numbers of workers in a single factory, the penetration of individualistic ideology among the workers, the recent rural origins of so many workers, the direct and personally exercised authority by employers in the factory, and employment of private police in town and cities were the most potent mechanisms of social control. The English state in the late eighteenth and early nineteenth centuries was weak, decentralized, and nonprofessionally administered, and its positive programs of social control were few and reactive.

The English state's most important role in industrialization was consistent with *laissez faire* principles: it vigorously enforced the "rules of the game" (that is, protected property relationships) when necessary; and it got out of the way of the market mechanism that, with the intense competition among small units of production, generated the market price signals indicating where factor and product sales would be the most remunerative, and, thus, rewarded perspicacity, innovation, and capital formation by the industrial bourgeoisie.

GERMANY: FINANCE
CAPITALIST INDUSTRIALIZATION

The sketch of English history in Section II suggests the reasons that wage goods never became the source of general and sustained competitive capitalist industrialization in Germany in the early nineteenth century. German agriculture was commercialized in that large quantities of its products were sold in domestic and foreign markets, but the organization of agricultural production (semifeudal east of the Elbe and small-holding peasants in the south and west), slow population growth, and, less important, the destructiveness of the Napoleonic wars and political fragmentation combined to retard the development of large domestic consumer goods markets and the migration of people from agricultural to industrial occupations.[4]

But probably the most decisive constraint on competitive capitalist industrial growth was the presence of a vigorous system of aristocratic privilege vested in the landowning Junkers of the east and symbiotic with a powerful central state. The decisive failure of the 1848 revolution demonstrated the resolution and ability of preindustrial elites to prevent the liberal reforms necessary for competitive capitalist industrialization. Another political lesson that 1848 forcefully taught German liberals was that the industrial working class could not be counted on as reliable allies; important segments of the workers threatened to carry the revolt beyond reformist objectives, and this experience revealed to the industrial bourgeoisie new advantages in the Prussian state with its aristocratic and military pillars. (Marx, 1848; Tilly, 1956)

Germany became an industrial power, but not until the second half of the nineteenth century when another type of industrial growth became feasible. Table 5 demonstrates that German industrial development was based not on consumer goods as in England but rather on producer goods—intermediate products like steel and chemicals and on machine-building industries and other steel-using products. These products were not important in English industrial development because their very existence or the way in which they were produced or both reflected the economic progress that occurred in the century between the beginning of English industrialization and German industrialization. The major features of this progress were technological change, the mid-nineteenth century railroad boom, and in regard to machine-making firms, increased backward-linked specialization resulting from the expansion of the market. For all intents and purposes. England in the eighteenth century did not

Table 5
The Structure of German Industrial Growth

Year	Real National Income	Industrial Production		
		Consumer Goods	Producer Goods	Total
1871	100	100	100	100
1913	357	286	625	476

Source: G. Bry, *Wages in Germany, 1871–1945* (Princeton, NJ: Princeton Univ. Press for NBER, 1960), p. 17.

	Distribution of Industrial Value Added		Rates of Labor Productivity Growth
	1846/61	1913	1875 to 1913
Foodstuffs & Beverages	16.0	15.0	0.9
Textiles	23.5	12.2	2.1
Clothing & Leatherwork	26.3	17.1	1.6
Woodworking	11.7	10.3	1.6
Paper products	1.0	3.1	3.5(a)
Metals production	1.9	4.7	2.4
Metal working	10.2	20.0	2.2
Chemicals	0.9	3.0	2.3
Stones and Earth	5.6	8.5	1.2
Other	2.9	6.1	n.a.
TOTAL	100.0	100.0	1.6

(a) 1882 to 1913
Source: W. G. Hoffmann, *Das Wachstum der Deutschen Wirtschaft Seit der Mitte des 19. Jahrhunderts*, pp. 68–69.

possess a capital goods sector; it was not unusual for workers recruited to work in a new plant to build both the plant and the capital equipment before operating it. Factories using machines to build machines resulted from the success of factories using machines to produce consumer goods.

The military value of intermediate and capital goods production, including the railroad, made them attractive to the Prussian state and other powerful groups, and the technical conditions of their production made industrial growth less threatening to those with substantial stakes in the preservation of the preindustrial social order.

These intermediate and capital goods were produced in establishments that utilized the most advanced technologies in the world, initially drawn from England and Europe and later developed within Germany. As a consequence of the scale and capital intensity of the firms in the most dynamic lines of production (see Table 6), German industrial growth did not diffuse economic power among a large number of owner-operators of diverse backgrounds; instead, it constituted the basis for new concentrations of economic power controlled by those who had access to the considerable financial resources necessary for establishing an enterprise on an economically viable scale. This did not mean that firms were founded exclusively by family fortunes or by the state. While a large part of Germany's industrial capital was financed by the German government(s) and by English investors in the 1820s and 1830s, financial capital was increasingly supplied by joint-stock investment banks from the beginnings of rapid industrial growth of the 1850s.

These banks did not merely perform the passive function of financial intermediation; by the late 1840s external sources of funds were not important, and through their own retained profits and by credit creation the banks financed, directed, and even established industrial enterprises. The banks also encouraged coordination of production and pricing decisions among industrial enterprises through mergers and agreements. Instead of open, competitive determination of market prices, centralization of industrial production and mutual recognition of interdependence led to the formulation and administration of production and marketing decisions by negotiation among interested parties. Industrial cartels—the adaptation of an organizational form with a long history in Germany—embraced most of the firms that constituted the dynamic core of German industrial growth, and, although they did not completely suspend market forces (particularly for exporters), cartels did substantially reduce competition among producers.[5]

The labor market in which the large industrial firms operated also was considerably less than free. Workers in the leading industrial firms, undoubtedly helped by the large scale of the plants in which they worked, formed stronger labor unions at an earlier stage of industrial development than did their English counterparts, and negotiations between them and cartelized employers was closer to the conditions of bilateral monopoly than of competition.

The lower "living" labor-to-output requirements of steel, coal, chemicals, and machinery production meant that the formation of an industrial labor force was a considerably more modest endeavor than for English wage goods production. There was no functional need to remove the legal barriers on

Frederick Stirton Weaver

Table 6
Great Britain and Germany: Some Comparisons

	Gross Domestic Capital Formation (% GNP)		Government Consumption (% GNP)	Entrepreneurs & Self-Employed (% Labor Force)	Return on Entrepr. Equity (% GNP)
	Total	Prod. Equip. & Non-Res. Constr.			
United Kingdom					
1860/69	9.4	6.3	4.8	13	10
Germany					
1871/90	18.9	10.6	5.9	n.a.	n.a.
1891/1913	23.0	14.2	7.1	26 (1913)	31 (1913)

	Incremental Capital-Output Ratios (constant prices)		% Total Production in Sector Divided by % Total Employment in Sector	
			Agric., Forestry, Fishing	Manufacturing
United Kingdom		United Kingdom		
1860/69 to		1801	0.905	0.788 (a)
1880/89	3.5	1851	0.935	0.800 (a)
Germany		Germany		
1871/80 to		1882	0.775	0.839
1891/1900	4.5	1907	0.707	1.320
1881/90 to				
1901/13	4.8			

(a) These figures include production and employment in mining and construction as well as manufacturing. If mining and construction employment were excluded from the denominator of the 1851 figure, the ratio would be 1.04. In 1851, British mining employment was 4.1% of total employment, construction 5.2%, and manufacturing 33.0%. Other separate manufacturing totals are not available.

Sources: S. Kuznets, *Modern Economic Growth: Rate, Structure, and Spread* (New Haven, Conn.: Yale University Press, 1966, pp. 168, 236, 252; P. Deane and W. A. Cole, *British Economic Growth, 1688–1959*, pp. 142, 143, 146; W. A. Hoffman, *Das Wachstum der Deutschen Wirtschaft Seit der Mitte des 19. Jahrhunderts,* p. 33; B. R. Mitchell, *European Historical Statistics, 1705–1970* (New York: Columbia University Press, 1975), p. 156.

geographical mobility by agricultural workers on eastern latifundia nor to destroy the freeholding peasantry in the south and west to supply the factories with vast numbers of people. In a similar manner, population growth did not make a vital contribution to industrial development. The strength of the industrial workers' unions, their relatively few numbers, and their productivity compared with agricultural workers and those producing consumer goods (in which artisans and handicrafts were prominent), set them apart from the general working population in income as well as work life experience. Thus, although modern sector workers possessed considerable political influence at an early stage of industrial growth, their position with respect to other German workers helps to explain the style of German working-class politics and its ultimate inability to push German social and political change in different directions. The dogmatic character of the Social Democrats' agricultural reform program, which had virtually no appeal to agricultural workers, is a prime example of this ineffectiveness. (Gerschenkron, 1943: 28–32; Mitrany, 1961: 40–51).

The types of products that constituted Germany's leading industrial lines also had far-reaching implications for the nature of industrial product demand. The military usefulness of these products made them valuable to the German state, which was determined to reassert its military superiority on the continent and to resist the threat from the English. The state directly and indirectly was an important source of demand for these products (for example, in the construction and operation of railroads) before exports became significant (see Table 6 for government consumption), and promoted militaristic nationalism into the dominant ideology of industrial development.

The patterns of factor mobilization and market development required by this style of industrial growth were the general economic ingredients for the "revolution from above," a process by which industrial development was possible without disrupting and supplanting Germany's preindustrial social and cultural forms with liberal institutions and values. The fact that these economic ingredients were present did not make the outcome easy nor inevitable, but it is a matter of historical record that it did happen.

The centralized and bureaucratic Prussian state and the ideology of German nationalism were specifically German components to the success and the character of late nineteenth century industrial development in Germany. It was this powerful state that mediated the conflicts between the Junkers and the agents of industrial growth and convinced both that national corporate aspirations transcended their short-term interests. This was a protracted and difficult process, but the relatively few industrial leaders, the acceptability of their backgrounds and value to the aristocracy, and revolutionary agitation among the best organized workers facilitated the "marriage of iron and rye" that was consummated in the 1870s. (Barkin, 1970; Lebovics, 1967).

The industrial bourgeoisie and (nationalist) ideology were, as in England, important in containing the working class, but the political strength of the workers required considerably more positive state participation in social control. Bismarck's creative mix of brutal repression and sweeping social insurance and welfare legislation (Rimlinger, 1966: 565–567) was very effective, principally because of the industrial workers' advantaged position relative to the situations of the majority of German workers, which made making them vulnerable to nationalist appeals in times of crisis.

A final contrast with competitive capitalist industrialization is illustrated by German agriculture, which lagged far behind industry in output and productivity growth. Because it was not required to be a source of labor or product market demand, it could remain backward. Industrialization and urbanization did increase domestic market demand for agricultural products, but the demand was met principally by switching from foreign to domestic markets and by imports rather than by increased domestic production. German agriculture by the end of the nineteenth century did show some dynamism, but as in the case of industrial consumer goods, agricultural growth was the result of industrial development (for example, application of domestically produced farm machinery and chemical fertilizers) rather than a source of that development.

Germany in 1913 was a conservative industrial society that combined the conservatism of its own past with the general change in the nature of industrial capitalism, which, in its late nineteenth century, finance capitalist phase, enabled retention of key preindustrial social and cultural elements. I wish my argument about how this occurred to be especially clear on two central points. First, the social and cultural configurations of industrial Germany were not determined by finance capitalist industrialization but flowed in a relatively smooth, nondialectical manner from preindustrial society. That is, finance capitalism did not force Germany into conservative industrialization; it was simply that Junkers and allied elites would go along with industrialization only as long as it was conservative. The abortive revolution of 1848 and the reaction of the 1850s demonstrated rather clearly another dimension of historically cumulative change: the influential and powerful strata of German society understood the origins of English liberalism and of the French Revolution sufficiently well to ensure, at least as a veto group, that the liberal competitive path of industrial development simply was not an exercisable option. (Hamerow, 1958: 199–255)

Having emphasized the essentially permissive nature of economic forces, I turn to the second point, which comes from another direction. No matter how strongly the Prussian state, the Junkers, the peasants, and others may have wanted conservative industrialization, their desire would not have been enough to create it had there not been an alternative to competitive capitalism. Returning to my introductory remarks on standard approaches to the comparative study of industrialization, German preindustrial society did not simply add a conservative patina to a competitive capitalist industrialization (compare Rostow, 1971); the politically dominant forces in Germany took advantage of fundamental changes in the character of industrial capitalism that were the direct legacy of earlier competitive industrializations.

Comparing late nineteenth century Germany with England of the same period (rather than with England of one hundred years before as I have done) underscores the global character of the finance capitalist phase. The same features that I have emphasized in Germany—the relative importance of producer goods industries, heavy participation by banks, a centralized state, economic power concentrated in a few large enterprises often organized into cartels, and a segmented working class—were apparent, at least as strong tendencies, in late nineteenth century England. (Ashworth, 1960; 1962:86–101; Hobsbawm, 1964)

The expansion of capital and intermediate goods production with the attendant organizational features (for example, prevalence of corporate forms) in England worked against the atomistic conditions that characterized the formative period of competitive capitalism of earlier decades. But because of this context, centralization did not reach the degree it did in Germany—probably to England's economic disadvantage. By the turn of the twentieth century, liberal institutions were already ineffective in coordinating and stimulating what had become the leading branches of industrial growth, and the liberal heritage was a disadvantage in competing with the economically more dynamic Germany.

In Germany, England, and the United States, the finance capitalist phase, with the rise of capital and intermediate products firms, encouraged a skewed distribution of income, the monopolization of raw material sources to maintain product market monopolies, creation of an "aristocracy of labor" that had the organizational coherence and resources to serve as the vanguard of the working class, and chronically destabilizing effects of crises of proportion and surplus realization problems. All of these features indicated the need for a strong state apparatus to manage a more complex and unstable economy and to contain working-class aspirations. Although these forces were in differing relationships in the two nations, they had common roots, and when one adds the observation that there was more than one industrialized nation in the world at the turn of the twentieth century, they account for all the elements of classical theories of the "new imperialism." Militarism, colonization, and racism all served very real functions for these economies, and the export of *real* capital (for example, rails and machinery) served as the necessary centerpiece for the entire system. (Weaver [1980: 42–45] develops this argument more fully.)

BRAZIL: MONOPOLY
CAPITALIST INDUSTRIAL GROWTH

The explanation for Brazil's lack of industrial development in the nineteenth and early twentieth centuries is straightforward when one uses the sketches of competitive and finance capitalist industrial development as guides. Although it did not experience the convulsive wars of independence that wracked continental Spanish America in the early decades of the nineteenth century, Brazil was a sparsely populated agricultural nation with sugar, its principal commercial crop, produced by a decaying slave labor system. The slaves clearly were not a source of effective domestic demand for industrial wage goods, nor were they free to leave agriculture for industrial work even if there had been opportunities for such employment. Moreover, there was little in the realms of politics and culture to encourage competitive capitalist industrialization.

By the end of the nineteenth century, much of this had changed. Slavery had been abolished, coffee was the leading export crop, and its production employed large numbers of wage laborers. European immigrants supplied wage labor to coffee plantations as well as to rapidly growing urban activities, and considerably more flexible and decentralized political institutions had replaced the colonial and immediately postcolonial monarchies. In this milieu, a variety of entrepreneurs—middle-class immigrants, members of coffee planter families, importers, and so forth—established wage goods factories that were afforded some protection from imports by transportation costs and by tariffs placed on imports of wage goods to raise governmental revenues by taxing the working classes. By 1920, industrial production employed about 13% of the Brazilian labor force, and it was overwhelmingly in wage goods.[6]

Even those categories in Table 7 that sound like heavy, large-scale industry were, in 1920, principally repair shops, small factories making harsh soaps, and the like. But it was already more than 50 years too late for wage goods to be the dynamic core of national industrial development, and manufacturing remained dependent on coffee export earnings to expand local consumer goods markets and to supply the foreign exchange for needed imports of capital and intermediate inputs.

Market forces did not promote local production of capital and intermediate goods. First of all, transportation costs for such goods were a smaller proportion of final selling price than for cheap consumer goods, thus affording less protection to potential domestic producers. (Merhav, 1969: 36) Moreover, local

Table 7
The Structure of Brazilian Industrial Growth (value added)

	1920	1950	1970	1976 Index of Industrial Production (1972 = 100)
Food Products, Beverages, Tobacco	32.0	25.5	17.1	125.7
Textiles, Clothing, Shoes, Textile and Leather Products	39.6	25.7	13.2	113.6
Timber and Furniture	7.8	5.6	4.6	n.a.
Paper and Paper Products	1.5	2.1	2.6	118.3
Printing and Publishing	—	4.2	3.7	n.a.
Rubber Products	0.2	2.1	2.0	138.7
Chemicals, Plastics, Pharmaceuticals, Cosmetics	6.0	9.4	16.7	151.8
Non-metallic Minerals	4.7	7.4	6.9	159.6
Metallurgy	4.3	7.4	11.6	119.5
Machinery and Electrical Equip.	2.0	3.9	12.5	137.4
Transportation Equipment	—	2.3	8.0	153.0
Miscellaneous	1.9	1.9	2.1	n.a.
TOTAL	100.0	100.0	100.0	133.8

Sources: W. Baer, *Industrialization and Economic Development in Brazil* (Homewood, Ill.: Irwin, 1965), p. 269; *Anuário Estatística do Brazil, 1976,* v. 37, pp. 179, 201.

factories' demand for backward-linked inputs was small and erratic, and, although considerable investment had occurred in transportation (particularly railroads, tram lines, and dock facilities) and urban utilities, the bulk of this activity was financed by foreign capital with strong ties to foreign producers of steel, machinery, and fuels.

The lack of market incentives to produce capital and intermediate goods was and is a common situation in nonindustrial economies in the twentieth century, and the fact that the Brazilian state was neither in the fiscal nor political position to offset this pattern is also not surprising. Its taxes were only meager proportions of national income in the early twentieth century, and it was not free to find the resources to channel into steel mills and refineries.

Coffee planters were the most powerful political group in Brazil at the time, and domestic development of steel, machinery, and fuel production to supplant imports would have raised the costs of producing, processing, and transporting coffee exports. In addition, domestic industrialists were in a similar situation, and they added their slight political weight against even tariffs on capital and intermediate goods.

A strong, militaristic type of nationalism would have helped to unite these factions behind an expanded central state able to sponsor a large domestic armaments sector, but this variant of nationalism was far too weak to justify to the Brazilian elite either the economic costs of an expanded state and import-substituting production or the political risks of reduced influence over a powerful, centralized bureaucratic state. Positivism was a strong ideology among those who counted politically in Brazil of that period ("Order and Progress" is still the motto on the national flag), and while the state was an active force in the economy, the state's activities were primarily devoted to supporting Brazil's place in the international division of labor—a program that included an elaborate coffee price support system.

Not until the 1930s did social and political conditions in Brazil change enough to allow the promulgation of policies that significantly encouraged industrial growth. The economic and political position of the coffee planters was severely eroded by the effect of the depression on coffee exports, and the depression's discrediting of *laissez faire* liberalism removed ideological obstacles. The Brazilian central state, under the leadership of Getulio Vargas, assumed the responsibility of economic regulation and coordination that the market system seemed unable to perform, and with these functions, the state grew in size and authority.[7] A serious challenge to the new political order was mounted by the coffee planters in 1932, and it was decisively crushed by Vargas in a military campaign that included the aerial bombardment of the city of São Paulo.

Although the coffee elite continued to receive governmental subsidies, they had become clients of the state rather than the power behind it. The social bases of the Brazilian state had changed, and Vargas worked with an eclectic constituency of urban middle and working classes, rural and urban small proprietors, the military, and urban masses. Nevertheless, Vargas was definitely not at the head of a social revolution. The government maintained property relations, made repeated efforts to improve foreign markets for export staples, and continued the subsidies of coffee price supports. Urban worker unrest was contained by social legislation, repression, and the effectiveness of efforts to minimize urban unemployment. In attempting to counteract urban unemployment, the government used tariffs and exchange controls to channel scarce foreign exchange toward imports of capital goods and other needed inputs necessary to maintain domestic industrial production and employment.

The curtailment of luxury imports and the preservation of local patterns of income distribution (and, thereby, the composition of demand) created new domestic opportunities for the production of luxury goods. Little could be done for frustrated consumers of French perfume and wine, but by supporting incomes for the prosperous and cutting off imports, the local production of luxury goods of a new type, which I called "modern consumer goods" in the first section, was feasible. In Brazil, consumer durables and other modern consumer goods were and continue to be predominantly luxury goods, but like the United States, over the next 40 years such items as automobiles, radios, phonographs, pharmaceuticals, washing machines, vacuum cleaners, processed foods, and eventually television sets and other electronic consumer goods (along with backward linked branches producing inputs) became the leading product lines of Brazilian industrial growth.

This pattern of industrial growth requires substantial state support: maintaining the distribution of income underlying consumer demand for these products; establishing domestic productive capacity in backward-linkage industries like steel, fuel, and power to insulate local production of modern consumer goods from the uncertainties of international staples markets; investing heavily in infrastructural projects (for example, electrification and transportation); encouraging foreign investment that contributed much of the needed capital, entrepreneurship, and technology for this type of production; and containing working and lower classes' political activities.

Despite the vagaries and manipulative populism of Brazilian politics from the 1930s to the early 1960s, the state's performance of these functions was adequate for considerable, though uneven, industrial growth, but only after the military *coup d'état* of 1964 did the state vigorously, intelligently, and above all, ruthlessly promote the "Brazilian economic miracle" of monopoly capitalist industrial growth. From the end of 1965 to the beginning of 1975, industrial production grew at an average annual rate of 11% and GDP at 9% (6% per capita). As Table 7 shows, the industry groups leading this growth were chemicals, machinery, and metallurgy, electrical and communications equipment, and transportation equipment, while wage goods lagged behind. (also see Tyler, 1976: 863–864) The pattern of consumer demand was highly influenced by upper-income receivers and reinforced by imaginative credit schemes to include middle-class consumers.[8] Although the pace of economic expansion slowed in the latter half of the 1970s, the average annual rates of growth over the 15 years between 1965 and 1980 were 9.8% for manufacturing and 9.0% for GDP (World, 1987: 205), and substantial progress was registered in high technology industries. (Tigre, 1983)

The revitalization of parastatal firms, the tight control of wages, and the reorganization of the banking system were three important elements of Brazilian industrial policy. (See Trebat, 1983 for an excellent study of state sector firms.) The centralization and expansion of the banking system, with large-scale state participation, was crucial, although to a large extent these financial institutions were acting less as financial intermediaries for domestic borrowers and lenders than as vehicles for tapping foreign savings. Private and public banks' foreign indebtedness rose from the mid-1970s and accelerated in the early 1980s, and nonfinancial state enterprises' foreign indebtedness was especially striking. Of the 200 largest firms in Brazil, nonfinancial state enterprises' capital rose from 69% of the total in 1969 to 84% in 1984. (And multinational firms' share declined from 28% to 9% in the same period.) In 1981, 64% of these enterprises' debt was held by foreigners. (Frieden, 1987: 104–115)

This set the stage for the miracle of the 1970s to become the crisis of the 1980s, and Table 8 shows a bleak picture in which the massive foreign debt became a threat to the Brazilian financial and production systems. The economic recovery of the United States in 1984 increased the demand for Brazilian exports that began to pull the Brazilian economy out of the worst of the decline, and Brazilian GDP grew at an annual average rate of five percent in 1984 and 1985.

On the upside or on the downside, whether one classifies Brazil as being industrialized, newly industrializing, semiperipheral, or whatever, it seems clear that by industrial structure and urban economic organization Brazil in the 1980s is a full-fledged member of the genus Monopoly Capitalism. Industrial production is characterized by a sharp technological and organizational dualism in which the leading portion is populated by a few large, technologically sophisticated firms (private and public, domestic and foreign) with relatively well-organized and well-paid work forces, and the wage goods side contains many small firms that use simpler, more labor-intensive techniques and operate in competitive markets with atomized and low-wage work forces. (Schmitz, 1982) Industrial accumulation and output growth are led by firms using production processes that offer few additional employment opportunities. The state "services" (which camouflage high levels of urban under- and unemployment) and wage goods firms absorb those unable to find jobs in progressive, high-wage

Table 8
Brazil: Indices of Manufacturing Production

	1970	1975	1980	1981	1982	1983
Total Manufacturing	100.0	165.6	236.4	212.9	213.2	199.8
Types of goods						
Consumer						
non-durables	100.0	134.6	175.1	171.2	174.3	165.3
Consumer durables	100.0	235.3	369.9	269.2	290.8	279.3
Intermediate	100.0	165.3	250.7	224.5	225.5	218.7
Capital	100.0	224.7	303.1	296.5	219.8	175.3

Brazil: Annual Growth Rates of Manufacturing Production

	1980	1981	1982	1983
Total Manufacturing	7.6	−9.9	0.1	−6.3
Types of Goods				
Consumer				
non-durables	5.2	−2.2	1.9	−5.2
Consumer durables	10.7	−27.2	8.0	−4.0
Intermediate	8.3	−10.5	0.5	−3.0
Capital	6.5	−18.7	−10.8	−20.2

Source: *Economic Survey of Latin America and the Caribbean, 1983* (Santiago de Chile: U.N., Economic Commission for Latin America and the Caribbean, June 1985)

firms, and large proportions of the economically active urban population are professionals and salaried white collar workers (the "modern middle class") employed by public and private bureaucracies in managerial and clerical capacities.

With large firms controlling markets for modern consumer goods, including their inputs of capital and intermediate goods, the state setting most wages, white collar workers protected by social legislation covering wages, job security, and work conditions, and the government regulating a wide range of economic activity, the competitive market as an allocative and control mechanism is important only for the activities and products of the poorest and most economically marginal strata of the urban population. Government policies underwrite modern firms' profits and accumulation through cheap credit, grants, tax breaks, and below-cost pricing of publicly produced inputs, and the consequent inflations, in the face of structural and technological rigidities, do little to reduce high rates of unemployment. As in the other more industrialized nations of Latin America, "stagflation" is not an anomaly in Brazil; it has been a recurring phenomenon for decades.

During the 1970s and 1980s, all of these elements in varying degrees can be seen in the United States and other "mature" industrial capitalist nations, but this should not obscure the significant species differences between nations becoming industrialized under conditions of monopoly capitalism and nations that were industrialized prior to entering the monopoly capitalist phase. First of all, low per capita incomes in Brazil mean that a distribution of income highly skewed toward top income receivers is necessary for sustaining, much less expanding, markets for consumer goods and backward-linked products made by the leading industrial firms.

The crucial link between income distribution and demand is badly blurred when the discussion is cast in the overly aggregated terms of Keynes' effective demand or Marx's surplus realization; what is at issue is not the general question of sufficient demand or realized surpluses but rather the specific conditions for the sufficiency of a particular pattern of demand and the realization of particular firms' surpluses that, in the context of low per capita incomes, depends on a highly inequitable distribution of income. In a similar way, the central influence of the distribution of income on economic activity is confused and even inverted in neoclassical economic theory of income distribution in which the pattern of consumer demand is seen to be determined primarily by individual consumer preferences and relative prices.

In Brazil, the distribution of income—the outcome of the political struggle among competing groups—occurred prior to and has governed the pattern of consumer demand and, thereby, the technical conditions of production that, in turn, has required a particular amount and type of productive factors. The centralization of property ownership in the Brazilian economy creates some self-reinforcing tendencies of income distribution: economic growth, whether from modern industry or staple exports, generates extremely unequal income distributions. Similarly, power among contending groups is such that inflation also contributes to the skewed distribution of income. (Georgescu-Roegen, 1970)

But there is no natural or automatic process that can be relied upon, and sustaining and reproducing the market conditions for monopoly capitalist industrial development requires a powerful and vigilant state. This is a different and more formidable task than that faced by the state in the late nineteenth century Germany or in the mid-twentieth century United States. German industrial growth was not highly sensitive to patterns of consumer demand, and in the United States, high per capita incomes, comparatively homogeneous consumer cultures, and a more equitable distribution of income allows concessions to working and lower classes in the form of income redistribution and income maintenance policies that contribute both to market demand for modern consumer goods and to social peace.

In Brazil, however, even a modest redistribution of income from the top to the bottom can curtail demand for modern consumer goods and slow economic growth, and Table 9 shows that this certainly has been avoided.[9] As a consequence, the state engages in outright repression rather than welfare as the more effective device to promote industrial growth with political stability, but even with considerable help from the United States, the inability of the regime and

Table 9
Brazil: Size Distribution of Income
and Purchasing Power of Income-Receiving Groups

	% of Economically Active Population					Gini Coefficient
	0–60	61–80	81–90	91–95	96–100	
Proportion of Income						
1960	22.7	20.4	16.4	11.6	28.9	0.57
1970	16.5	16.9	15.0	13.0	38.6	0.64
Purchasing Power of Income in 1960 Prices (100 = purchasing power of 1960 income)						
1960	37.8	102.0	164.0	232.0	578.0	
1970	36.4	112.0	200.0	344.6	1023.1	

Source: Derived from Richard Weisskopf and Adolfo Figueroa, "Traversing the Pyramid: A Comparative Review of Income Distribution," *Latin American Research Review*, vol. 11, No. 2 (1976), page 91.

Brazil: Size Distribution of Income

	% Share of Household Income by Percentile Groups of Households					
	Lowest 20 percent	Second Quintile	Third Quintile	Fourth Quintile	Highest 20 percent	Highest 10 percent
1972	2.0	5.0	9.4	17.0	66.6	50.6

Source: *World Development Report, 1987* (New York: Oxford University Press for the World Bank, 1987), page 253.

social order it represents to legitimate itself in the eyes of the poorest half of the population through income redistribution policies places great strains on political institutions.

Although repression can work, at least in the short run, to neutralize dissent from the poorest and least organized, the military regime could not rely solely on terror, and it drew positive support from some important parts of Brazilian society. Evans (1979) analyzes with impressive insight and documentation the alliance among the military government, multinational corporations, and large-scale local capital. Brazilian industrialists operating medium-sized and small firms in the competitive sector, however, have frequently protested vigorously against the rise in effective taxation, foreign investment, and the unparalleled expansion of public enterprises. (Gall, 1977; Mendonca de Barros and Graham, 1978)

Although I do not disagree with Evans' analysis of the ruling triumvirate, I believe it to be incomplete. Another vitally important base of political support for the Brazilian military government and its policies can be more readily understood by looking at income-receiving strata rather than at roles in the process of production. Higher income receivers, who were able to purchase modern consumer goods, were the major pillars of support for the Brazilian state and the social order. This group, of course, includes the entire propertied class (as consumers), but it also includes the veritable armies of clerks, accountants, managers, lawyers, sales representatives, public officials, teachers, and associated technical personnel needed to record, regulate, coordinate, and justify the economy and society in its myriad detail. These functions are required by the increasing complexity of industrial production and distribution and of the surrounding social and political relationships, and, although much of this work has had only very little directly to do with commodity production, it is vital for sustaining and reproducing the conditions of monopoly capitalist production and is duly rewarded. The point here, though, is that these modern middle classes are important as consumers, and consumption for them is a source of status and integral to their life-styles.

So in addition to protecting the privileges and incomes of these strata, the post-1964 Brazilian regime consolidated its political support by creating an imaginative set of consumer credit arrangements, and the upper stratum of the working class was also susceptible to being brought into the fold by this means. The ideology of this powerful group is adequately expressed by the rubric "consumerism," and these people's allegiance to the regime depended principally on its ability to deliver the goods.

The strain of the downturn in the 1980s led to the dissolution of the alliance among the most powerful factions in Brazilian society and also alienated the middle classes and the upper stratum of the working class from the military government's efforts to maintain international credit worthiness at the expense of domestic recovery. The pressure for the return to democratic forms, which had been sporadic and uncertain during prosperous times, became irresistible and was led by local industrialists. Opposition political parties won the election and assumed office in 1985, and the character of this return to democracy and the intentions of its principal advocates are graphically illustrated by the fact that a central element of the opposition parties' campaign was to lower interest rates[10] (Frieden, 1987: 116–122; also see Pereira, 1984: 212–213 on local industrial bourgeoisie.) Stepan (1988: 68–145) shows that the military have retained significant political control in the civilian government and that their share of the national budget has risen substantially since the election.

As a final note on Brazil, manufacturing was the principal focus of governmental efforts to stimulate economic growth, but public policies also promoted complementary sectors like mining, construction, agriculture, and transportation that supply necessary inputs to industrial production. Agriculture is especially important, because it also produces food for the urban population at prices low enough to allow other purchases from consumer budgets, and although manufacturing exports have become very important, agricultural exports continue to contribute much of the foreign exchange needed to import industrial inputs.

As already noted in the case of Germany and as will be discussed more fully in the next section, however, agricultural transformation and development are not necessary for later industrializations, and this certainly has been the case for Brazil. (See Kutcher and Scandizzo, 1981.) Table 10 shows how the productivity of Brazilian agriculture has lagged behind that of industry, and, for comparative purposes, the table reproduces the corresponding figures for the United Kingdom and Germany from Table 6.

SUMMARY AND CONCLUSIONS

The historical example of competitive capitalist industrialization profoundly influences our conceptions of what industrialization is all about. Some of this influence in English-speaking nations is exerted by the emphasis placed on study of English and U.S. history, but its most subtle and pervasive route is through generalizations abstracted from that history and embodied in purportedly universalistic theoretical principles. Both liberal and Marxist theories of economic growth and change are direct products of English history, and through such theories, competitive capitalist industrialization has indelibly colored our perceptions and the organization of our thinking about industrialization processes in general.

Table 10
Relative Productivity of Labor in Agriculture and Industry

	% Total Production in Sector Divided by % Total Employment in Sector					
	Brazil		Germany		United Kingdom	
	1940	1970	1882	1907	1801	1851
Agriculture	0.53	0.40	0.78	0.71	0.91	0.94
Industry	1.24	1.35	0.84	1.32	0.79	0.80

Sources: Werner, Baer, *Industrialization and Economic Development in Brazil,* pp. 18, 27; James R. Wilkie and P. Turovsky (eds.), *Statistical Abstract of Latin America,* Vol. 17 (Los Angeles: UCLA Latin American Center Publication, 1976), pp. 33, 135; Table 6.

The recognition that a net product (that is, a product whose value is greater than the value of its inputs) could be produced in a sector other than agriculture is clearly one of the most important principles extracted from late eighteenth and nineteenth century industrial growth, and it contains the strong corollary that material gains enjoyed by one nation or one group within a nation need not necessarily have occurred at the expense of other nations and groups. Although older conceptions about the nature of economic growth can still be found in recent scholarship, and resource and environmental concerns have qualified optimism about unlimited economic expansion, the essentially technical principle of net gain has not been falsified, and, indeed, has been confirmed, by subsequent industrializations.[11]

Not so with theoretical tenets. Important examples include the following, which are found in various mixes in both liberal and Marxist theories: there is an "economy" with its own laws of motion distinct from political institutions (Wood, 1981); industrial growth is a natural and ineluctable consequence of capitalist organization and economic "freedom" (the stronger, pre-Soviet statement that such organization and freedom are necessary for industrial growth still appears occasionally); and industrial growth is a powerful social and cultural force that can reshape all dimensions of preindustrial society, promoting liberal social and political forms and ideologies. Because these theoretical convictions and expectations are based on the historical experience of the "truly revolutionizing path" (Marx, 1894: 334) of competitive industrial capitalism, it is worth reviewing some key aspects of later phases of industrial development.

Under the conditions of finance and monopoly capitalism, the necessity of the industrial bourgeoisie as an active agent of social and economic change (a class for itself as well as in itself) has been sharply reduced. Such features as the predominance of large-scale enterprise, state sponsorship and guidance, and foreign ownership in leading, industrial firms have diminished the need for widespread, aggressive, private entrepreneurship in industrial growth. Although it is too early for firm conclusions, the Brazilian case does suggest that an active industrial bourgeoisie may be created by a successful industrial growth that was importantly initiated and conducted by other agents (for example, the state and multinational corporations).

Entrepreneurship has not been the only factor so affected. The mobilization of an industrial work force has become a much more modest process and no longer requires reaching into every sector and region of the nation to free labor power from precapitalist social and geographic restrictions. But in finance and monopoly capitalism, capital has become the factor required at an increased rate, a rate that precludes the casual, rather *ad hoc* arrangements that prevailed in the early stages of English industrial growth. Institutions and procedures have to be created to ensure the adequate availability of capital, and large banks, the state's fiscal powers, and foreign investors can perform this function.

Furthermore, in later industrializations, agriculture's relationship to industrial development can be qualitatively different from that of English agriculture in eighteenth and nineteenth century competitive industrial development. Virtually the only role for the agricultural sector in both German and Brazilian industrialization has been to supply produce, and this function can be performed even if agriculture is noncapitalist and stagnant in output and labor productivity. Nevertheless, it is clear that the more agricultural produce per rural inhabitant, the less harsh, efficient, and costly the political controls over agricultural workers (be they sharecroppers, wage laborers, peasant proprietors, or whatever) needed to wrest from them sufficient produce both to feed the urban population and to export.

So agricultural development, as it is commonly understood, can make important contributions to monopoly capitalist development but, unlike the case of England, financial and monopoly capitalist industrial growth do not necessitate the transformation of the countryside so that it can serve as a source of labor power and of demand for consumer goods. In later industrializations, the countryside does not have to become like the city in organization, culture, and prosperity, but the consequence is not liberal industrial capitalism, as would be expected from the experience of competitive capitalism. (Moore, 1966)

The patterns of factor mobilization required for industrialization, then, have changed to reduce the requirements for large-scale inputs of entrepreneurship and labor—extremely disruptive aspects of competitive capitalist industrialization—and to emphasize the inputs of capital mobilized by centralized, stabilizing institutions. Because large consumer goods markets were not necessary to support finance capitalist industrial growth, and as relatively few, well-to-do consumers constitute the key private markets for monopoly capitalist industrialization, demand conditions support and extend these centralizing tendencies.

It is these related and mutually reinforcing changes on the supply side and demand side, inherent in developments of industrial production, that have inexorably altered the nature of industrialization as a social process. Industrialization no longer has to come from below, transforming all dimensions of preindustrial social life, but can come from above, preserving and strengthening traditional hierarchies and cultural forms. (for example, Geertz, 1963) The functional relationship between industrialization and liberalism, among industrial capitalism and individualism, democracy, and an open, decentralized market economy has thus been broken.[12] The bourgeois revolution, as the dialectical consequence of competitive capitalist industrialization, can be seen as a historically restricted phenomenon that by its very success created its own negation.

The differences between competitive capitalism and later phases are more dramatic than those between financial and monopoly capitalist industrialization, but recognizing the distinction between the last two is still vital. For instance, in monopoly capitalist development (compared with that of finance capitalism) the domestic industrial bourgeoisie can play a less significant economic and political role, and a powerful, dirigistic central state is the source of more initiation and control. These differences are a matter of degree, but when embedded in the markedly different natures of the leading product lines, we see the emergence of a qualitatively different form of industrial growth. In all three phases of industrial development, those benefiting from the production of leading categories of industrial goods could be counted on to support industrial expansion, but these constituencies change over time.

For instance, from our examples of competitive and finance capitalist industrialization, we see a shift in political importance from those producing industrial products to those using them. And the shift from finance capitalism, led by intermediate and capital goods, to monopoly capitalism, led by modern consumer goods, signified key changes in who, as users, have a stake in industrial growth. I have characterized the corresponding ideological difference as between a militaristic nationalism versus consumerism. As I have described in the third and fourth sections of this chapter, these labels imply profound differences in the social and cultural milieu appropriate for industrial growth as well as significant differences in the types of policies required to promote growth.

Table 11 summarizes the differences among the three historically successive kinds of industrial development, as derived from the case studies.

All of these differences are either ignored or subordinated to insignificance by liberal and Marxist stage theories of economic growth, modernization theory, and any attempt to extract lessons from history by analogy or use of universalistic theories emphasizing similarities of industrial development.[13] In addition, efforts to account for differences in experiences with industrialization by attributing them to the peculiarities of individual national histories are seriously incomplete.

As I mentioned in the introductory pages, the historical conception of industrial development I propose here is a more cumulative notion of historical change, where each phase builds on preceding ones and contains important elements from the earlier ones. This approach is best represented by the metaphor of dual historical movement: national configurations of social, cultural, and political life in nonindustrial societies continually change; and the processes of capitalist industrial production also change. The conditions necessary for competitive capitalist development were not even approximated in early nineteenth century Germany and Brazil, and those necessary for finance capitalist development were not present in Brazil during late nineteenth and early twentieth centuries. Capitalist industrial development occurred only when local conditions were sufficiently consistent with the requirements of the phase of industrial production current at the time that some domestic groups were able to seize the opportunities of industrial development.

We can quibble over how much consistency is sufficient, but the principal point is that the "prerequisites of economic development" have changed historically and continue to change. I have presented an interpretation of those changes, based on the way in which the technical and sectoral changes in capitalist industrial production have enabled a considerably wider range of social formations to experience significant and sustained material advancement than previously. Even some seemingly archaic social formations, which would have had no chance for successful industrial development during the era of competitive capitalism, may have real potential for undergoing large-scale industrialization in the late twentieth century.

On a methodological level, I argue that by focusing on dual historical movements in a flexible manner (that is, as a way to ask questions rather than to deduce answers), we can better distinguish the particular from the general and construct historical models of industrial development without either flattening

Table 11

Competitive, Finance, and Monopoly Capitalist Industrial Development: Characteristics, Conditions, and Mechanisms

	Competitive	Finance Capitalist	Monopoly Capitalist
Characteristics of leading product lines			
Type of product	Wage goods	Intermediate and Capital goods	Modern consumer goods
Production processes and industrial structure	Labor-intensive technology; many small firms	Capital-intensive technology; few large firms	Capital-intensive technology; a few large firms
Necessary conditions for growth of leading product lines			
Factor mobilization	Need for large numbers aggressive entrepreneurs and availability of massive labor and modest capital inputs	Need for some entrepreneurs sensitive to social and political parameters and availability of modest labor and massive capital inputs	Need for some technically competent managers and availability of modest labor and massive capital inputs
Product markets	Wage workers, domestic and foreign	State, other productive enterprises, and foreign investment	Modern middle class, other high income receivers, and state
Social and cultural order	Unrestricted geographical and sectoral mobility of productive factors	Unrestricted geographical and sectoral mobility for *industrial and urban productive factors*	Unrestricted geographical and sectoral mobility for *industrial and urban productive factors*

	Considerable occupational and social mobility	Some limited opportunities for occupational and social mobility	Some limited opportunities for occupational and social mobility, principally within the middle class
	Status derived largely from position in private production process	Some status from control over large-scale productive assets, although other factors may continue to exert decisive influence	Status largely determined by position in private and public bureaucracies, linked to income levels and consumption patterns
	Ideology of aggressive, competitive individualism; industrial bourgeoisie's drive to accumulate productive assets unencumbered by government regulations and cultural restraints of social responsibility or "irrationality"	Ideology of nationalism, which may mitigate industrial bourgeoisie's drive for private accumulation	Ideology of consumerism, pervasive even among the high-level bureaucrats in charge of leading production lines
Political order	Decisive political influence exerted by industrial bourgeoisie as a class, expressing its economic power, supported at crucial junctures by working class	Considerable political influence wielded by owners of large scale industry, and the conflicts within the propertied class (e.g., agriculture vs. industry) both require and are a source of significant independent political power vested in central state	Political power centralized in state and the most substantial influence from outside the political apparatus is exercised by the literate, articulate, modern middle class with organizational skills

(*Table continues on next page*)

Table 11

Competitive, Finance, and Monopoly Capitalist Industrial Development: Characteristics, Conditions, and Mechanisms (*Continued*)

	Competitive	Finance Capitalist	Monopoly Capitalist
Mechanisms			
Coordination of economic activity	Decentralized market system	Cartels and state	State planning
Principal agents of social and cultural change	Industrial bourgeoisie	Industrial bourgeoisie and state, the latter able to negotiate the minimum changes necessary to accommodate industrial growth without destroying the pre-industrial social and cultural order	State regulates and monitors slight changes needed
Social control	Industrial bourgeoisie at production sites and liberal ideology; state enforces private, "free" contracts	Industrial bourgeoisie and nationalist ideology; state redistributes income for social and political stability, not economic stimulus, and uses police powers when necessary	Consumerism; state assumes principal responsibility for social control by use of police power and by distributing income and subsidizing firms so certain groups receive increasing amounts of modern consumer goods

and distorting individual national experiences or introducing special *ad hoc* explanations to account for diversity. This enables us to see both material success and failure as well as the past and the present through a unified, consistent analytical framework that does not press data into rigid, preformed categories.

By way of example, without straying from the guidelines in Table 11, I believe that the differences between competitive and finance capitalism help considerably in understanding the properties of French industrial development during Louis Bonaparte's reign and the nature of Japanese industrial growth in the late nineteenth and early twentieth centuries. Capitalist Russia, Bulgaria, and northern Italy can be seen as either failures or only partial successes for reasons outlined in Table 11, and the "socialist" industrial development in the first two is strikingly similar to the German-Prussian model and would not have been possible under the technical conditions of industrial production during the competitive capitalist phase.

Moreover, the political power and consumerism of Kenyan and Indian public employees, and (in Argentina) the anachronistic wage goods emphasis of Peronist policies and post-Peron stop-go monopoly capitalist industrial growth (Allen and Weaver, 1979) can be fruitfully studied as examples of dual historical movements. Some of the patterns seen in the "newly industrializing countries" (such as, Hong Kong, Taiwan, South Korea, Singapore), however, are somewhat different from those listed on Table 11, because they have been used as cheap labor reserves by industrially developed nations and, at least until recently, levels of domestic consumption have been restrained. Those patterns are not in themselves incompatible with those listed on Table 11 (Lipietz, 1982; Harris, 1986), but the rapid increases in the international integration and coordination of industrial production may indicate new directions of worldwide (and, thereby, national) capitalist industrialization.

Notes

1. Throughout the paper I use such terms as industrialization and industrial development interchangeably. What I mean by these terms is the purely quantitative phenomenon of industrial growth to the point that somewhere between 30% and 40% of national output is produced by the sector. I eschew more multifaceted and qualitative definitions of industrialization, because it is precisely these other aspects of industrial growth that I argue have changed significantly over the last 150–200 years, and I do not want the relationship among different facets of the social order to be confused by including them in a too-comprehensive definition of industrialization.

2. The shift in the composition of industrial production, along with some of its implications, is described in virtually all U.S. economic history textbooks. For perhaps the most respected (*not* for pedagogical reasons), see the one written by Lance Davis

and all-star cast of new economic historians (Davis, and others, 1972: 419–453). Chandler (1977: 240–376) is far richer in scope and detail, relating changes in industrial output to changes in technique, firm organization, and market power. Wolman (1924: 110–118) shows that the pattern of union growth in the late nineteenth century is consistent with the pattern I mention in the text, and Nutter and Einhorn (1969: 132) present useful data on industrial organization around the turn of the twentieth century.

3. Dean (1967) and Landes (1969: 41–123) contain most of the information necessary to confirm my arguments about leading sectors, firm scale, productive technology, population growth, the roles of agriculture and of the state, and the importance of eighteenth century England's relative social and political openness. In addition, see Gatrell (1977) for cotton textile industrial structure in the early nineteenth century; Bergier (1973: 404–412), Mantoux (1961), and Marglin (1974) for the origins and qualities of the industrial bourgeoisie; Crouzet (1972) for the volume and sources of industrial capital; Bergier (1973) for agriculture; Lazonick (1974) and Mantoux (1961: 136–180) for the Enclosures: Thompson (1963) for the working class and social control; and MacDonagh (1977) for the halting beginnings of government centralization in the 1830s and 1840s and governmental ineffectiveness as a regulator of the economy through the middle of the century. Mokyr (1985) has an interesting and intelligent review of recent economic scholarship and debates about the industrial revolution. Polanyi (1944) is an invaluable guide for understanding the meaning of these events and processes.

4. "Germany," as a notion, did not exist before the unification of 1871, but the Prussian provinces contained well over half of the 1861 population and employed work force of what would become Germany ten years later. Moreover, Prussia was politically and economically dominant with respect to the other German states throughout the nineteenth century. Prussian predominance after unification is illustrated by the frequency with which people simultaneously held top posts in both the Imperial and Prussian governments and by the fact that in 1913, Prussian fiscal revenues were over 40 times the revenues of the Reich and almost twice that of all of the other provinces together. (Stolper, 1967 and others: 17)

5. See Gerschenkron (1943) and (1952), Henderson (1975), Hoffman (1965), Landes (1969: 193–358), Millward and Saul (1977: 17–70), and Stolper (1967) for the composition and technology of the most progressive lines of industrial production, agricultural organization and stagnation, slow growth and backwardness of consumer good industries, the sources of financial capital, and the role of the state. Borchadt (1973) is best on interpreting the meaning of these economic processes. Dahrendorf (1969), Gillis (1968), Hamerow (1958 and 1969), Tilly (1956), and Wehler (1970) are good treatments of the state in general and its labor policies in particular, including the revolution of 1848 and the subsequent reaction. For more specifics on particular facets of German industrial growth in this period, see Landes (1965) and (1966) for industrial structure in comparative perspective; Tilly (1969) for banks; Wehler (1969: 112–193) on ideology; Sagarra (1977: 175–227) on social and cultural continuity; Henderson (1954) for early transfer of industrial technology to Germany; Maschke (1969) on cartels; and Wunderlich (1961) on agricultural labor. Table 6 should be consulted for some important contrasts with English industrial growth.

6. For the early years of Brazilian economic history, see Baer (1965), dos Santos (1974), Furtado (1965), and especially Dean (1967) and Topik (1987).

7. The Vargas period has been the subject of considerable study; in addition to the citations in footnote 6, see Erickson (1977), Leff (1986), Skidmore (1967), Teixeira Vieira (1951), and Wirth (1970).

8. In addition to previously cited works on Brazil, the following consider the economics and politics of the post-1964 regime from various perspectives: Flynn (1974), Furtado (1973), Martins (1974), Mendes de Almeida and Lowry (1976), Morely and Williamson (1974), Pereira (1984), Roett (1976), Stepan (1973), and Tyler (1976). As important as these works are, however, Evans (1979) and Frieden (1987) together represent the key interpretations of Brazilian political economy in the last 25 years, and I draw heavily from their works.

9. A 1972 input-output study by Francisco Lopes concludes that a redistribution of income from the top to the bottom in Brazil would severely curtail demand for transportation equipment, petroleum products, rubber, and electrical equipment while substantially increasing markets for wage goods, including food, textiles, apparel, leather goods, beverages, and tobacco. Cited in Tyler (1974: 874–875)

10. See Frieden (1987: 116–122) for these points and Pereira (1983: 212–213) on the domestic bourgeoisie. Stepan (1988: 68–145) is especially interesting about the politics of the military. He shows that the military has retained considerable institutionalized and effective power in the new civilian government and that its share of the national government's budget has risen substantially since the election. In his discussion of the military's commitment to a domestic arms industry and his advocacy of the military's defining their nationalist role in respect to groups outside of Brazil, it seems as though he may be suggesting a Prussian solution for Brazilian economy and policy.

11. Brenner (1977) criticizes Immanuel Wallerstein's and Andre Gunder Frank's conception of underdevelopment that retains "fixed pie" notions of economic growth. (In Marxist terms, such analyses are said to depend on "absolute surplus" rather than "relative surplus.") Brenner's article is an excellent interpretation of fifteenth and sixteenth century economic growth, although it is marred by overgeneralization. Weaver (1978) argues against economic interpretations of U.S. racism that employ conceptions of capitalist growth similar to those used by Wallerstein and Frank.

12. In a frequently quoted sentence, Marx (1867: 8–9) unequivocally stated that "The country that is more develop industrially only shows, to the less developed, the image of its own future." Trotsky (1932: 3–15, 463–470) ably criticizes this view from a perspective related to my own, and whether or not the viewpoint expressed by the sentence was belied by Marx's own historical and theoretical writings, it accurately sums up conventional uses of history characteristic of both Marxist and liberal traditions. Although the confines of the paper prevent me from pursuing this point, it should be clear that my conception of historical change implies the converse proposition: the less industrially developed (but developing) nations show the more developed some indication of their future. The features of late nineteenth century German industrial growth were apparent as strong tendencies in England and the United States at the same time, and, despite the differences in analysis, language, and intentions, the conclusions in a study for the Trilateral Commission by Crozier, and others (1975) is similar to what I say about Brazil with respect to the

absence of a functional relationship, and the presence of tension, between monopoly capitalist economic growth and liberal freedoms.

13. The most profitable economic sectors under monopoly capitalism do not operate in "an open, decentralized market economy"; principal markets are controlled by large firms. Participatory political regimes in Latin America, responding to popular demands, tend to limit this privately exercised market power, and economic "freedom" (that is, deregulation) is often practiced by repressive regimes that control the population by terror. This relationship, and the phenomenon of "market-authoritarianism", is discussed by Sheahan (1987: 313–327).

References

Allen, Julia Coan, and F. S. Weaver. 1979. "The Fiscal Crisis of the Argentine State" *Latin American Perspectives,* 6 (Summer): 30–45.

Ashworth, William W. 1960. *An Economic History of England. 1870–1939.* New York: Barnes & Noble.

——. 1962. *A Short History of the International Economy Since 1850.* 2d edition. London: Longmans.

Averitt, Robert T. 1962. *The Dual Economy.* New York: Norton.

Baer, Werner. 1979. *The Brazilian Economy: Its Growth and Development.* Columbus, Ohio: Grid Publishing, Inc.

Baran, Paul, and Paul Sweezy. 1966. *Monopoly Capital.* New York: Monthly Review Press.

Barkin, Kenneth D. 1970. *The Controversy Over German Industrialization. 1890–1902,* Chicago: Chicago University Press.

Baumol, William J. 1967. "Macroeconomics of Unbalanced Growth: The Anatomy of Urban Crisis" *American Economic Review* 57: 415–426.

Bergier, J. F. 1973. "The Industrial Bourgeoisie and the Rise of the Working Class, 1700–1914." In C. Cipolla (ed.) *The Fontana Economic History of Europe,* Vol. 3, pt. 1, London: Fontana Books, pp. 397–451.

Borchadt, Knut. 1973. "Germany 1700–1914." In C. Cipolla (ed.), *The Fontana Economic History of Europe,* Vol. 4, pt. 1, London: Fontana Books, pp. 76–160.

Braverman, Harry. 1974. *Labor and Monopoly Capital: The Degradation of Work in the Twentieth Century.* New York: Monthly Review Press.

Brenner, Robert. 1977. "The Origin of Capitalist Development: A Critique of Neo-Smithian Marxism" *New Left Review* 104.

Chandler, Alfred D., Jr. 1977. *The Visible Hand: The Managerial Revolution in American Business.* Cambridge, MA: Belknap Press of Harvard University Press.

Crouzet, F. 1972. *Capital Formation in the Industrial Revolution.* New York: Barnes and Noble.

Crozier, Michel, Samuel P. Huntington, Joli Watanuki. 1975. *The Crisis of Democracy. Report on the Governability of Democracies to the Trilateral Commission.* New York: New York University Press.

Dahrendorf, Ralf. 1969. *Society and Democracy in Germany.* Garden City, New York: Anchor Books.

Davis, Lance, and others. 1972. *American Economic Growth.* New York: Harper & Row.

Deane, Phyllis. 1965. *The First Industrial Revolution*, Cambridge, MA: Cambridge University Press.

Deane, Phyllis and W. A. Cole. 1967. *British Economic Growth. 1688-1959*. 2d edition, Cambridge: Cambridge University Press.

dos Santos, Theotonio. 1974. "Brazil" in *Latin America: The Struggle with Dependency and Beyond*. Cambridge, Mass: Schenkman, pp. 409–490.

Erickson, Kenneth P. 1977. *The Brazilian Corporate State and Working Class Politics*, Berkeley and Los Angeles: University of California Press.

Evans, Peter. 1979. *Dependent Development: The Alliance of Multinational, State, and Local Capital in Brazil*. Princeton, N.J.: Princeton University Press.

Flynn, Peter. 1974. "Brazil: Authoritarian and Class Control" *Journal of Latin American Studies* 6: 315–333.

Frieden, Jeffrey A. 1987. "The Brazilian Borrowing Experience: From Miracle to Debacle and Back." *Latin American Research Review* 22 (1): 95–131.

Furtado, Celso. 1965. *The Economic Growth of Brazil*, Berkeley and Los Angeles: University of California Press.

———. 1973. "The Post-1964 Brazilian 'Model' of Development" *Studies in Comparative International Development* 8: 115–127.

Gall, Norman. 1977. "The Raise of Brazil" *Commentary* (January): 45–55.

Gatrell, V. A. C. 1977. "Labour, Power, and the Size of Firms in Lancashire Cotton in the Second Quarter of the Nineteenth Century" *Economic History Review* 30, (1)(February): 95–139.

Geertz, Clifford. 1963. *Peddlers and Princes*. Chicago: University of Chicago Press.

Georgescu-Roegen, Nicholas. 1970. "Structural Inflation-Lock and Balanced Growth" *Economics et Societes* (4): 557–605.

Gerschenkron, Alexander. 1943. *Bread and Democracy in Germany*. Berkeley and Los Angeles: University of California Press.

———. 1952. "Economic Backwardness in Historical Perspective." In *The Progress of Underdeveloped Countries*, ed. B. Hoselitz. Reprinted in Gerskenkron, *Economic Backwardness in Historical Perspective*, Cambridge, Massachusetts: Harvard University Press, 1966, pp. 5–30.

———. 1966. "The Approach to European Industrialization: A Postscript." In his *Economic Backwardness in Historical Perspective*, Cambridge, Massachusetts: Harvard University Press, 1966, pp. 353–64.

Gillis, John R. 1968. "Aristocracy and Bureaucracy in Nineteenth-Century Prussia," *Past and Present* No. 41 (November): 105–129.

Gordon, David M. 1972. *Theories of Poverty and Underemployment: Orthodox, Radical, and Dual Labor Market Perspectives*. Lexington, Mass.: D.C. Heath.

Hamerow, Theodore S. 1958. *Restoration, Revolution, Reaction: Economics and Politics in Germany, 1815-1871*. Princeton, New Jersey: Princeton University Press.

———. 1969. *The Social Foundations of German Unification 1858-1871*. Princeton, N.J.: Princeton University Press.

Harris, Nigel. 1986. *The End of the Third World: Newly Industrializing Countries and the Decline of an Ideology*. New York: Penguin Books.

Henderson, W. O. 1954. *Britain and Industrial Europe. 1750-1870*. Liverpool: Liverpool University Press.

————. 1975. *The Rise of German Industrial Power. 1834–1914.* Berkeley and Los Angeles: University of California Press.

Hewlett, S. A. and R. S. Weinert, eds. 1982. *Brazil and Mexico: Patterns in Late Development.* Philadelphia, Pa: Institute for the Study of Human Issues.

Hirschman, Albert O. 1968. "The Political Economy of Import-Substituting Industrialization in Latin America." *Quarterly Journal of Economics* 82 (1)(February): 2–32.

Hobsbawm, Eric J. 1964. "The Labour Aristocracy in Nineteenth Century England." In his *Labouring Men: Studies in the History of Labour.* London: Widenfield & Nicolson.

Hoffman, Walther G. 1965. *Das Wochstumder Deutschen Wirstschaft Seit der Mitte des 19. Jahr hunderts.* Berlin: Springer-Verlag.

Kelley, Allen C., and others. 1972. *Dualistic Economic Development: Theory and History.* Chicago: University of Chicago Press.

Kolko, Gabriel. 1967. *Triumph of Conservatism: A Reinterpretation of American History, 1900–1916.* New York: Quadrangle Books.

Kronish, R. and K. S. Mericle, eds. 1984. *The Political Economy of the Latin American Motor Vehicle Industry.* Cambridge, Mass: MIT Press.

Kutcher, G. P. and P. L. Scandizzo. 1981. *The Agricultural Economy of Northeast Brazil.* Baltimore and London: Johns Hopkins University Press for the World Bank.

Kurth, James R. 1979. "Industrial Change and Political Change: A European Perspective." In D. Collier (ed.), *The New Authoritarianism in Latin America.* Princeton, N.J.: Princeton University Press, pp. 319–362.

Landes, David S. 1965. "Japan and Europe: Contrasts in Industrialization." In *State and Economic Enterprise in Japan,* ed. W. W. Lockwood, Princeton, N.J.: Princeton University Press, pp. 93–182.

————. 1966. "The Structure of Enterprise in the Nineteenth Century: The Case of Britain and Germany." Reprinted in *The Rise of Capitalism,* ed. D. S. Landes, New York: Macmillan, pp. 99–111.

————. 1969. *The Unbound Prometheus.* Cambridge: Cambridge University Press.

Lazonick, William. 1974. "Karl Marx and Enclosures in England" *Review of Radical Political Economy* 6 (2): 1–59.

Lebovics, Herman. 1967. "'Agrarians' vs. 'Industrializers.' Social Conservative Resistance to Industrialism and Capitalism in Late Nineteenth Century Germany" *International Review of Social History* 12: 31–65.

Lerner, Daniel. 1964. *The Passing of Traditional Society.* New York: Free Press.

Leff, Nathaniel. 1968. *Brazilian Capital Goods Industry. 1929–1964.* Cambridge, Mass.: Harvard University Press.

Levine, David P. 1975. "The Theory of the Growth of the Capitalist Economy" *Economic Development and Cultural Change* 24 (October): 47–74.

Lewis, W. Arthur. 1954. "Economic Development with Unlimited Supplies of Labor." Reprinted in *The Economics of Underdevelopment,* eds. A. Argawala and S. Singh, New York: Oxford University Press. 1963, pp. 400–449.

Lipietz, Alain. 1982. "Towards Global Fordism?" *New Left Review* 132 (March-April): 33–47.

Luxemburg, Rosa. 1913. *The Accumulation of Capital,* London: Routledge and Kegan Paul, 1951.

MacDonough, Oliver. 1977. *Early Victorian Government, 1830–1870*, New York: Holmes & Meier.

Mantoux, Paul. 1961. *The Industrial Revolution in the Eighteenth Century.* Rev. ed., New York: Harper and Row.

Marglin, Stephen A. 1974. "What Do Bosses Do? The Origins and Functions of Hierarchy in Capitalist Production". *Review of Radical Political Economics,* 6 (2): 60–112.

Marins, Carlos E. 1974. "Brazil and the U.S. from the 1960s to the 1970s." In *Latin America and the U.S.: Changing Political Realities,* eds. J. Cotler and R. Fagen, Stanford, Ca.: Stanford University Press, pp. 269–300.

Marx, Karl. 1848. "The Bourgeoisie and the Counter-Revolution." In Marx and Engels, *Selected Works in Two Volumes,* Moscow: Foreign Languages Publishing Hosues, 1958, pp. 66–69.

———. 1857–1858. *Grundrisse,* New York: Vintage, 1973.

———. 1867. *Capital,* Vol. I, Moscow: Progress Publishers, 1965.

———. *Capital,* Vol. III, Moscow: Progress Publishers, 1965.

Maschle, E. 1969. "Outline of the History of German Cartels, 1973 to 1914." Reprinted in *Essays in European Economic History 1789–1914,* ed. F. Crouzet, W. H. Chaloner, W. M. Stern. London: St. Martin's Press, pp. 226–58.

Mendes de Almeida, Angela and Michael Lowry. 1976. "Union Structure and Labor Organizations in Contemporary Brazil" *Latin American Perspectives* 3 (98): 119.

Mendonca de Barros, Jose R. and Douglas H. Graham. 1978. "The Brazilian Economic Miracle Revisited: Private and Public Sector Initiative in a Market Economy" *Latin American Research Review* 13: 5–38.

Merhav, Meir. 1969. *Technological Dependence. Monopoly and Growth.* Oxford, London: Pergamon Press.

Milward, Alan S. and Saul, S. B. 1977. *The Development of the Economics of Continental Europe. 1840–1914.* Cambridge, Mass.: Harvard University Press.

Mitrany, David. 1961. *Marx Against the Peasant.* New York: Collier Books.

Mokyr, Joel. 1985. "The Industrial Revolution and the New Economic History" in his *The Economics of the Industrial Revolution.* Totowa, N.J.: Rowman and Allenheld.

Moore, Barrington. 1966. *Social Origins of Dictatorship and Democracy.* Boston: Beacon Press.

Morley, Samuel A. and Williamson, Jeffrey G. 1974. "Demand, Distribution, and Employment: The Case of Brazil." *Economic Development and Cultural Change* 23: 33–60.

North, D. C. and R. P. Thomas. 1973. *The Rise of the Western World: A New Economic History.* Cambridge: Cambridge University Press.

Nutter, G. Warren and Henry A. Einhorn. 1969. *Enterprise Monopoly in the United States 1899–1958.* New York: Columbia University Press.

O'Conner, James. 1973. *The Fiscal Crisis of the State.* New York: St. Martins.

Pereira, Luiz Bresser. 1984. *Development and Crisis in Brazil. 1930–1983.* Boulder, Colo: and London: Westview Press.

Polanyi, Karl. 1944. *The Great Transformation,* Boston: Beacon, 1957.

Rimlinger, Gaston V. 1971. *Welfare Policy and Industrialization in Europe. America and Russia.* New York: Wiley.

Roett, Riordan ed. 1976. *Brazil in the Seventies.* Washington, D.C.: AEI.

Rostow, Walter W. 1971. *The Stages of Economic Growth.* 2d edition. Cambridge: Cambridge University Press.

Sagarra, Eda. 1977. *A Social History of Germany. 1648–1914.* New York: Holmes & Meier pp. 175–227.

Schmitz, H. 1982. *Manufacturing in the Backyard: Case Studies on Accumulation and Employment in Small-Scale Brazilian Industry.* Totowa, N.J.: Allanheld, Osmun Publishers.

Sheahan, John. 1987. *Patterns of Development in Latin America: Poverty, Repression, and Economic Strategy.* Princeton, N.J.: Princeton University Press.

Skidmore, Thomas. 1967. *Politics in Brazil 1930–1964.* New York: Oxford University Press.

Steindl, Joseph. 1952. *Maturity and Stagnation in American Capitalism.* Oxford: Basil Blackwell.

Stepan, Alfred. 1988. *Rethinking Military Politics: Brazil and the Southern Cone.* Princeton, N.J.: Princeton University Press.

——. ed. 1973. *Authoritarian Brazil: Origin, Policies, and Future.* New Haven, Conn.: Yale University Press.

Stolper, Gustan, and others. 1967. *The German Economy, 1870 to the Present.* New York: Harcourt, Brace and World.

Survey of Current Business. 1974. "The Input-Output Structure of the U.S. Economy, 1967" 54, (2)(February): 24–56.

Teixeira Vieira, Dorival. 1951. "The industrialization of Brazil." In *Brazil: Portrait of Half of a Continent,* eds. T. L. Smith and A. Morchant, New York: Dryden Press, pp. 244–264.

Thompson, Edward P. 1963. *The Making of the English Working Class,* New York: Vintage.

Tigre, P. B. 1983. *Technology and Competition in the Brazilian Computer Industry,* New York: St. Martin's Press.

Tilly, Richard. 1956. "The Political Economy of Public Finance and the Industrialization of Prussia, 1815–1866" *Journal of Economic History* 26: 487–97.

——. 1967. "Germany: 1815–1870." In Cameron, and others. *Banking in the Early Stages of Industrialization.* London, New York, Toronto: Oxford University Press, pp. 182–238.

Topik, Steven. 1987. *The Political Economy of the Brazilian State, 1889–1930,* Austin, TX: University of Texas Press.

Trebat, T. J. 1983. *Brazil's State-Owned Enterprises: A Case Study of the State as Entrepreneur.* New Haven, Conn: Yale University Press.

Trostsky, Leon 1932. *The History of the Russian Revolution,* Vol. 1. New York: Simon and Schuster.

Tyler, William G. 1976. "Brazilian Industrialization and Industrial Policies: A Survey". *World Development* 8: 863–882.

U.S. Department of Commerce, Bureau of the Census. 1975. *Historical Statistics of the United States, Colonial Times to 1970,* Part II. Washington, D.C.: Government Printing Office.

Vatter, Harold. 1967. "Has There Been a Twentieth-Century Consumer Durables Revolution?" *Journal of Economic History* 27 (March): 1–16.

Warren, Bill. 1980. *Imperialism: The Pioneer of Capitalism.* London: New Left Books.

Weaver, Frederick Stirton. 1970. "Growth Theory and Chile: The Problems of Generalizing from Historical Example." *Journal of Inter-American Studies and World Affairs* 12 (January): 55–61.

——. 1974. "Relative Backwardness and Cumulative Change: A Comparative Approach to European Industrialization". *Studies in Comparative International Development* 9 (Summer): 70–97.

——. 1976. "Capitalist Development, Empire and Latin American Underdevelopment, An Interpretive Essay on Historical Changes". *Latin American Perspectives* 3, (4)(Fall): 17–53.

——. 1978. "*Cui Bono*? and the Economic Function of Racism". *Review of Black Political Economy* 8, (3)(Spring): 302–313.

——. 1980. *Class, State, and Industrial Structure: The Historical Process of South American Industrial Growth.* Westport, Conn: and London: Greenwood Press.

Wehler, Hans-Ulrich. 1969. *Bismarck und der Imperialismus,* Cologne and Berlin: Kiepenheur U. Witsch.

——. 1970. "Bismarck's Imperialism, 1862–1890". *Past and Present* 48: 119–55.

Weinstein, James. 1968. *The Corporate Ideal in the Liberal State: 1900–1918.* Boston: Beacon Press.

Weisskoff, Richard and Adolfo Figueroa. 1976. "Traversing the Social Pyramid, A Comparative Review of Income Distribution in Latin America". *Latin American Research Review* 11: 71–112.

Wirth, John D. 1970. *The Politics of Brazilian Development 1930–1954.* Stanford, Calif: Stanford University Press.

Wood, Ellen Maksins. 1981. "The Separation of the Economic and the Political in Capitalism." *New Left Review* 127 (May-June): 66–95.

Wolman, Leo. 1924. *The Growth of American Trade Unions. 1880–1923.* New York: NBER.

World Bank. 1987. *World Development Report, 1987,* Washington, D.C.: World Bank.

Wunderlich, Frieda. 1961. *Farm Labor in Germany 1810–1945. Its Historical Development Within the Framework of Agricultural and Social Policy.* Princeton, N.J.: Princeton University Press.

Chapter 5

Toward a Relevant Psychology

Leonard Bloom

AGAINST A DEFEATIST PSYCHOLOGY

Can there be a psychology relevant to the Third World? Should there be? There both should and can be such a psychology. We must create one. The alternative is that psychology professions will continue to stagnate—remaining conservative and satisfied with merely maintaining their scientific and political respectability. A revivified psychology could emerge from comparative research and the cross-fertilization between Western techniques and methodology with the individual and collective problems of the Third World.

Kagitcibasi (1982) pleads for an independent, socially relevant and policy-oriented social psychology, staffed by Third World psychologists and working in interdisciplinary teams of social scientists. But his position conceals rarely examined problems. Are Third World psychologists more independent than others? Are they exceptionally sensitive to local problems? I am not as optimistic as Kagitcibasi that a new and more policy-oriented breed of psychologists is maturing. A major problem in establishing a relevant psychology is developing a professional identity and confidence that supports the professional in holding at bay suspicious and authoritarian administrators, who too often lack knowledge of the social sciences and who are too interested in immediate solutions to problems that they have themselves defined. (Bloom, 1988) Moreover, many Third World psychologists are as firmly locked into technologically biased, antihumanist and uncommitted philosophies of science as their Western colleagues.

I have another misgiving about Kagitcibasi's optimism. Some psychologists have spent too much ingenuity in demonstrating the dangers of the exportation of the social sciences and on attacking the colonial mentality of Western psychology. (see, for example, Moghaddam and Taylor, 1986). It would be more useful if they began to create a critical and constructive psychology.

It is depressing to find only one major professional paper with the word relevant in its title. Yet, as long ago as 1973, the Pan African Conference of the International Association of Cross-Cultural Psychology (held in Ibadan, Nigeria) was almost entirely devoted to the problems and prospects in Africa for a young but relevant profession. It is, however, encouraging to read a paper published in a South African journal, *Psychology in Society,* which advances a theory and practice of a relevant psychology and doubts that the ideological and institutional foundations of psychology are appropriate and directed to "do work relevant to the vast problems posed by our own needs as a Third World society" (Dawes, 1988). Dawes describes how South African psychologists (and related workers) work among the poor and the persecuted—both children and adults. They use their professional skills to strengthen those whom we chillingly call "subjects" to protect their integrity against the assaults of a violent society. Most South African psychologists are white. Most "subjects" and "clients" are black. One might cynically observe that even the most uncommitted white psychologist could gain professionally by working in a huge and largely ignored population. Dawes argues for a self-questioning psychology, collectively concerned pragmatically with transforming itself from a discipline largely constrained by the concepts, values, and problems of the urban industrialized one-third of the world, into one responsive to the massive problems of the nonurban, nonindustrialized two-thirds.

Abdi (1975), flatly asserts that "the concepts of psychology, its theories and methods as understood by Westerners are alien to the thinking of Africa"—and a fortiori to the thinking of other non-Western people. This is cryptoracism. Africans, and other peoples of the Third World, are no more aliens to Western people than they are to other people of the Third World. Many Westerners "think" and "feel" Africa. Many Third World people think and feel both Western and Non-Western! One of my African friends crisply observed to me: "I think like an African. I think like a Westerner. I think like Memoye!" A relevant psychology will be remodeled from both Third World and Western thinking. It will happen only if psychologists reject the racism of those who claim that there are such gross divergencies between the affective and cognitive processes of different peoples that mutual understanding is, if not impossible, then, at best, difficult.

Other Third World scholars have argued that psychology is essentially so detached from the problems of the Third World that it is pointless to discuss ways in which it might be made more relevant. A detached and alien psychology must forever remain so. In a tendentious and bitter paper, Mehryar (1984), consigns his own profession to the rubbish bin. He writes that the problems of the Third World are, by their very nature and etiology, unlikely to be solved by psychology, because the problems are economic, political, and sociocultural.

Not only are psychologists irrelevant to the Third World (Mehryar excepted, no doubt), but they are also agents of colonialism. Mehryar writes: "The social sciences in general, and psychology in particular, have in practice turned into another means of cultural dependence and colonialism." Contradictorily, he rejects psychology in the Third World as insignificant in numbers and influence! He ignores the living influence of Frantz Fanon who seized Western psychiatric and psychoanalytic insights and transformed them into a potent social philosophy and psychology of resistance to colonialism. Fanon used a Western notion to create a Third World and liberating psychology.

Mehryar evades the real problems of a relevant psychology, which is not to exert social and political influence directly, but, rather, indirectly to influence national ideologies and policy by demonstrating that political and social problems may be better solved by professional research and skills than by political passion. Psychology may, moreover, reduce the influence of colonial dependency by showing what can be done during the early years of childhood to encourage independence.

Ardila (1983) is as defeatist as Mehryar. Ardila, a Latin American psychologist, rejects Western psychology because it is, he claims, "an Anglo-Saxon discipline" and "alien to the Latin American way of thinking." He does admit that there is psychology *in* Latin America, "meaning the investigation and application of psychological principles in a particular context." But all psychology refers to particular contexts. The important question is consistently to compare what we learn from one context against what we have learned in other, comparable, contexts. Ardila makes much of the complexity of Latin America, but fails to see that complexity is a challenge to the investigator. Latin America has 20 nations, three major languages, many ethnic groups, and peoples at many different levels of socioeconomic and political development—an excellent opportunity for cross-cultural research!; an opportunity for a liberating psychology to evolve! The Third World, as indeed the rest of the world, offers similar and challenging opportunities for research at once relevant and possibly theoretically significant.

A non-Eurocentric psychology dates back to the early 1900s, yet these pioneering efforts have been almost totally ignored. The work from the 1920s onward of Bartlett, Nadel, and Margaret Mead, for example, already indicated (on the basis of experimental or observational studies) that affective-emotional and cognitive-intellectual processes are essentially universal, although influenced by social and cultural variations. If the pioneers had been within the mainstream of the development of psychology, we might have had a relevant and culturally sensitive social psychology a generation earlier than it appeared in Otto Klineberg's highly original *Social Psychology* in 1940.

I am, I believe, following an old trail that is now largely hidden by the flourishing of a narrowly conceived scientistic psychology. I argue for a contrasting approach—for a committed psychology that neither patronizes people nor surrenders to the cryptoracism of those who reify social and cultural differences into a somewhat outmoded quasi-biological determinism. I insist (perhaps a little too obsessively), that there is no place in a relevant psychology for either Abdi's barely concealed racism, or for its Western counterpart that limits psychology to the known parameters of the Western, urban world.

FOUR ISSUES

Four issues will recur in my critique of nonrelevant psychologies, in my exposition of relevant psychological issues, and in my suggestions for a relevant psychology.

1. Should Western-trained psychologists extend their professional and political interests to Third World problems? Are there any gains for Western psychology from such extension, or would this be little more than adding an exotic but marginal element? I strongly believe that a relevant psychology is an essential and central part of all psychology, and that the comparison between mainstream Western psychology and Third World contributions may productively unsettle Western psychology.

2. Some psychologists have attempted to construct a relevant psychology, and, although I welcome their attempts as far as they go, I am skeptical about whether they add much to either our approach to Third World problems or to extending the aims and methods of mainstream psychology. Their essential deficiency is the result of their lack of involvement with their subjects in their subjects' real world. This is not a radical notion: Kurt Lewin pleaded for such a relevant social psychology in the 1920s.

3. Western psychology is, I maintain, inadequate because of its overly behavioristic and psychometric methodology. Many contemporary, Western-trained psychologists are timid about approaching such complex areas as motivation and socioemotional development. They also tend to reduce to psychometrical studies the complexities of the relationships between individuals and society. Whatever is difficult to shape in a statistical and testable form tends to be banished from mainstream psychology and to be regarded as unworthy of scientific psychology. So, out goes the psychodynamic perspective! But it is not essential to be a committed Freudian to adopt the psychodynamic perspective with its insights into

the universal process of domesticating the antisocial (or asocial) human infant into the more-or-less socialized human adult.

4. I have been influenced by three complementary psychological perspectives: humanistic, psychoanalytic, and social-gestalt. Early on, I adopt the positions that people are often motivated by goals and hopes, and that psychologists would do well never to ignore nor minimize individual strivings toward finding meaning to their lives. The psychoanalytic perspective contributes two related emphases. It is essential to understand the unconscious conflicts and anxieties that motivate much human behavior. It is equally important to trace the emotional origins of behavior and experience. A relevant psychology depends on these three perspectives, and is, thus, far away from most of mainstream psychology.

SHARING PSYCHOLOGIES

Internationally, psychology has been grossly wasted. The American Psychological Association has more than sixty thousand members. The British Psychological Society has nearly ten thousand members. It is most unlikely that there are even twenty thousand fully qualified and trained psychologists spread throughout the Third World, and the number and range of social and individual problems that might be better understood and alleviated by professional psychologists are immense and largely neglected. Yet, not one major association of psychologists has made an open social and political commitment to sharing collectively the skills and experience of its members with the handful of psychologists in the Third World. On the one side, the associations placidly wait for governments to ask for help. On the other side. Third World governments are reluctant to ask to help—partly because few governments have any idea that psychological research could help in understanding and solving social problems, and partly because most governments are politically sensitive to accusations that they might be depending on outsiders for help. But a major reason is that no professional association has declared boldly: "We have skills and experience. We have mutual problems. Can we get together, learn from each other, and see what can done to understand the problems and mitigate them?"

Owing to the passive indifference of the Western professional associations, the latent belief that Western psychology is the Westerner's personal magic, and Third World suspicions, psychology has been almost totally isolated from the problems of the majority of the world's peoples.

This almost total apartheid within psychology is regrettable because of the universality of some psychosocial problems, such as (1) alienation and the development of a sense of identity, meaningful to individuals and not in conflict with their societies; (2) the control of aggression and of sexuality; (3) the most useful form of education for the development of cognitive skills and for the development of independence; and, most broadly (4) the contribution of childrearing to the mitigation of tendencies toward learned helplessness, the readiness to attribute decisionmaking to individuals and groups over which the individuals feel that they have little or no control; and (5) the little recognized problem of encouraging cooperative and nonauthoritarian social and political relationships. None of the attempts to define a relevant psychology shows much awareness of the gravity of these problems, much less to investigate them with our sophisticated research techniques.

Possibly this neglect is a result of the attitude that the Third World has been little more than a theater of operations—a convenient and interesting venue for research. Sharing psychology has meant no more than using Western research skills and experience to investigate specific empirical questions in which Western-trained psychologists have been interested. The resulting studies have usually been technically competent, but have rarely been applied to Third World problems. Western experimental design decorated by Third World palm trees remains Western-oriented psychology.

Connolly (1985) proposes that "if we are to grow a psychology for the Third World . . . such a programme would . . . lead to the development of 'appropriate psychological technology'." But is this enough? Psychology is more than skills and techniques. It must also generate insight into the human condition and stimulate sympathy for the pains of living, even though the pains may be caused by socioeconomic and political factors. The essential and almost totally neglected basis of a relevant psychology is the study of the obstacle-bestrewn journey "from metaphor to meaning" (Stein and Apprey, 1987). We live within an atmosphere of metaphor that gives meaning to the goals and relationships of individual and collective life. A relevant psychology must, therefore, share more than its skills. It must even share more than the spirit of a scientific psychology. To share skills is not difficult. To communicate how it feels to think as a mainstream psychologist is more difficult but still not impossible. It is almost unheard of to explore the implications of extending psychology beyond mere "appropriate psychological technology" to incorporate the enthusiasms of humanism's approach to working with people rather than with subjects, for people are not subjects. A Third World psychology must become actively involved in the neglected question of the assessment and evaluation of the actual and potential psychological hurt or damage that policies may inflict. Western psychologists should lead the profession internationally to become the professional advocates for the more vulnerable members of society—the poor and the uprooted, those who are regarded as politically or socially dangerously deviant, the mentally disturbed, the ill-treated, and ill-educated children.

So dramatic a shift in orientation will expose psychology to accusations that it is subversive or radical, and, in both cases, politically tainted and, therefore, unscientific. But psychology is already implicitly political in being detached from the more urgent contemporary issues as well as in its hesitation and moderation when it does criticize social policies. But are not "subversive" and "radical" any more than synonyms for what is socially and politically disturbing? No psychology can be relevant to the Third, or any other, world unless it does unsettle those whose policies affect the happiness and welfare of the community.

From the psychoanalytic-cum-anthropological perspective, Stein (1985) suggests that there are theoretical reasons to share psychology. It is, maintains Stein,

> . . . essential to understand what is now a mystery: how feelings come to be articulated in social institutions, symbols and rituals, and are enacted in social policy. The study of a society's psychodynamic process and structure [is] a springboard for studying unconscious influences upon cultures.

Very little is known about how emotional influences and relationships in childhood shape adult relationships, although the broad principles are clear. Broadly the relationships and social sentiments that we acquire during childhood determine our adult relationships and social sentiments. We lack specific insights into what is probably the key variable—identity. One universal problem is learning how identity is formed in societies that are experiencing rapid change and, consequently, dual processes of disintegration and new forms of reintegration.

Moghaddam and Taylor (1986), in their critique of Western psychology observe that Third World psychology must consider the "dualism" of Third World countries. They define dualism as "the presence of a modern and a traditional sector functioning alongside each other in the same society." Ignoring for the moment the objection that these sectors interact rather than operate independently, identity formation is a particularly painful process in such riven societies, and, therefore, a particularly central feature of a relevant psychology.

QUESTIONS OF METHODOLOGY

The methods of psychology are as important as its content. Although psychology was introduced to the Third World from the Western and more urbanized-industrialized part of the world, this does not, in itself, justify the argument that psychology is irrelevant to the Third World.

The basic scientific methods of proposing testable questions and hypotheses, gathering data or evidence and evaluating its relevance, validity, and reliability apply to all kinds of psychological questions and societies.

But this view is not without its critics, who appear to deny that the Third World should even consider how far these principles are applicable and worth sharing. Asante (1987) has a persuasive, although not fully convincing, argument for a specific research methodology for Africa, and, by implication, for the Third World. Asante criticizes the Eurocentric perspective of both classical and radical streams of social analysis. Marx, Freud, Habermas, and Marcuse are dismissed as "captives of a peculiar arrogance, the arrogance of not knowing that they do not know what it is that they do not know." Their views of reality are limited and are, therefore, of limited significance to the Third World.

And what is it that Europeans do not know that they do not know? It is nothing less than that "the African perspective [is] a part of an entire human transformation." Asante's "search for an Afrocentric method" is succinctly expressed in a section almost at the end of his book, entitled "Other ways of knowing," and has three strands. First, "Western . . . objectivity has often protected social and literary theory from the scrutiny that would reveal how theory has often served the interests of the ruling classes." Second, and "more damaging still has been the inability of European thinkers, particularly of the neopositivist or empricist traditions, to see that human actions cannot be understood apart from the emotions, attitudes, and cultural definitions of a given context." Third, "the Afrocentric thinker understands that the interrelationship of knowledge with cosmology . . . and traditions [is a] principal means of achieving a measure of knowledge about experience." Asante seems to forget that Marxism and psychoanalysis meet many, if not most, of their criteria for the study of human transformation. It is, however, timely to have Asante's 212 pages that add from a non-Eurocentric perspective to widely accepted caveats about the sociocultural limitations of much of contemporary psychology.

No startling novelty here! But it is startling to read Asante's ambivalence about the reality (or otherwise) of two worlds—one black and the other non-black. He writes that although "it would be nonsense to . . . claim uniformity in black behaviour, the variance among blacks is less than between blacks and non-blacks." (Asante, 1987:37) It would, indeed, be an "entire human transformation" if the Afrocentric view taught Western thinkers that a common humanity can be found concealed by the apparant variance between blacks and non-blacks. An Afrocentric research methodology would, I believe, be based upon the postulate that universality and variance are equally significant features of humanity.

A more radical methodology than Asante's would describe and analyze the immense range of variance within both black and nonblack societies so that we might better appreciate their essentially common humanity. We might also investigate ways in which specific economic, social, and political contexts create specific stresses and frustrations—regardless of the skin color of individuals. We should be questioning what there is in common and what is divergent among, for instance, inhabitants of a Kalahari Bushmen community, unemployed and undereducated black youths in a deteriorated inner city, and professional blacks in a leafy suburb of New York. We should be asking the same questions of, for instance, members of a Greek peasant community, white youths in deteriorated Liverpool District 8, and professional whites in London's green suburbs.

Contemporary psychology underestimates the common human responses to social contexts, and finds it difficult to appreciate the rich variety of psychologies among blacks and whites. An Afrocentric perspective should be destroying the stereotypes that whites have about blacks and that blacks have about whites. Any philosophy that fails to object to categorizing whites *as a group* and blacks *as a group* is an antihuman foundation for psychological enquiry.

An essential question of methodology is the difficulty that individuals have in understanding other individuals. Black and nonblack psychologists are unscientific if they fail to explore both the emotional and cognitive bridges and barriers between individuals and communities. The psychoanalytic discussion of positive and negative transferences bears directly on this problem.

Mainstream psychologists such as Connolly and Moghaddam and Taylor ignore the problems of transference in research. Others too readily assume that there are such strong emotional antipathies between blacks and whites that investigations of blacks by whites (and whites by blacks) predictably arouse negative transferences. But is this necessarily so? Psychologists still have to test the limits of this pessimistic notion, and my experience leads me to doubt its universal applicability. I have, for example, found it easier to evoke a transference in therapy with young Africans than with young English clients. As an outsider to my African clients I was considered safe: I was outside the authoritarian family structure and relationships. I did not belong to a threatening kinship, ethnic, or national group. I was unlikely to possess supernatural powers that I might use to punish or control my client. Above all, my concern and interest was highly charged emotionally. I am a white man committed to helping an African in trouble or distress! And when I have an insight that leads to a meaningful interpretation, the cathartic release of tension is often dramatically stronger than for a white client.

It is a methodologically significant question to ask: To what extent and in what ways can people move through the intangible barriers of collective identity—the familiar and accepted contrasted with the alien and unaccepted. We are not helped by the metaphysical assumptions of "human nature" of Dixon and Foster (1971), that Asante quotes with approval. Dixon and Foster describes what they call the "black referent." This includes six factors: "humanism, communalism, the attribute of oppression/paranoia, emphathetic understanding, the importance of rhythm and the principle of limited reward." It seems (but it is uncertain), that these generalizations were drawn from the experiences of American blacks, both during slavery and in reaction from its lingering, postfreedom trauma. But does not "referent" apply to the black and brown people in the postcolonial Third World? I am not concerned by the "attribute of oppression/paranoia." Is this an ineradicable characteristic of Third World blacks? It is a diminishing characteristic? Increasing? Impervious to changing social, political, and economic conditions? There can only be a relevant and comparative psychology if we can reasonably assume that human nature is universal and that people can perceive other people in a nonparanoid manner, and that they can reach others emotionally, although, perhaps, at a less intimate and informal level than one might wish and be familiar with. Yet, paradoxically, Dixon and Foster do not see that "empathetic understanding" may exist across collective boundaries. The methodological question is how to create a true crosscultural or comparative psychology that explores "emphathetic understanding"—escaping from the inverted ethnocentrism that assumes too unquestioningly that we are imprisoned within our own cultures and suspicious of others.

THE THIRD WORLD CONTRIBUTION

An exclusively Third World psychology would cut off a vast segment of humanity and seal it into its own world, which is as racist in its implications as the most overtly Eurocentered psychology. It is equally invalid. My position is that there is as wide a variation within Third World peoples as within peoples in the urban-industrialized world. There is a wide, indeed, probably total, psychological overlapping between the Third World and the rest of the world. The historical experiences and socioeconomic changes that have affected all communities in our brief human history—and continue to influence hitherto untouched communities—make a scientific psychology a psychology of change. Yet, change is rarely directly addressed in mainstream psychology. The contribution of the Third World is to compel psychology to apply its theories and techniques to the universal phenomena of change. The contribution is positive, creative, and likely to generate a new and realistically comparative cross-cultural psychology. There are three broad possibilities of the Third World contribution.

The Importance of Symbolism and Ritual

All peoples, whether Third World or Western, dwell in a "forest of symbols." All peoples "pride [themselves] on being realistic, pragmatic, rational . . ." (Stein, 1985). But this reality exists in terms of their own collective definitions. . . . The individual and collective working realities of everyday life—the myths of the past and the hopes and expectations of the uncertain future—may be far from the rationality that most psychologists feel themselves competent to investigate. Psychoethnology is bolder. Turner (1967), for example, has beautifully and sympathetically described the forest of symbols that define the world of the Ndembu of East Africa. The Ndembu live in a colorful environment that is rich in trees and plants, which offer them the resources of survival. But survival is emotional no less than physical. The objects with which the Ndembu live together with their natural qualities, acquire qualities, meanings, and emotional coloring. These qualities are as powerful determinants of Ndembu behavior and experience as the natural qualities themselves. The objects of the Ndembu world differ from the same objects as perceived by their non-Ndembu neighbors—to say nothing of enquiring social scientists! The objects are embedded in rituals and evoke deep, symbolic inner significances and relationships with the Ndembu. The *mudyi* tree is more than a tree. It secretes a milky white juice if it is cut. The tree and its life-fluid are used in rituals and symbolize an astonishing variety of things and relationships. It is not surprising that it may represent the mother's breast milk, which extends to the social activity of nursing the baby and the mother-child relationship. More difficult to appreciate intuitively for the non-Ndembu is that it also symbolizes the abstract (but far from immaterial) pattern of matrilineal descent.

A psychology relevant to the Ndembu would be inadequate and thin if it failed to appreciate the rich texture of the Ndembu people's cognitions and interpretations of the objects in their world. Development studies too often ignore these considerations. A proposal, for example, to exploit the natural resources of the forest and to destroy the *mudyi* tree for its fruit or timber would provoke an emotional and social disruption, and no amount of compensation could recreate the shattered community, which is held together by the web of meaning and belongingness spun from this real but magical tree.

A more recent example is from my experience. In the late 1970s a social anthropologist and I were consulted by a government about the possible consequences of moving villagers to clear space to build a new federal capital city. A new site for the village had been offered, discussed, and apparently accepted. Monetary compensation had been paid. The villagers had materials for their new houses and transportation for the move. All seemed well, but the villagers refused to move at the appointed time, despite the authority's pleas and threats. It was not surprising. The planners had shifted trees and boulders to the new site to give the villagers a familiar environment. But the trees and boulders were not simple trees and boulders. They were also the homes of the ancestors, who had not been adequately consulted and were, therefore, annoyed. The trees and boulders belonged to the ancestors. Their descendants lived in a world in which the past and the present were equally real and inextricably intertwined.

Even Westerners have not totally torn the present from the past, nor have fantasy and the symbolic been abolished. But few Western psychologists seriously acknowledge such potent, if intangible, variables. The symbolic and emotionally ambivalent qualities that are latent in many relationships influence much human cognition and perception. The psychometric, experimental, and narrowly positivistic methodology of mainstream psychology is ill-fitted to investigate these most significant motivations. In the late 1980s, a century since Wundt and James founded modern psychology, it is high time to emerge from the constraints of an immature psychology.

Although Stein (1985) has pioneered in exploring the interactions between individuals and the symbolic milieux that they have created, this theme has not (as far as I am aware) been applied to the problems of socioeconomic development. It is typical of this hiatus in the center of contemporary psychology that the imaginative text of Bock (1988)—a study of continuity and change in the study of human action—has only one five-page section about psychology and cultural change in a text of 215 pages. There is very little discussion about the relationships of the social psychology of change and development with the symbolic world that has been created and that must itself change if socioeconomic development is to evolve. Naturally, we do not live exclusively in a world of metaphor and symbols any more than we live solely in a network of relationships and social structures. But Bock, Connolly, and others who confine their analyses to the latter and ignore the former, offer an inadequate account of the resistance to change and what facilitates it.

One of the most thoughtful contributions to the debate: "Can there be a psychology for the Third World?" (Connolly, 1985) exemplified how mainstream psychology is indifferent to the complexity and density of the worlds in which development in the Third World takes place. Connolly pessimistically argues that "much suffering is an irremediable part of the individual human condition," despite the massive achievements of the technological and scientific revolutions of this century. He, therefore, argues that the competence of psychology is limited in scope, although valuable as far as it goes, but it does not go very far. The massive problems that arise from the economic, social, political, and technological changes in the Third World, the changes and conflicts of ideology, epistemology and life-space are, implicitly, beyond the reach of psychology. He, therefore, favors the same piecemeal approach in the Third World that has been successful in limited professional areas in the more industrialized world. Microtheories, microskills, and microtechniques must be applied to the analysis or ameloriation of microproblems. Western psychology avoids questioning the assumption that "much suffering is irremediable." A relevant psychology, rooted in the Third World, will note that the area of the irremediable has erratically but notably shrunk. It will examine the consequences of the meeting of the scientific metaphor with other metaphors. It will take heed of how the nature of the web of metaphor and myth changes in all communities. The changes have both harmonious and dissonant aspects—a relevant psychology examines the precise cognitive processes at work in different social-cultural contexts and in different individuals.

The Importance of Spiritual Enrichment

The Third World contribution will reform psychology to include as central topics the more spiritual and dynamic aspects. Western psychology has evolved as a technologically sophisticated discipline within a materialistic socioeconomic system. It has been almost wholly behaviorist in orientation and psychometric in technique.

But there have always been alternative movements within psychology. Since the beginning of the century, psychoanalysis has kept alive the interest in the complex emotional states that influence our behavior and color our experience. And, by its interest in the irrational, psychoanalysis has kept alive the study of unconscious motivations that influence our behavior, relationships, and sense of self. More recently, cognitive psychology has revived the interest in the processes of "adjustment," although these are often difficult to quantify. For example: Kagan and Segal (1988), in their mainstream survey describe the contemporary trend of modern psychology. It is "cognitive, referring to all the ways in which we learn about our environment, store the knowledge in memory, think about it, and use it to act intelligently in new situations . . . to help us think, understand, and solve problems." Western psychology is increasingly a study of these processes. It is less and less a catalog of supposedly measurable categories such as intelligence. Western psychology is now not impervious to insights from humanism, psychoanalysis, and many striking developments in psychobiology.

It has the beginnings of a new identity as "the science of mental life, both of its phenomena and their conditions." (James, 1950)

Little of the Third World is intensively urbanized and industrialized, and spiritual values have not been buried beneath the materialist values of Western urbanism. Few observers of the Third World fail to be struck by the creative, artistic, and spiritual spontaneity of mental life, which even poverty only partly suppresses. It is disappointing that even the "radical" advocates of a Third World psychology write as though they were oblivious of the cognitive, artistic, and spiritual effervescence that characterizes many aspects of life in the post-colonial Third World. The Third World psychologist needs more than the politicized Western psychology of, for example, Moghaddam and Taylor (1986).

The main thrust of Moghaddam and Taylor's reasoning centers about the consequences of the "exportation of the social sciences." They argue, contrary to Connolly, that there has been a considerable and harmful exportation. The harm arises from the incorrect perception of Third World societies. Western psychology has been divorced from the needs of the vast majority of people in Third World countries, who are part of the traditional sector of dual-sector societies. Psychologists are (with few exceptions) isolated from the traditional, rural sectors. The peasantry is ignored and psychology is developed within the urban-industrialized sector. It is, therefore, directly or indirectly for the benefit of new economic organizations and more closely linked with metropolitan psychology and values than to the values and problems of the Third World. It is argued that the role of psychology is both limited and distorted by sharing and encouraging the scientific and cultural subordination of the Third World. The Third World cannot be culturally liberated until its scientific subordination has dwindled and it has begun to create its own values in response to its own collective needs, aspirations, and values.

Moghaddam and Taylor make much of the tendency to "see all things Western as superior and necessarily better than anything comparable from the developing world." This reverence for things Western includes psychology in its behaviorist and psychometric forms. They argue that Connolly is typical of many Western psychologists who assume that, if we apply Western psychology to Third World problems, it will be as intellectually profitable to the West as it will be economically profitable for the people of the Third World, or, as critics believe, as profitable for elite groups in the Third World.

What, then, should psychology be doing for the Third World? Moghaddam and Taylor see psychology as problem-centered, but not limited to Western methodological purity. They believe that psychologists actively learn from the indigenous people as equal partners in the development of psychology. They insist that psychology must be politicized so that it may "deal with the question of how feasible it is to implement a given type of psychology" and to test psychology's suitability to indigenous needs and values.

Moghaddam and Taylor (1986) propose six guidelines to a relevant psychology, but do not go far enough in exploring how these guidelines can be enriched by asking how Third World contributions may not merely complement but transform them. The criteria are self-reliance, needs responsiveness, cultural compatibility, institutional feasibility, economic suitability, and political practicality. Not all are likely to be familiar to the average psychologists, even if they are working in the Third World, because few are aware of the political implications of their psychological research, and probably fewer still recognize that their subjects are people, too.

The psychology of self-reliance is, I believe, the most crucial problem for psychologists in creating a relevant psychology. Fanon (1986) was preoccupied with the problem of how to encourage a self-reliance in peoples whose colonial experience daily demonstrated their political and social impotence. Postcolonial Third World peoples still must acquire a healthy sentiment of self-reliance. Self-reliance depends upon growing up in a society that encourages it by providing many and varied experiences of autonomy. On a social level, this may include the growth of pride in the spiritual and cultural sides of life—it is possible to be economically poor but have a cognitive and emotional life that is rich in significance for the community. Poverty and political persecution obviously depress the spirit. The Third World context can teach Western psychology how varied are individual and collective resistances to hostile societies. It can more positively suggest questions that are largely ignored by Western psychology about how adversity may be transformed by individuals into the construction of an alternative worldview. Parin and others (1980) have analyzed the tendency of groups to respond to stress by regressing to more childlike or primitive types of emotional bonding. Their research suggests the broad question about ways in which the different patterns of childrearing prepare individuals to deal with the antiself-reliant roles of adulthood? How do children learn that they are distinct individual identities, despite the oppressive and often claustrophobic and alienating circumstances in which they are raised in many societies?

The Third World peoples' struggles to make sense of changing social and cultural worlds, and to establish a satisfactory sense of self-reliance suggests a question that Western psychology has barely touched. What is the emotional price that is paid for resisting authority and for attempting to establish our individual, and emotionally satisfying personal boundaries?

Government Policymaking and the Individual

Western psychology works within a traditional pattern of seeking the determinants of behavior—patterns of association between events that suggest patterns of cause and effect. There are such dizzying changes occurring throughout the Third World, and there are such varied collective and individual responses to the changes, that Western psychology's simple search for causes is arguably out of place. Is inevitability a false philosophy? In the Third World, it may well be. Both classical and operant (or instrumental) theories of conditioning are too tidy and deterministic, and too static, and are unable to make sense of the human propensity to respond to novelty. I am not convinced that people react to social circumstances passively because the complexity of social circumstances permits them to do little else but to respond. It seems truer that individuals often respond to the unpredicted with unpredictable understanding.

Popper (1988) has long held the view that a narrow and strict determinism does not apply to humanity. At the World Congress of Philosophy, he declared that "the world is no longer a causal machine. It can now be seen to be an unfolding process, realizing possibilities and unfolding new possibilities." The unpredictability of change in the Third World is a challenge to psychology to explore the cognitive techniques with which we plan and create possibilities, deal with the uncertainties of change, and search for meaningful consistency in a world in which consistency is not always, nor even often, apparent.

The Western theory that seems most sensitive to the problems of change at both an individual and collective level is psychoanalysis. Popper's view is consistent with the 'determinism' of psychoanalysis, which is based upon the not unreasonable suppositions that there is a meaningful continuity between childhood and adulthood, and that the individual's emotional and social development in childhood continues with adult social behavior and attitudes. Both Popper's view and the philosophy of psychoanalysis are directed to how the filaments of consistency may be distinguished within the muddles of individual and collective life. The psychoanalytic oppositions—conscious versus unconscious, rational versus irrational, creativeness versus destructiveness, love versus hate, sociability versus privacy—are together a system of metaphors that illuminate many (if not most) of the darker corners of the human mind. But how does this apply to the problems of the Third World?

Psychoanalysis is permeated by the theme of how social relationships and structures both shape individual lives and are variously interpreted, and reacted to, by individuals. As long ago as 1921, Freud was exploring the tense and complementary relationships of individuals and society in *Group Psychology and the Analysis of the Ego*. He wrote:

> In the individual's mental life someone else is invariably involved, as a model, as an object, as a helper, as an opponent; and so from the very first, individual psychology, in this extended by entirely justifiable sense of the words, is at the same time social psychology as well. (Freud, 1985).

Freud might have added that the someone else might be lover, oppressor, or alter ego. These relationships are relationships that may satisfy or dissatisfy the individual; they may enrich or frustrate; liberate or constrict. They may nourish individual narcissism or enable the individual's gratification in affiliation with others to flourish. No nation-state through its government and administrative system has yet investigated how their policies either liberate or constrain the individuals who constitute the nation-state. No government seems to have the remotest awareness that policies affect people in both their social relationships and their individual wants, needs, and goals. In the Third World, the readiness with which ideological positions and policies are switched, as emergencies come and go, blinds government to the possibly harmful effects of their policies. And neither governments nor the people are emotionally prepared, either consciously or unconsciously, to cope with the uncertainties that are created by society or by society's sometimes ill-advised interference with nature.

Society lives by fantasy as well as by reality. One aspect of fantasy is what the future might be. Education to deal with the uncertain future, to cope with the collective and individual fantasy life may at present be fanciful, but cannot much longer be ignored.

Hartmann (1964), discussing the concept of health, considers the fundamental issues of adaptability and freedom. All peoples have a limited capacity to adapt to change. This capacity depends upon structural factors, upon individual ego strength, and upon the nature and strength of the unconscious and irrational drives that motivate the individual. The other issue, freedom, is not the traditional philosophical problem of Free Will versus Determinism, but the practical problems of the extent to which, and in what ways, individuals and collectives are free from anxieties and irrational drives? To what extent are they free to perform their daily tasks, and what, if any, emotional satisfaction do they derive from them? The human child's long period of immaturity can socialize the child to be free and adaptable. Socialization is not necessarily a training for subordination and helplessness. A relevant educational and developmental child psychology could gather the mass of comparative material that relates patterns of child socialization and adult personality, and maybe tentative findings might emerge about how certain patterns and policies are liberating and others are not.

Freud himself, concluded his speculations about the future of the human condition with the hope that where Id was shall Ego be—if civilization survives. The psychoanalytic message to the Third World might be, therefore, to introduce no policies unless they might strengthen the Ego—the rational and the component aspects of reasoning. And to introduce none that strengthen the Id. Alas, the makers of policies are no more rational than the rest of us.

RETHINKING AND REFEELING PSYCHOLOGY

Paradoxically, both mainstream psychology and its politicized critiques are only partially correct. The insistence on meticulous methodology is essential. We can also agree that there is no psychology that is either ethically or politically totally neutral. However, both are limited approaches that conceal the unspoken assumption that the Third World is helpless and psychology is either utterly irrelevant or feeble. Three examples illustrate these two views.

Biesheuvel (1958), while Director of The National Institute of Personnel Research (South Africa), was involved in the assessment, selection, and training of Africans then being integrated into an urban-industrial socioeconomic system. His two research aims were "to gain an understanding of the behavior of African peoples" and to test "the general validity of psychological hypotheses concerning human behavior." Biesheuvel seemed little concerned with human experience! Not surprisingly in those politically insensitive times, he considered that "African research programmes should . . . be preferably directed towards the measurement of limits of modifiability of African behaviour, and towards a definition of the environmental factors that determine those limits." This static and pessimistic view persists in those theories that doubt the capacity of people in the Third World to adapt themselves to Western industrial organization, or to adapt Western industrial organization to Third World needs.

The defeatism of self-styled radical critics usually bluntly asserts that Western psychologists "mismatch First World psychology and Third World problems" (Jordan, 1985), or "psychologise" Third World economic, political, and social problems. (Mehryar, 1984). Both types of argument lead to the view that psychology is impotent at best, and evil at worst because (according to Jordan) it is a factor in "the creation of perpetuation of poverty." But why, if psychology is feeble and irrelevant should it contribute to anything or need to be actively rethought? Why if, as Jordan complains, psychology is one of the invalid "voluntarist theories of change" should psychology have the slightest concern in policy issues? There is no way to destroy another's philosophical assumptions without exposing oneself to counterassertions that are no more objective and testable than one's own. The debate is time-wasting and irrelevant. Connolly argues that the "failures of western psychology and its inadequacies are . . . not a cause for despair or despondency but a challenge." I shall now boldly present the elements of a committed psychology. I shall not trouble myself with speculations about the possibility that I have a latent colonial mentality, nor whether I am trying my readers' patience by bemoaning the theoretical impotence of the social sciences.

RELEVANT PSYCHOLOGY IS SOCIAL AND DYNAMIC

C. Wright Mills contends that the social sciences are about the nature and significance of milieux. Psychology, one of these sciences, investigates the many environments within which people live and to which they respond. At times, the responses are passive and accommodating; at others, they are active, and the environment is modified and assimilated to individual needs, wants, and goals. Individuals, however, always behave in a specific yet changing life-space—resisting its constraints and utilizing its opportunities. Individual and collective needs, wants, goals, and fantasies define our perception of the environment, which is, therefore, never neutral nor totally external to individuals. A mainstream experimental and positivistic psychology—a politicized psychology—is equally bound to understand the interaction between the individual and the sociocultural.

The milieu or the environment is not a thing like a plough or a railway system. It is a changing relationship between a people and their ploughs and their railway system—what they make with them, and what they fear, love, respect, and expect of them. This position pushes mainstream psychology toward questions and issues that it has been reluctant to face. This social psychology—committed and challenging—is already creeping into mainstream psychology (Gergen, 1975), and although Lewin's plea for relevant psychology is now of historical importance, his dynamic, cognitive position has reappeared in the form of a more interactionist position. Society and the individual are increasingly seen as a unit.

There is a convergence between the radical and sociological criticisms of mainstream psychology and mainstream psychology itself. They all denigrate psychology as a humanity by reducing its scope. The pioneering psychoanalyst Otto Rank wrote in a study of psychology and social change that "the tendency of our times to minimize the importance of all psychological explanation of human behaviour seems indicative of the failure of our rationalistic psychology [and sociology—L.B.] to account for the increasing power of irrational forces operating in modern life." (Rank, 1958) By "irrational" Rank referred to "powerful ideologies" that appear to be uncontrollable because they have deep emotional roots underlying their manifest cognitive and intellectual content. Racism is an example of such an ideology.

The convergence is a paradox: "social integration is largely, if not overwhelmingly achieved by psychological process" (Stein, 1985). Even the socially erratic transition from colonial dependence to postcolonial independence has been created and experienced by individuals. Those individuals have been influenced as much by wishful thinking and their unconscious feelings and attitudes as by the realities of economic, political, and social problems.

One crucial psychosocial problem of independence that illustrates the paradox is identity. Motivating many political conflicts and misunderstandings are such questions as: Who are we, the Utopians? How do we differ from our neighbors? Are we one people or many? Are we one family of peoples, or many competing families thrown together by the accident of our colonial past? Connolly (and others writing from within the mainstream and radical perspectives in psychology) ignore this fundamental problem of identity. I believe that until the nation-states in the Third World acquire a sense that they are communities, then economic and technological innovations are doomed to benefit one section of the state; thus, the seeds are sown for a vigorous growth of secessionist or regional fragmentation or conflict. Because few countries have succeeded in creating a paramount sense of identity, cultural fragmentation tends to become highly politicized and unstable.

Therefore, in explaining social problems, psychologists must never forget that individuals are variables too, and that it is insufficient to confine research and understanding to the behavioral level. Thinking and feeling that one is a member of a society means both learning that one belongs to it, and feeling accepted by it. The culture and society about which one learns is not a network of events and relationships as solid and unambiguous as the pyramids. Cultures and societies are interpreted, understood, loved, feared, and even hated by individuals whose peculiar relationships and socialization refract their sociocultural perceptions. Little Muyunda and little Sikota live within the same culture? But what is this "sameness"? The external and superficial definition of nationhood, ethnic membership, even of family, kin, and village membership, and their behavioral and emotional demands, is far from identical with Muyunda's and Sikota's inner, personal, and idiosyncratic defenses against the anxieties and frustrations of their lives. Society and culture are often muddled. Relationships are often unsatisfactory Our socially defined identity does not always foster our self-esteem.

Let us return to the forest of symbols to examine in detail how these convergences and conflicts between sociocultural and psychodynamic views suggest a new direction for understanding the human problems of surviving emotionally in a changing world.

PSYCHOLOGY IN THE FOREST OF SYMBOLS

Western psychology has tended to be at more home with describing human skills and the measurable aspects of personality, and finds faintly raffish the concern with the unmeasurable and subjective conscious and unconscious feelings of identity. Yet, unless individuals live in a world in which they can mature from helplessness to self-determination, that world will probably be stagnant or even regressive. I agree with Winnicott (1974) who has argued that "the fear of breakdown" or of failure is a major factor in inhibiting individuals from dealing rationally with their world. Individuals are unconsciously vulnerable to two kinds of fear of failure. Some people fear the breakdown of ego-organization—they struggle to deal with the sense of having no meaningful identity, or they resist an imposed identity. The imposed white masks of colonialism have sometimes distorted or damaged the black faces that they conceal. Other people fear the pains of reality and resist growing up and having to accept the demands of adult responsibility in both cases, Winnicott's patients tended to regress to the emotional relationships of childhood and repeated, in those relationships, the contradictions of love and hate that characterize childhood. As children, less is expected of them than of adults, and, if they are fortunate, they may be protected emotionally where adults are left exposed. But, as children, they are more emotionally vulnerable than adults are expected to be. In the Third World unsettling fears of failure exist collectively as well as in individuals, and they converge and exacerbate each other.

Durkheimians would describe the economic, social, and political uncertainties, deprivations, and conflicts of societies struggling to develop a practical, working sense of being a society. The economic and political relationships of the Third World with the donor nations has done little to reduce these uncertainties to emotionally bearable levels. For individuals, there are deep uncertainties about how to cope with the plethora of problems and the unpredictability of their social, political, and economic worlds. The emotional problems of independence are many. Not least is vulnerability to the fear of feeling that one's society is weak and is perceived as such by the powerful outside world. Colonization, slavery, and other forms of exploitation, damage individuals and societies alike. Individuals are socialized into learned helplessness—they learn to depend upon helping hands. These hands, however, often do not help but strike indifferently or angrily. The expectation of helplessness is accompanied by expectations of erratic help. Panic results from living in situations and relationships that are unpredictable and uncontrollable. Individuals are forced, individually and collectively, to create emotional defenses against a destructive world. Sometimes these defenses are positive, anticolonial sentiments are generated, and political movements are formed. At other times, however, groups retreat regressively into a quasi-family with emotionally and culturally closed boundaries. Internal security and fear of failure is bought at the price of isolation from wider and, therefore, stronger loyalties. The problem of the Western world and of the Third World is the dissolution of community. The Third World also faces the resistance to change of communities that are motivated by insecurity and that limit the growth of wider-ranging social sympathies and loyalties. Declining villages and swelling cities create vast problems.

For development studies, three aspects of the fear of national failure and sheer survival seem to be particularly important:

1. There is a fear of the annihilation and death of the society with its emotional and social bonds corroded by the acids of ideological and technological change. Many communities in the Third World oscillate uneasily between a sense of defeat and self-pity and an extravagant sense of self-reliance and rejection of the need for outside help. The realities of economic, social, and political problems are grave. They are not solved by the capricious shifting from superficial euphoria to deeply rooted self-doubts. The fear of annihilation is often unconsciously expressed by a search for the political magician who will radically restore the society's former vigor and purity, renew its collective sense of purpose, and expel the evil forces of corruption. The dramatic nature of grand political gestures by would-be saviors are fundamentally attempts to postpone the death of the society, and are often strongly infused with depressing omens of the terrible fate of the society if the savior fails to save. Another attempt to deny annihilation is the angry rejection of bits of society feared as worthless or as evil. Self-torturing and hypercritical punishment or destruction of "worthless" individuals, groups, or ways of life, lead to suicidal economic and social policies that lead to the very weakening of social bonds that is feared.

2. There is often a sense of inner emptiness, both individually and collectively, expressed in sentimental regrets for bygone times and long past glories. More significant are widespread expressions of feelings of alienation and of complaints that the society offers nothing to the masses while providing wealth and power to the elites. There is a manic flight from the overwhelming problems of society into a numbing defeatism. No one

would deny the reality of many problems, because poverty and drought or flood are tragically real, but much social policy degenerates into manic, meaningless diversions—masquerades that give the sensation of accomplishment but that are rooted in desperation. An obsessive concern with forms of government and systems of economic and social organization and an illusory sense of reassurance that is fostered by yet another paper new world, breed and increase a sense of emptiness. Failure to overcome failure deepens the feeling of impotence, and impotence destroys the consciousness of an inner confidence, competence, and self-esteem.

3. V.S. Naipaul has cruelly described the world of "the mimic men." The mimic men run those countries that have nothing of their own. They do not exist to provide a permanent sense of satisfactory belonging and meaningful activity for the masses but for external symbols of power and wealth. These symbols are owned and manipulated by the elite, but they are vicariously enjoyed by the masses. The country of mimic men (and women) exists by mimicking the ways of life of more successful countries. The mimicking nations have names, flags, heads of state, and nominal, legal independence, but little else. A sense of emptiness pervades them, and they are characterized by ambivalence toward the mimicked countries, which are blamed and repudiated, resented for their influence, yet, nevertheless, mimicked.

Of course, the outside world does exist. It is the world with food, shelter, education, and security. It may even be perceived (erroneously) to have an enviable sense of community. This world demonstrates what the deprived country lacks and is a reproach and a source of envy not unlike a distant and wealthy relative. There is often an unhealthy deterioration that moves from regrets that "We have no collective ego, no identity" to "We don't want *your* collective ego, your identity, now that colonialism has passed by." The unconscious and ultimate surrender is: "But the ego that you show us, your success and your wealth, though they may be terrible and alien to use may be the best that we can effectively mimic."

The Third World, because of the overwhelming burdens of reality, is always dangerously close to increasing the risks of real social breakdown by the fear of breakdown. Reality is bad enough. There is, alas, no realistic reason to expect that the Third World can be any more certain than the rest of the world of finding political and social leaders who are able to meet the challenges and sooth the anxieties of a reality that is often interpreted as malignant—and with some justification. But there is nothing so deeply rooted in the sociology of the

Third World that it is condemned forever to flee to empty mimicry from painful reality. An African friend asked me rhetorically: "Why must the Third World be so anxious to build a bubble-gum world?" Winnicott would perhaps reply that a mimicked identity is a substitute for a badly damaged one. The spurious identity and sense of belonging of the bubble-gum world symbolizes success, power, and economic autonomy. The West can never break down! It is secure and predictable—established. It has long had nationhood and a history of over-coming the turmoil of war and economic and political failure. The mimic men and their mimic societies display "flight . . . from internal reality" (Winnicott, 1975)—the inner reality of learned helplessness and disappointments. Politics become daydreams of wealth, of fantasies of power and status. But daydreams do not for long check the depression that is caused by a surfeit of the burdens of reality. T.S. Eliot observed that " Mankind cannot bear much reality." When reality is too much to bear, mankind retreats into fantasy. The life experiences of many Third World people fail to offer them a world where a realistic sense of self-determination is possible. Confidence in the predictability of situations, relationships, and values is frequently erratically shattered. But "a personal continuity of existence" (Winnicott, 1966) is an essential condition of healthy emotional maturity, and, if the development of a sense of continuity and integrity is denied to the growing child, it will not be easily developed in adulthood. If societies promote fears of breakdown, of impotence, and of bewilderment, then the capacity to deal with reality is diminished. It is crucial, therefore, to interpret social relationships and systems on both the realistic, pragmatic level, and on the level of unconscious fantasy about that society and its relationships. Winnicott (1966), as a clinician, explored the experiences of children in coming to terms with reality, and persuasively argues that children's styles in dealing with emotionally favorable and unfavorable experiences will influence how they deal with them in adulthood.

Two areas of adjustment to reality are, I believe, central to the problems of development—achievement orientation and the opposing sentiments of optimism and pessimism. Weiner (1974) is one of many psychologists who stress the importance of the orientation toward either failure or success. This orientation is seen on both individual and collective levels, and seems to depend upon two sources. First, do we perceive causes to be within our control or outside it? Do we, therefore, feel that we must rely upon our own efforts for success or that we are the pawns of some sort of fate or superhuman agency? Second, how predictable are the causes? To what extent and in what way can we influence them? A major part of religion and of magic is the attempt to influence causes that are perceived as beyond normal human control, and, thus, in need of specialist intervention.

The relevance of these considerations is easily seen in everyday life, and on both a supernatural and social level. For example, in many Third World societies, it is important to have "long legs" or access to influential relatives if one is to succeed. Similar contacts are not unknown in the industrialized world! If we believe that we have no such access and that we are, therefore, doomed to fail, then we are likely to be failure oriented. If, on the contrary, we have such access, then we are more likely to grow up optimistic and success oriented. We live in a changing and an imperfect world where virtue is not as frequently rewarded as one might wish. If children learn that they are members of a success-oriented group, then they are more likely to succeed than if they are brought up in a failure-oriented group. The ignored question in psychology and sociology is: how do individuals and communities compensate for the built-in encouragement to failure? Alas, often by withdrawing into a supernatural world or into political fantasies in which their virtue *is* rewarded.

A relevant psychology is, therefore, a developmental psychology that focuses on the paths that children find through the forest of symbols. I have suggested that optimism or pessimism, defeatism or a sense of competence, are acquired through relationships and may be realistic or unrealistic. Few psychologists who work in the Third World have tried to unravel these complicated aspects of growing up. Almost none have tried to relate patterns of childhood optimism and pessimism to the orientation of adulthood. Children use adults as their models of success or failure, which are intermingled in most adults. I have been unable, however, to find any studies of the precise areas of optimism and pessimism in Third World studies, so there is little but intuition to guide the student of the Third World about what patterns of child socialization and education might increase rational realism and optimism. Individual children have their own needs for success and their own fears of failure, however, so they will unconsciously or consciously select models of adult behavior or fantasies about them. Children, too, may consciously or unconsciously oppose adult influences, and, in so doing, they are opposing the social and cultural values and practices of which adults are the models. Children, thus, hew from the raw human material of family, kinship, and other primary groups their own meaningful cultural experience and orientation toward their world. This experience may be happy or unhappy. It may lead to children's developing an orientation toward success and failure that is characteristic of their society—or it may not. It often leads to the tense, often violent, confrontations between the younger and the older generations. The older generations assume or openly claim that they have earned the right to a monopoly of authority and wisdom and, therefore, of the opportunities for success. But those who are assumed or asserted to be destined for subordination and failure consciously or unconsciously resist.

Slaves, members of inferior castes, women, certain "ethnic" or minority groups may be imprisoned throughout their lives in a failure-oriented position. For these subordinated groups, technological and economic development is inconceivable unless it is associated with liberation from their lowly status, and, thus, a little explored consequence of technological and economic development is the disruption of many authoritarian relationships. Behind many sociopolitical conflicts of the Third World—and the others—is the unconscious, symbolic warfare between the generation of authoritarian fathers and their subordinate, but rebellious, children.

ELEMENTS OF A RELEVANT PSYCHOLOGY

The elements of a relevant psychology cohere about the emotional, developmental, and irrational-unconscious social-psychological aspects of psychology that are now largely ignored. If any one aspect be crucial it is identity or the self. The major psychological dilemma of the postcolonial and postslavery period is that of the restoration of the self (Kohut, 1977) The dilemma is how to restore the self without either retreating into a mythical past or adopting an equally mythical and facile "Western" identity. The Western and the Third worlds have been haunted by the questions: "Who am I? Who are my people? What type of people are we? What is our nature, our uniqueness?" The factors that facilitate the development of a sense of collective and individual identity, and those that inhibit it, are at the heart of a relevant psychology. I wonder whether identity is a problem that did not exist in precolonial times. One of my students once explained passionately during a debate: "I am *not* an African! I am *not* a Nigerian! I am *not* a Hausa! I'm Danladi Umaru! *That's* who I am!" I doubt if even a decade ago so powerful a defense of the integrity of the self could have been made to an audience without being met with silent or stormy outrage and incomprehension. Now, in the late 1980s such a statement vibrates with significance. Yet, I do not doubt that an inner ambivalence about identity in the Third World troubles many introspective younger people, who feel that they both belong to the Third World and to the increasingly influential Western. This ambivalence is delicately evoked in Act Four of *The Tempest*. Prospero, the magician prince, has given orders to his sprite, Ariel, who acknowledges his orders and asks: "Do you love me, master? No?" To which Prospero replies: "Dearly, my delicate Ariel." Prospero continually promises Ariel his freedom and continually postpones it. Ariel continually demands his freedom, yet never rebels, and, in the end, is touchingly reluctant to leave his beloved, yet resented, master. His master is—or seems to be—reluctant to let him go.

The restoration of the self is, I believe, a psychopolitical problem for both the Third World and the Western. Mehryar (1984) and Jordan (1985) smother the point in tendentious political cotton wool by insisting that if psychologists analyze Third World problems, they are indulging in irrelevant "psychologizing." The questions of development—of wealth and poverty—are, of course, economic, political, and technological, but why do we yearn to abolish poverty and insecurity? Surely only to liberate people so that they may individually and collectively develop emotionally satisfying identities and a sense of a worthwhile self. Mehryar and Jordan (and most self-styled radical critics) write as though the Third World were not populated by people. They "externalize" individuals by reducing them to mere images of sociopolitical constructs.

One of the most powerful motivating forces during the struggles for independence has been the rise of black consciousness or other ethnic-based parties and movements. All Third World peoples—Africans in South Africa and those scattered by the diaspora—have fought to restore their collective sense of self. This, I believe, is far more than an effective emotional resistance to colonialism or other forms of discrimination; nor is it only a response to racism or to the deeply disturbing effects of cultural and political change. It is an active assertion of identity, and as with all assertions of identity and selfhood, it is emotionally ambivalent.

The belief persists commonly in the Third World—often manifestly, but sometimes unconsciously—that the emotional legacy of colonial mentality inhibits the growth of an independent national sense of identity. Dividing and ruling had emotional results beyond their administrative outcomes. Many countries are still oscillating between past and present. There may be an obsessive search for emotional roots of a collective selfhood, for a myth of origins, for a utopian past. Such a search can be dangerously regressive, however. If a community is too obsessed by searching for a past that has never existed except in the collective imagination that needs it, this obsession prevents the group's developing a contemporary, forward-looking sense of self. I doubt the emotional wisdom of encouraging a determination to adopt uncritically the ways of the Western world. The Western world's diminishing sense of community, its widespread alienation, its harmful hierarchical structures, and the consequent racism, sexism, and economic inequality, are better avoided than mimicked.

Both regressing to a mythical past and trying to profit from the West have similar dangers: communities are drawn from the realities of change and of self-determination. The "exhumation" of the past is as unrealistic as the "group fantasy according to which people are scrambling for belonging and security" (Stein, 1985), by claiming the identity and raison d'etre of different worlds with their own problems of anomie and insecurity.

Writing of the Western world, Lasch (1985) remarks that "identity has become uncertain and problematical . . . because [people] no longer inhabit a world that exists independently of themselves." I wonder whether the Third World has begun to experience a similar problem with the weakening of village and other local or regional emotional ties? Once a sense of identity and of belonging was firmly rooted in, and constrained by, life in small, localized, clearly defined social units that are easily imagined and identified with. Children were socialized to be sensitive to the boundaries of these units, and so their place in their social world was unambiguous. Children learned who they were, to what groups they belonged, and what behavior was expected of them. They grew sensitive to relationships, both with their contemporaries and with their past.

The social boundaries, however, are now beginning to dissolve and to become ambiguous—the Third and Western worlds. On a cultural level, the Western world is being influenced by the Third World. Technologically, economically, and politically, the Third World is more and more tightly integrated within the Western world. Collective views of identity and selfhood are changing and are increasingly tinged with inconsistency and conflict. Individual and collective definitions of the self are losing their sharpness, and conflicts result. Moreover, the universal and primitive conflicts between age and youth, the sexes, the individual, and the collective, have acquired a new and growing intensity in the Third World. These conflicts are more and more openly directed to the strivings for individual identity in societies in which the collective constraints persist to conflict with the growing influence of opportunities and constraints that arise from outside the Third World. It is unfortunate that the behaviorist and psychometric psychologists have not yet turned their attention to the methodologically difficult question that arise from these problems.

It is surprising that in the section of his book entitled "The Liberation" Asante (1987) does not discuss the self or identity. Yet in the "Afrocentric discourse" he proposes three fundamental themes, of which one is "human's relationships to their own being." The three pages on "personalism" are a Blakean rhapsody to mankind's harmony with nature and to relationships. Asante writes that "The African finds energy and life in the midst of persons. . . . Ours is preeminently a tradition of remarkable encountering with others. . . . I know myself only in relation to others . . . ." Later, he makes much of the notion of "possession" by the gods of Africa. Africans search actively to achieve harmony with their collective experience by becoming possessed by the collective gods, by music and dancing, rhetoric and prayer. The Western "logical positivist tradition" that dominates Western thought and relationships for Asante starkly contrasts with African spirituality. Unfortunately, I feel that Asante's romantic views are uncomfortably close to the romantic racism of for example, Mannoni (1956) and Jung.

RELEVANT PSYCHOLOGY IS ANTI-RACIST

One of my Nigerian friends commented with some bitterness: "this undead colonialism is self-colonialism." The residual colonial mentality is a preoccupation of many Western psychologists. Even those who are concerned about sharing psychology with the Third World have tended to be unaware of the racist implications of constructing a psychology of the Third World that assumes—or openly asserts—that dominated peoples remain unyieldingly dominated, self-colonized, and dependent. Although overtly racist psychologies are less influential than they were 20 years ago, the latent racism of such psychologists as Jung and Mannoni has not vanished. A relevant psychology, therefore, must counter these views that influence Western immigration policies and are dangerously divisive in the Third World.

Mannoni (1956) practiced as a psychiatrist in Madagascar, and generalized from his experience to the Third World. He argued that there are two basic personality types—the dominator and the dominated. He applies this theory to colonial situations where the colonized people have a need to be dominated and the colonizers (nearly always Europeans) have a corresponding need to dominate. This becomes a symbiotic relationship. Collectively and individually social relationships develop that are analogous to sadomasochistic relationships. Indeed, the violence of some master-servant relationships is very close to sado-masochism. Mannoni criticizes the economic interpretations of colonialism as inadequate. The colonist is not simply seeking profit; he is greedy for psychological satisfaction. This, Mannoni suggests, imprisons the colonist in the colonial situation that satisfies his inner needs to dominate others. Profits are frequently sacrificed for the sake of emotional satisfactions, because an economically more profitable system might well have educated and trained the colonial people, although this would raise their status and enable them to feel independent. According to Mannoni, however, the dominated people demand independence, but when they receive it, they readily return to sociopolitical systems that are as hierarchical and authoritarian as the colonial regimes.

Certainly the history of colonialism has been marked by perverted sexual and sadistic behavior by colonists—both individually and collectively—that in other situations would probably have been regarded as pathological. The colonized peoples have often been stigmatized as immature or even subhuman creatures, who exist only to be exploited for profit and emotional satisfaction. *Robinson Crusoe,* and the hundreds of stories of adventure and exploration have consciously or unconsciously been used by Europeans as vehicles for the baser fantasies of power and domination. There are a mere handful of stories in which a non-European is treated as an equal. One of these is Samuel Johnson's *Rasselas, Prince of Abyssinia,* which was written as a moral essay in 1759. Prince Rasselas expounds what is probably Johnson's own philosophy of life and is far from being portrayed as a "noble savage."

Mannoni believes that the European restlessness and the collective impulse to find people to dominate is related to sexual guilt and frustrations. Guilt and frustration are transformed into manic flight—the mad itch to explore and to exploit the significantly named "virgin" lands. The colonized peoples are emotional scapegoats onto whom unconscious guilts can be projected. The colonized people are felt to be wild, unpredictable, sexually attractive, yet forbidden, malevolent (and to be feared), yet childlike. This primitive is a projection of the colonizer's own wild, unpredictable restlessness, malevolence, childishness and sexuality. In Jungian terms the colonized peoples symbolize the dark side of human nature—a dangerous side that both attracts and repels. Further, the individual is subordinate to the "collective" or "racial" unconscious: this is a mythical entity, the origins of which are lost in an archiac nature that distinguishes one people from another. So, for example, blacks are distinguished from whites, Jews from Aryans, the colonizers from the colonized, because of their collective unconscious.

The hidden agenda of white racism is that the peoples of the Third World are locked in dependency relationships and are, therefore, slow to change—if they can significantly change at all. This latent racism is, however, abated by a psychoanalytic approach to personality development, in which insights from cultural anthropology are integrated. In all societies there are "key integrative systems" (Kardiner and Ovesey, 1951). Human beings share the same basic psychobiological needs and characteristics, which only appear superficially to differ in different cultures, because to develop from an asocial infant to a socialized adult entails the same developmental tasks in all societies. Underlying cultural differences, there may be recognized similar emotional sensitivities—needs for self-esteem and social respect. Although the opportunities and constraints of one community differ from those of another, there is a universality of human emotions that belies the glib racist assumption that there is more than one kind of human being.

A realistically relevant psychology has, therefore, to search for the universals as a corrective to those psychologies that overemphasize the superficial differences between communities.

There is of course, more than one version of the integrative systems. I propose the following because I think that they are arguably fundamental:

1. In all societies the human infant is helpless and needs care, nurturance and protection. The quality of care varies: in some cultures it is erratic, in others it is consistent; in some it is given reluctantly or with hostility, in others it is given freely and with pleasure. But the tendency of all infant care is to make dependency in infancy a motivation for relationships in adulthood. The dependency relationships described by Mannoni are not, therefore, peculiar to the colonized people. Establishing a sense of independence in adulthood is an emotional problem in all communities.

2. In all societies relationships between children and adults are reciprocal; infants provoke adults to relate to them. Adults are more or less individually responsive to their infants. The norm for relationships in a community may be warm, open, honest, and intimate, or they may be chilly, distant and wary. There may be an emphasis upon cooperation and reward, or upon obedience and punishment. In no society can there be so deep a mutual sense of distrust between children and adults that no socialization into society's norms is possible.

3. Children's sibling relationships shape adult relationships. The norms within families of controlling or sublimating rivalries and aggression, cooperation and competition, ways in which the younger generation defers to the elders or unites in silent opposition to them, have never been described and related to problems in larger social units.

4. We need to know far more than we now do about what holds societies together and what stimulates conflict and disintegration. No society is without conflict between groups and individuals, any more than families are. Some families seem to be so preoccupied with their internal rivalries and conflicts that these is little emotion remaining for the betterment of the family. Indeed, some families thrive on rivalry and conflict, which are their raison d'etre. Likewise with societies: an outsider may despair at the emotional extravagance of societies locked in draining civil wars or where exhausting poverty exists side-by-side with an ostentatious wealth. How, we must ask, do societies (from the family to the nation-state and beyond), socialize their members so that potential conflict and disintegration is sublimated into action that permits cohesion to continue—until the disintegrative latent conflicts can no longer be contained? All societies are a network of constraints and of acceptable relationships, which both shape socioeconomic development and are influenced by it. The interaction between existing and changing patterns of integration and disintegration in Third World societies has barely been recognized as the urgent problem that it is.

5. Influencing the social systems and relationships are the beliefs and attitudes of members of the community. We ignore the reality of the fantasy
   worlds inhabited by the many different groups within a society: young
   and old, females and males, urban dwellers and rural, believers in different religious or philosophical systems, those identified with Western values and those who reject some part or all of them, and the rich and the
   poor. It is dangerously simplistic to describe any society as though it were
   one more-or-less uniform unit without its internal divisions that development often exacerbates.

It is peculiarly puzzling that social scientists have almost totally neglected
the arts, crafts, and traditional techniques of societies. Herskovits (1949) wrote
that ". . . art is to be thought of as any embellishment of ordinary living . . .
any manifestation of the impulse to make more beautiful and thus to heighten
the pleasure of any phase of living that is so recognized by a people." He even
writes of "the aesthetic drive" and was eloquent in the tradition of many earlier
cultural anthropologists who interpreted dance, oratory, storytelling . . . as activities that forever remind the observer that a functional and pragmatic view of
social life is an impoverished view. Beyond the degree of technical virtuosity in
inventing or elaborating a dance, making a raffia house or decorating abode
dwellings, the content of artistic and creative activity says much about the
emotional preoccupations of society. Besides, much creation and construction is
collective, bringing people together and symbolizing comradeship, whether it is
temporary or prolonged. The fears, hopes, anxieties, complex emotions, fantasies, and group relationships within a society are as real in their artistic expression as they are in the "real" world.

Radin and Herskovits have described the American Indian interest in the
"trickster-transformer," and the elaborate creation myths of the South East
Pacific are as well known as the universal myths about families of supernatural
animals or humans. These fantasy worlds are more than fancy. Bettelheim
(1986) has analyzed those myths of, and about, childhood that we call fairy
tales, and has shown how the fears and wish-fulfillments that they contain are
related to everyday fears and preoccupations. The fairy tale, according to Bettelheim, is one expression of the "existential predicament:" "the psychological
problems of growing up—overcoming narcissistic disappointments, oedipal dilemmas, sibling rivalries; becoming able to relinquish childhood dependencies;
gaining a feeling of selfhood and self-worth, and a sense of moral
obligation . . ." People in the Third World, as in every other world must, bring
order into the chaos of emotional personal life and into the relationship chaos of
social life. Bettelheim has distinguished more than 30 fairy tale themes, the

most common of which is "the struggle for meaning" in life. In the Western and the Third World our identity and relationships are dramatically transformed. Fairy tales present children with emotional and relationship problems, offer symbolic solutions and encourage them with happy—or fairly happy—endings. Similarly, many artistic activities reveal emotional and social problems and offer hope, relief, and control of the more destructive emotions and relationships.

CONCLUSION

A relevant psychology for the Third World is, therefore, not irrelevant to the Western world. Too much of contemporary psychology is accurate but limited, far distant from what motivates men, women, and children in their everyday lives. But the attempts to construct a relevant psychology for the Third World must be sensitive to the dangers of a pitying "inverse racism" which is racism, nevertheless. Bruckner (1983) warns bitterly:

> 'Take care! Throughout the argument about the current term "Third World" there is a current controversy: that of the mental space that we reserve for the future for non-European peoples. When we speak about the Third World as though it were a hospice, it shrinks the psychological horizons of our fellow human beings. It disqualifies four billion people from future generations'.
>
> (L.B.'s translation).

Can there be a psychology relevant to the Third World? Yes! It should be a psychology with no covert racism. It must be, therefore, a psychology that is addressed to the emotional and social problems of growing up in all worlds. Fanon (1980) has, from the Third World, attacked those simplistic descriptions of the world as though it were composed of black people and white. Such descriptions may be emotionally comforting and politically motivating, but they are a mystification of reality. Fanon pioneered a psychology of the Third World, and rejected any suggestion that this could be based upon stereotypes: there is no justification in lumping together as a few undifferentiated masses the billions of people whose experiences and emotional and cultural resources differ. The diversity and complexity of the Third World is as essential a characteristic as its postcolonial struggles for economic, political, and emotional independence.

Psychologies of all worlds must rectify the simplicities of those mainstream exercises that blandly ignore the complexities of individuality and of human society. There are many worlds within the Third World in which billions of individuals strive throughout life to make sense of their experiences and to express their feelings about them. A relevant psychology must be far more enterprising in studying the dilemmas of emotional, cognitive, and social survival. Relevant psychologists will have to abandon part of their scientific detachment, and substitute it with an all too rare empathy and identification with the world's (euphemistically termed) underprivileged.

Relevant psychologists must begin to examine historically their professional philosophy and practice. Is psychology meeting the challenge of the times? On whose side is the profession? What is the profession doing to break out the "thick membrane of technocracy, which deflects any questioning in advance, indeed, rules out the possibility of questioning, the 'pure, value free, and scientific' pursuit" (Kovel, 1988) of a committed, humanistic and practical psychology?

ACKNOWLEDGMENTS

I am deeply grateful to Mr. Memoye Ogu for his acute, fair, patient, and frank discussions with me. He has helped me, an outsider, immeasurably to understand that part of the Third World known as Africa. I am also grateful to Dr. Egwu U. Egwu who, in his own teaching and research, is a relevant psychologist. Above all, I am grateful to Dr. Rosemary Galli who persuaded me to attempt the formidable task of meeting her academic and human standards.

Notes

1. My own attempts to carry psychology beyond the Western world are, I hope, apt: "Some values and attitudes of young Zambians, studied through spontaneous autobiographies," *African Social Research,* December 1972, 14, 288–300.

"Values and attitudes of young Nigerians: Responses to social change," *West African Journal of Sociology & Political Science,* 1978, 2, 99–115.

"Cultural fragmentation and mental distress: A psychoethnographic perspective." *Psychopathologie Africaine,* 1984/5, 20, (1): 7–96.

"Obstacles of socio-economic change: Human beings the forgotten variable." *Nigerian Journal of Psychological Research,* 1985, I, (1): 21–32.

"Social science in Africa: Problems and prospects." *Journal of Social Development in Africa.* 1988. 3, (1): 55–71.

References

Abdi, V. O. 1975. "The Problems and Prospects of Psychology in Africa." *International Journal of Psychology* X (3): 227–234.

Ardila, R. 1983. "Psychology in Latin America Today." In M. R. Rosenzweig and L. W. Porter (eds.). *Annual Review of Psychology, 1982* 33. Palo Alto, Calif: Annual Review Press.

Asante, M. K. 1987. *The Afrocentric Idea.* Philadelphia, Pa: Temple University Press.

Bettelheim, B. 1986. *The Uses of Enchantment: The Meaning and Importance of Fairy Tales.* Harmondsworth, UK: Penguin Books.

Biesheuvel, S. 1958. "Objectives and Methods of African Psychological Research." *The Journal of Social Psychology* 47: 161–168.

Bloom, L. 1988. "Social Science in Africa: Problems and Prospects." *Journal of Social Development in Africa* 3 (1): 55–71.

Bock, P. K. 1988. *Rethinking Psychological Anthropology.* New York: W. H. Freeman.

Bruckner, P. 1983. *Le Sanglot de l'Homme Blanc: Tiers Monde, Culpabilite, Haine de soi.* Paris: Editions du Seuil.

Connolly, K. 1985. "Can There Be a Psychology for the Third World?" *Bulletin of the British Psychological Society* 38: 249–257.

Dawes, A. 1988. "The Notion of Relevant Psychology with Particular Reference to Africanist Pragmatic Initiatives." *Psychology in Society* 5: 28–49.

Dixon, V., and Foster, B. 1971. *Beyond Black or White.* Boston, Mass: Little, Brown.

Fanon, F. 1986. *Black Skin, White Masks.* London: Pluto Press (original edition 1967).

Gergen, K. J. 1978. "Toward Generative Theory." *Journal of Personality and Social Psychology* 36 (11): 1344–1360.

Hartmann, H. 1964. "Psychoanalysis and the Concept of Health." In H. Hartmann, *Essays on Ego Psychology.* New York: International Universities Press.

Herskovits, M. J. 1949. *Man and His Works.* New York: Alfred A. Knopf.

James, W. 1950. *The Principles of Psychology.* New York: Dover Books.

Jordan, J. 1985. "And a Psychology of the First World?" *Bulletin of the British Psychological Society* 38: 417–418.

Kagan, J., and Segal, J. 1988. *Psychology: An Introduction.* San Diego, Calif: Harcourt, Brace & Jovanovich.

Kagitcibasi, C. 1982. "The Relevance of Social Psychology for Development." Paper presented at the 6th International Congress of the International Association for Cross-Cultural Psychology, Aberdeen, TX, July 1982.

Kardiner, A., and Ovesey, L. 1951. *The Mark of Oppression.* New York: Meridian Books.

Kohut, Heinz. 1977. *The Restoration of the Self.* New York: International Universities Press, Inc.

Kovel, J. 1988. *The Radical Spirit.* London: Free Association Books.

Lasch, C. 1985. *The Minimal Self: Psychic Survival in Troubled Times.* London: Pan Books.

Mannoni, O. 1956. *Prospero and Caliban: The Psychology of Colonization.* New York: Praeger.

Mehryar, A. H. 1984. "The Role of Psychology in National Development: Wishful Thinking and Reality." *International Journal of Psychology* 19: 159–167.

Moghaddam, F. M., and Taylor, D. M. 1986. "The State of Psychology in the Third World: A Response to Connolly." *Bulletin of the British Psychological Society* 39: 4–7.

Parin, P., and others. 1980. *Fear Thy Neighbour as Thyself: Psychoanalysis and Society among the Anyi of West Africa.* Chicago, Ill: University of Chicago Press.

Popper, K. R. 1988. Reported in the *Times.* London, August 25, 1988.

Rank, O. 1958. *Beyond Psychology.* New York: Dover Books.

Stein, H. F. 1985. *The Psychoanthropology of American Culture.* New York: The Psychohistory Press.

————, and M. Apprey. 1987. *From Metaphor to Meaning: Papers in Psychoanalytic Anthropology.* Charlottesville, Va: University Press of Virginia.

Turner, V. W. 1967. *The Forest of Symbols.* Ithaca, NY: Cornell University Press.

Weiner, Bernard. 1974. *Achievement Motivation and Attribution Theory.* Morristown, New Jersey: General Learning Press.

Winnicott, D. W. 1966. "The Location of Cultural Experience." *International Journal of Psychoanalysis* 48: 368–372.

————. 1974. "Fear of Breakdown," *International Review of Psychoanalysis* 1: 103–107.

————. 1975. "The Manic Defence." In D. W. Winnicott, *Through Paediatrics to Psychoanalysis.* London: Hogarth Press.

Index

About the Authors

Rosemary E. Galli being a descendant of Italian *coltivatori diretti,* has been concerned with the problems of smallholders for much of her adult life. Her PhD dissertation on the politics of the Common Agricultural Policy touched upon these problems within the framework of the European Community and against the background of international trade negotiations. She extended her research on international and state intervention in agriculture by looking at rural development programs in Colombia and in Guinea-Bissau. Her work on Colombia resulted in several articles in *Latin American Perspectives* and *Estudios Rurales Latinoamericanos* and the edited work, *The Political Economy of Rural Development: Peasants, the State and International Capital* [SUNY, 1981]. Galli has published work on Guinea-Bissau in *African Studies Review, Development and Change, Review of African Political Economy, Soronda, and Revista Internacional de Estudos Africanos.* She co-authored *Guinea-Bissau: Politics, Economics and Society* [Pinter Publishers, 1987] and compiled *Guinea-Bissau: an Annotated Bibliography* [CLIO Press, 1991]. She has worked as a consultant to the United Nations, U.S. Agency for International Development, and the European Communities, and designed a project training female extension agents in Guinea-Bissau.

Lars Rudebeck, born in 1936, is an associate professor of political science at the University of Uppsala, Sweden, and chairman of the Forum for Development Studies of that university. He has been active as a researcher and teacher in development studies since the 1960s and has published many books and articles over the years, in several languages, including the major work on the independence struggle in Guinea-Bissau (*Guinea-Bissau. A Study of Political Mobilization,* Scandinavian Institute of African Studies, Uppsala, 1974). His current work is on the transition from liberation movement to state power in Africa and on structural adjustment and democracy.

K. P. Moseley studied with T. K. Hopkins and Immanual Wallerstein at

Columbia University, and specializes in West African development and social change. Currently at the University of Connecticut, Storrs, Moseley for more than ten years was in West Africa, working on anticolonialism in Dahomey, rural-urban migration in Sierra Leone, and industrial and urban development in Nigeria. Forthcoming articles deal with the commercial links of precolonial West Africa with the European and Islamic world-economies, and the impact of the current debt crisis on West African industry. As a spin-off from her piece in this volume, Ms. Moseley organized a session on 'Indigenous Peoples in the Face of Development' at the African Studies Association meetings last year. A general concern running through these projects is the way in which economic forces are mediated by the structural features of specific collectivities, whether pre-capitalistic systems or modern nation-states.

Frederick Stirton Weaver is professor of economics at Hampshire College, Amherst, Mass. He earned his B.A. in economics from the University of California, Berkeley and PhD in economics from Cornell University. He is the author of numerous books and articles on Latin American economic history and development and on higher education in the United States.

Leonard Bloom is fellow of the British Psychological Society. Fifteen years of teaching, research and practice in several countries of Africa inform Leonard Bloom's essay on a relevant psychology for the Third World. His current interests include the application of psychoanalytic ideas to social and political issues. Two current examples of this are his papers, 'The Psychoanalysis of Money and Possessions' and 'Psychological Aspects of Wealth and Power'. His first book, *The Social Psychology of Race Relations* [Allan Unwin, 1974], has been translated into several languages. He has recently completed three textbooks for Macmillan: *Changing Africa: an Introduction to Sociology* [1987], *Psychology: an Introductory Text* [1989], and the forthcoming *Individuals in Society: a Social Psychology for the Third World*.

DUE DATE

~~NOV 1 6 1992~~			
~~MAY 0 8 1993~~			
~~MAR 3 0 1993~~			
~~MAY 0 8 1997~~			
			Printed in USA